Thesaurus construction and use:
a practical manual

Thesaurus construction and use:
a practical manual

Fourth edition

Jean Aitchison

Alan Gilchrist

David Bawden

Europa Publications
Taylor & Francis Group

LONDON AND NEW YORK

First published 1972

Fourth edition 2000

© Europa Publications

2 Park Square, Milton Park, Abingdon, Oxon OX14 4RN

Europa is an imprint of the Taylor & Francis Group, an informa business

ISBN 10: 0-85142-446-5
ISBN 13: 978-0-85142-446-0

Transferred to Digital Printing 2004

The Authors

Jean Aitchison is an independent consultant, specialising in thesaurus design and construction. Prior to taking up consultancy work, she held a number of posts in public and special libraries, including six years as head of a large industrial library and information service. She was compiler of an early edition of *UNESCO thesaurus*, and the pioneering *Thesaurofacet*, and was advisor on the *BSI ROOT thesaurus*. More recently she has been involved in the compilation of the *International thesaurus of refugee terminology*, and in the UK, with the thesaurus of The Royal Institute of International Affairs and the *Education and employment thesaurus* of the DFEE. She received the 1982 Recognition Award for her work on thesaurus development and the reconciliation of classification systems and thesauri.

Alan Gilchrist is a director of the CURA Consortium and Associate Consultant with TFPL Ltd offering consultancy in information management and all aspects of information systems design and implementation. He is a Certified Management Consultant, a Fellow of the Institute of Information Scientists and Editor of the *Journal of Information Science*.

David Bawden is a Senior Lecturer in the Department of Information Science at City University London. He is the author of numerous books and articles, and leads Aslib's training courses in thesaurus construction, organizing digital information, and knowledge organization for knowledge management.

Contents

Acknowledgements

Figure 3: Copyright by and reprinted with permission of the Medical Library Association. McCray, A.T. '*UMLS* knowledge for biomedical language processing,' *Bulletin of the Medical Library Association*, April 1993, 81 (2): 187.

Figure 5: From the *Engineers Joint Council system of roles*, Battelle Memorial Institute, 1964. Reproduced by permission of the publisher.

Figure 6: Reprinted with permission of Chemical Abstracts Service, a division of the American Chemical Society.

Figure 7: in Maron M.E. *et al. Probabilistic indexing: a statistical technique for document identification & retrieval*. Los Angeles, CA: Thompson Ramo Woodridge, 1959.

Figure 8: in *Chronolog*, November, 1996. Reproduced with the permission of Knight-Ridder. Knight-Ridder.

Figure 9: in *NASA thesaurus* from World Wide Web. This electronic version of the NASA thesaurus was developed by the NASA STI program in 1994 as an experimental Web resource.

Figure 10: *Guidelines for the construction, format, and management of monolingual thesauri*. ANSI/NISO Z39.19-1993 Bethesda, MD: NISO Press, 1993. Permission granted from NISO Press, 4733 Bethesda Avenue, Bethesda, Maryland USA 20814; www.niso.org.

Figure 11: 'Conventional alphabetical display,' in *Thesaurus of engineering and scientific terms*, 1967. Reproduced with the permission of American Association of Engineering Societies.

Figure 12: 'Multilevel alphabetical thesaurus' in *CAB Thesaurus*, 1995. Reproduced with the permission of CAB International.

Figure 13: Figure reproduced from KWOC Index of the *International thesaurus of refugee terminology*, 2nd edition, 1996 (560 p), published by the United Nations High Commissioner for Refugees (UNHCR) and distributed by the United Nations. Distribution and Sales Section (Geneva and New York). ISBN: 92-1-000052-8; Sales No. GV.E. 96.0.3.

Figure 14: 'Hierarchies generated from alphabetical display' in *INSPEC thesaurus*. Stevenage, Hertfordshire: IEE, The Institution of Electrical Engineers, 1995. Reproduced with the permission of IEE, The Institution of Electrical Engineers.

Figure 15: Reprinted from *Thesaurus of ERIC descriptors,* 13th edition, edited by James E. Houston © 1995 by the Oryx Press. Used with permission from the Oryx Press, 4041 N. Central Ave., Suite 700, Phoenix AX 85012 (800) 279-6799.

Figure 16: Reprinted from *Thesaurus of ERIC descriptors*, 13th edition, edited by James E. Houston © 1995 by the Oryx Press. Used with permission from the Oryx Press, 4041 N. Central Ave., Suite 700, Phoenix AX 85012 (800) 279-6799.

Figure 17: Reprinted with permission from *IBE thesaurus*, 4th edition, 1984. © UNESCO.

Figure 18: Page 471 of the *ILO thesaurus/Thesaurus BIT/Tesauro OIY*, 4th edition, 1992. Copyright International Labour Organisation 1992. Reproduced with the permission of the International Labour Organisation.

Figure 19(a): Viet, J. *et al. Macrothesaurus for information processing in the field of economic and social development* 3rd edition. New York: Department of Public Information and Organisation for Economic Development, United Nations, 1985. Reproduced with the permission of the United Nations.

Figure 19(b): Viet, J. *et al. Macrothesaurus for information processing in the field of economic and social development* 3rd edition, New York: Department of Public Information and Organisation for Economic Development, United Nations, 1985. Reproduced with the permission of the United Nations.

Figure 20(a): in *MeSH, Medical subject headings, Tree structures, 1997*. Reproduced with the permission of the National Library of Medicine.

Figure 20(b): in *MeSH, Medical subject headings, Annotated alphabetical list, 1997*. Reproduced with the permission of The National Library of Medicine.

Figure 21: from Aitchison, J., and others, *Thesaurofacet: a thesaurus and faceted classification for engineering and related subjects*, English Electric Co. Ltd., 1969. Reproduced by permission of GEC.

Figure 22(a): from the *Art and architecture thesaurus*, 2nd edition (*AAT*) The Getty Information Institute, 1994. Reproduced with the permission of The Getty Information Institute.

Figure 22(b): from the *Art and architecture thesaurus*, 2nd edition (*AAT*) The Getty Information Institute, 1994. Reproduced with the permission of The Getty Information Institute.

Figure 23: from *Root thesaurus*, 3rd edition 1985, British Standards Institute. Extracts from *Root thesaurus* are reproduced with the permission of BSI. Complete editions can be obtained by post from BSI Customer Services, 389 Chiswick High Road, London W4 4AL.

Figure 24(a): in Aitchison *et al. The Royal Institute of International Affairs Library thesaurus* Vol. 1, page 247. Reproduced with the permission of the Royal Institute of International Affairs.

Figure 24(b): in Aitchison *et al. The Royal Institute of International Affairs Library thesaurus* Vol. 1, page 113. Reproduced with the permission of the Royal Institute of International Affairs.

Figure 25: in P. Defriez's *The ISDD thesaurus: keywords relating to the non-medical use of drug dependence*, 1993. Reproduced with the permission of ISDD.

Figure 26: from Austin, D., *Precis: a manual of concept analysis and subject indexing*, 2nd edition, British library, 1984 British Library. Reproduced with the permission of the British Library.

Figure 28: Organization for Economic Co-operation and Development. 1985, *IRRD thesaurus*, 2nd edition. Reproduced with the permission of OECD.

Figure 29: in *European Education Thesaurus, 1991*. Reproduced with the permission of the Council of Europe and the European Communities.

Figure 30: Reprinted with permission from *UNESCO thesaurus*, 1995, page 19. © UNESCO.

Figure 31: from *BS 6723: 1985 British Standard guide to establishment and development of multilingual thesauri*. Extracts from British Standard publications are reproduced with the permission of BSI. Complete editions can be obtained by post from BSI Customer Services, 389 Chiswick High Road, London W4 4AL.

Figure 40: Reprinted with permission from 'Integrated thesaurus of the social sciences: design study' prepared for UNESCO by J. Aitchison, *UNESCO thesaurus*, page 198. © UNESCO, 1981.

Figure 41: from Knapp, S.D., 'Creating BRS/TERM, a vocabulary database for searchers', *Database*, December 1984. Reproduced with the permission of Online Inc., publisher of *Database* magazine.

Figure 42: Copyright by and reprinted with permission of the Medical Library Association. McCray, A.T. '*UMLS* knowledge for biomedical language processing,' *Bulletin of the Medical Library Association*, April 1993, 81(2): 187.

Examples from *Precis: a manual of concept analysis and subject indexing*, 2nd edition, 1984 on pages 46–47 are reproduced with the permission of the British Library.

Examples from *EMTREE thesaurus*, 1997, Volume 2 on page 115 are reproduced with the permission of Elsevier Science B.V., Amsterdam.

Alphabetical entry and hierarchy display examples on page 121 are reproduced with permission of the Getty Information Institute from *Guide to indexing and cataloging with the Art and architecture thesaurus*, edited by Toni Petersen and Patricia J. Barnett, New York: Oxford University Press, 1994, pages 14 and 15.

Compound Term Rules in Appendix A are reproduced with permission of the Getty Information Institute from *Guide to indexing and cataloging with the Art and architecture thesaurus*, edited by Toni Petersen and Patricia J. Barnett, New York: Oxford University Press, 1994, pages 27–31.

Introduction to the Fourth edition

The first and second editions of this work were published in 1972 and 1987; a fifteen-year period that saw a burgeoning of computerized databases around the world. The first edition of this work was translated into Portuguese, and the second into Japanese and French; while a Spanish work incorporated a translation into an extended text. Many of the new databases used thesauri, and clearing houses were established to hold copies, or details, of these compilations. The United Nations family had produced over 20 specialist thesauri during this period; most of the large database providers supplied thesauri; and most software suppliers integrated thesauri into their retrieval capabilities.

However, by the time the third edition appeared in 1997, there had been a dramatic change in the text retrieval scene. Full text retrieval had become the norm; the ugly word 'disintermediation' was coined as information providers targeted the far larger market of end-users; new software suppliers came to the market with new techniques, which they claimed obviated the need for such old-fashioned things as thesauri. Above all, the Internet and its use grew at a staggering pace and search engines proliferated. When the authors were approached by the publisher with a suggestion that they prepare a third edition, they experienced some trepidation. The choice lay between a relatively straightforward job of updating and a complete rewrite; considering, for example, the ways in which text retrieval software handled the language problem. Encouraged by the observation of Milstead (Milstead 1995) that thesauri were not obsolete, merely invisible, the authors opted for the update approach.

But, while still largely in agreement with Milstead, there has been a completely new development in the world of retrieval, brought about by the poorly organized glut of information available on the Internet and the growing number of intranets. This development is known as the 'corporate taxonomy', which in its fuller manifestation incorporates elements of both classification and thesauri: both of which may be made visible, in whole or in part, being displayed on the screen or in printed directories. One software supplier introduces the topic on its website with the following words: 'In one of the ironic twists of modern technology, the widespread acceptance of the Internet has led to a resurgence of interest in the much older, traditional study of knowledge classification. While the classification and categorization of information previously rested primarily in academia and the library sciences, today any large website or corporation finds itself facing the problem of how to organize and structure the information it provides to its users. The problem isn't a trivial one; Yahoo! employs hundreds of "surfers" to maintain its web directory, while corporations employ knowledge management architects to maintain corporate intellectual capital sites. The Internet may have automated the distribution of information, but it has created a new army of information categorizers doing manual, time-consuming work'. This same supplier (of automatic categorization software) goes on to suggest an architecture comprising the three layers of Ontology, Taxonomy and Thesaurus. An Ontology is usually regarded as the top level to one or more classifications, which can be used for switching; a Taxonomy is a classification or categorization; while a Thesaurus works mainly with semantics at the term level. Another example of the influence of the Internet is the use of thesauri in subject gateways (see, for example, Robinson and Bawden, 1999). We hope, then, that this updating of the third edition is particularly timely.

The aim of this Manual remains to provide a practical, concise and handy guide to the construction of thesauri for use in information retrieval. There are three problems to be faced in keeping a book on this topic as short as possible. First, a large amount of theoretical material has had to be omitted. Those readers who wish to dig deeper are recommended to refer to the items in the bibliography at the end of the Manual, and in particular to the second edition of *Vocabulary control for information retrieval*, by F.W. Lancaster (Lancaster, 1986). Second, lack of space dictated that not all possible construction techniques could be illustrated fully in Section J, which is a practical summary of the preceding theory. Consequently, there is a bias in that section to the use of faceted techniques. Few apologies are made for this decision, as experience over the intervening years since the first publication of this Manual has tended to confirm that facet analysis is used intuitively by many of those who attempt to determine thesaurus structure and the consequent relationships. Third, we have taken the conscious decision to separate the compilation of a thesaurus from its application within the many software packages now available, and using the different devices supplied with each.

The first Section after this Introduction (Section A) is partly definitional and is concerned with the 'Nature, purposes and use of thesauri'. This is followed by Section B which addresses the planning and design of thesaurus systems, including whether it is necessary to construct a thesaurus; and should a thesaurus be needed, what type would be most effective in a given situation. Section C presents the principal thesaurus construction standards, including, in this edition, the US Standard as well as the International and British Standards, whose tenets are adhered to fairly closely throughout the following chapters. The main and technical part of the Manual is contained in Sections D to G, dealing with: vocabulary control; specificity and compound terms; structure; basic relationships and classification; and auxiliary retrieval devices. This is followed by Section H, which describes and illustrates a number of possible forms of thesaurus presentation; and Section I which discusses the problem of multilingual thesauri. Section J deals with the practical problems of construction, using a worked example; and Section K addresses thesaurus management, including maintenance and updating. The last Section L considers thesaurus reconciliation and integration, a topic likely to grow in importance as the Internet and intranets bring more databases together.

This Manual, though not claiming to be more than an introductory text, should nevertheless be an adequate guide to the competent compilation of most thesauri, particularly if used with the standards with which it is closely aligned. In the remaining circumstances, it should provide enough of an introduction to a complex subject for the reader to approach the task with a better understanding of the inherent problems.

May 2000

Section A: Nature, purposes and uses of thesauri

The thesaurus, in the context of this Manual, is a 'vocabulary of controlled indexing language, formally organized so that *a priori* relationships between concepts are made explicit', to be used in information retrieval systems, ranging from the card catalogue to the Internet.

Items in the bibliography covering all aspects of the thesaurus include the classic *Vocabulary control for information retrieval* (Lancaster, 1986); *Thesaurus in retrieval* (Gilchrist, 1971); and more general overviews, namely Gilchrist (1994, 1997), Aitchison (1992), Dextre Clarke (2001), D.J. Foskett (1981) and Taylor (1999).

The purposes of thesauri will be described further in section B. While they are more diverse than was the case in the past, it remains true that the primary purpose of a thesaurus is for information retrieval, which may be achieved in various ways. Secondary purposes include aiding in the general understanding of a subject area, providing 'semantic maps' by showing inter-relations of concepts, and helping to provide definitions of terms. More unusual applications include the generation of keyword lists which form the basis for planning, priority setting and other research management tasks (Nestel et. al., 1992), and the support of computer-assisted abstracting (Craven, 1993).

A1. Thesauri in retrieval

The primary use, for information retrieval, may be achieved by using the thesaurus in the indexing (intellectual or automatic) of a database, and/or in its searching. This gives four possibilities:

- thesaurus used both in indexing and in searching (first case)
- thesaurus used in indexing, but not in searching (second case)
- thesaurus used in searching, but not in indexing (third case)
- thesaurus used in neither case

A1.1. The classic thesaurus

In the first case, the same thesaurus is used for indexing and for searching a database. (It is possible to envisage different thesauri being used for the two stages, but this would correspond to independent application of cases 2 and 3). This is the 'classic' use of the thesaurus (although, according to Roberts (Roberts, 1984), it only stems from the relatively recent date of 1947), and the one which has predominated in practice, and which still does predominate to a lesser extent; other approaches, particularly the searching thesaurus, are the focus for much research effort, and more limited implementation in the operational setting.

This approach permits a very close mapping of the indexing and searching process, particularly when indexing and searching is carried out by the same individuals, as in a database maintained in-house and accessed primarily by the information specialists who maintain it. More commonly, the thesaurus will be used in indexing by the database compilers, and for searching purposes by users who are motivated to use the thesaurus as a retrieval tool; this is typical of the use of online and CD-ROM systems by expert intermediaries. In either case, the thesaurus must be available to all users, in either printed or electronic form: the former requires explicit intellectual choice of terms, the latter allows for the possibility of automatic selection.

A1.1.1

A recent development is the application of the traditional thesaurus on the Internet and in some intranets. This is, of course, a natural progression for some information providers who have migrated their databases, complete with thesauri, to such networks from other media. At the same time, the thesaurus has acquired, along with knowledge classification, a new impetus as designers grapple with the information explosion occasioned by the new technologies. However, as was pointed out in the Introduction, a new approach is being tried with corporate taxonomies. A new generation of software, using such techniques as linguistic inference (using mainly statistical analysis and rule bases), is now capable of automatically generating subject categories from analysis of the text of documents in a database (see F4). Currently, though, it would seem that human intervention is still needed in the 'teaching' of the software, and in the editing and fine-tuning of the results. Consequently, it would appear that the basic tenets of classification and thesaurus compilation are still valid and that much, or perhaps all, of the current commercially available software could be regarded as computer assisted construction of classifications and thesauri.

A1.2. The indexing thesaurus

In the second case, the thesaurus is used for indexing, but not for searching: the 'indexing thesaurus'. This is characteristic of the use of computerized databases by 'characteristic' end-users, who, though technically able to use the system, have no inclination to consult search aids, and generally adopt simple search strategies. The value of the thesaurus here is in providing a rich set of terms, including especially synonyms and broader terms, to increase the chances of successful retrieval. This would dictate that either the full set of potentially useful terms were added, or that the retrieval system automatically mapped from the unpreferred to the preferred term. The latter dictates that the thesaurus is available in electronic form.

A1.3. The search thesaurus

In the third case, the thesaurus is used for searching, but not for indexing: the 'searching thesaurus'. This concept was introduced during the late 1980s (see, for example Bates, 1989; Strong and Drott, 1986). The role of the thesaurus here is usually to assist in the searching of a free-text database by suggesting additional search terms, especially synonyms and narrower terms. The 'suggestion' may be done explicitly, by offering the terms to the searcher for their choice, or automatically: this process is generally referred to as 'query expansion'. Either option implies that the thesaurus is available electronically. Kristensen gives a good example of this, with a thesaurus used to improve searching of a large full-text newspaper database; comparisons were made of the effect of retrieval of including synonyms, narrower terms and related terms, alone or in combination (Kristensen, 1993).

Cochrane (Cochrane, 1992) gives a thoughtful discussion of the distinction between 'indexing thesauri' and 'searching thesauri', suggesting that the aids to searching presented by computerized database interface necessitate new forms of search thesauri, no longer showing a symmetry with the indexing thesaurus, or the process of its application, as was the assumption with the 'classic' form of thesaurus use. Lambert (Lambert, 1995), Milstead (Milstead, 1995, 1997) and Neilson (Neilson, 1998) discuss the same issues from the viewpoint of the searcher (see also B1.2).

Searching thesauri are often somewhat different in nature from the 'traditional' thesauri which are the focus of this book, especially in providing a much wider set of terms as an 'entry vocabulary'; conversely, it has been demonstrated that the richness of semantic structures of different kinds in the traditional thesaurus may be of particular value (Jones et. al., 1995). Techniques of construction may also differ, with greater use of automatic and semi-automatic construction techniques, and techniques based on discourse analysis from a cognitive viewpoint (see, for example, Lopez-Huertas, 1997; Chen et. al., 1997).

A1.4. Search techniques

Search techniques using a thesaurus have received a good deal of attention in research environments, often with the intention of providing a degree of 'intelligence' into such systems, by incorporation of semantic relations. A good example is Jones' description of the inclusion of thesaural information into a probabilistic retrieval system (Jones, 1993; Jones et. al., 1995). Shapiro and Yan describe an interactive query expansion process based on publicly available ANSI Z39.19 standard thesauri (Shapiro and Yan, 1996). Beaulieu compares interactive and automatic query expansion, and explicit versus implicit use of a thesaurus, within the Okapi experimental text-retrieval system (Beaulieu, 1997).

The query expansion principle may be extended by allowing users to select thesaurus terms from documents retrieved and judged relevant; so-called 'relevance feedback', see, for example, Smith and Pollitt (Smith and Pollitt, 1996). This in turn is related to the similar idea of using thesaurus terms to provide a hierarchical browsing capability, aimed at guiding the user through a complex multi-level set of concepts, in so-called 'view-based' or 'frame-based' retrieval systems (Pollitt, 1994; Pollitt, 1996; Pollitt et al., 1996; Hanani, 1996).

Browsing using thesauri may also be supported by a hypertext format (see K4.2.3) (Johnson and Cochrane, 1995; Hanani, 1996).

A2. The thesaurus in indexing

In any of these three cases A1.1–A1.3 above, the thesaurus may be invoked automatically, at either indexing or search time. Terms may be added to the indexing of a record, or to a search statement, without the explicit knowledge of the indexer or searcher; a 'hidden thesaurus'. An example of this is Chemical Abstracts Service *SCIFINDER retrieval package*, which equates, for example, 'cancer' and 'neoplasm' for retrieval.

The ways in which a digitized thesaurus may be invoked automatically, or otherwise presented to the user, will depend crucially on the features of the database software, rather than the thesaurus itself. For example, Schoonbaert shows the distinct differences in user capabilities in three implementations of the same thesaurus (*MeSH*) to index the same database (*Medline*) in the same medium (CD-ROM) (Schoonbaert, 1996).

The way in which index terms are chosen, whether this be an intellectual or automated procedure, will depend on the indexing policies followed: in the case of intellectual indexing, the decision will be made, or confirmed, at each indexing episode; with automated indexing, the decision will be made initially, and then followed automatically. These decisions essentially relate to questions of how many hierarchically-related index terms are to be assigned: just the most specific?; most specific and broader to one level?; most specific and all broader?; etc. A discussion of the principles and practice of indexing is beyond the scope of this book, but a review of indexing problems may be found in a paper by Milstead (Milstead, 1994). It can be noted that the fuller and more accessible the thesaurus, the more scope will be offered to the indexer.

Section B: Planning and design of thesauri

Before starting work on the construction of a thesaurus, it will be necessary to establish whether a thesaurus is, in fact, needed; and if it is, what form it should take to meet the requirements of the system and its users. This investigation will necessitate a thorough understanding of the information system that it is anticipated the thesaurus will support. This will entail consideration of such things as the material to be stored, user requirements and the physical aspects of the storage and retrieval system; nowadays normally the hardware and software options.

B1. Is a thesaurus necessary?

With the growing deployment of online information systems including the Internet using free text (that is to say the natural language of words in the titles, abstracts and full text of the documents) as a means of retrieval, the usefulness of controlled language (that is classification systems, subject headings and thesauri) has to be reassessed. The role of the thesaurus is changing, but it is likely to remain as an important retrieval tool, though with some of its features modified and their mode of use changed. The change is likely to represent an expansion rather than a contraction of the thesaurus' utility (Milstead, 1997). The expansion may include not only a role of thesauri in performance enhancement in full text systems (see B1.1), but also as a tool for use on websites and in intranets, or for use for any or all of indexing, search statement expansion and visual organization.

B1.1 Natural versus controlled language

The controversy over the choice of controlled versus natural language was for many years at the heart of the question of the value of the thesaurus in retrieval.

In manual systems the usefulness of controlled language was undisputed, both in pre-coordinated systems such as card catalogues and printed indexes, but also in post-coordinate systems employing punched cards, using, for example, optical coincidence to correlate subjects mechanically. Manual systems are not capable of dealing with untreated natural language because of the large number of cards which would have to be manipulated to handle the words involved. The thesaurus is of use in computer-produced printed indexes to control synonyms and provide the basis of 'see also' references, although natural language title and title-enriched indexes with free-text assigned keywords are thesaurus-independent. In machine-readable post-coordinate systems, natural language is frequently the only retrieval language, but there are also databases which use controlled language alone, and databases using natural and controlled languages combined in two-level or hybrid systems.

Figure 1. Comparison of natural and controlled language

Natural language

Strengths

○ High specificity gives precision. Excels in retrieving 'individual' terms – names of persons, organizations, etc.

○ Exhaustivity gives potential for high recall. Does not apply to title-only databases.

○ Up-to-date. New terms immediately available.

○ Words of author used – no misinterpretation by indexer.

○ Natural language words and phrases used by searcher.

○ Low input costs.

○ Easier exchange of material between databases – language incompatibility removed.

Weaknesses

○ Intellectual effort placed on searcher. Problems arise with terms having many synonyms and several species.

○ Syntax problems. Danger of false drops through incorrect term association.

○ Exhaustivity may lead to loss of precision.

Controlled language

Weaknesses

○ Relative lack of specificity, even in detailed systems.

○ Lack of exhaustivity. Cost of indexing to level of natural language prohibitive. Also terms may be omitted in error by indexers.

○ Not immediately up-to-date. Time lag while terms are added to thesaurus.

○ Words of author liable to be misconstrued. Errors in indexing terms can cause losses.

○ Artificial language has to be learned by the searcher.

○ High input costs.

○ Incompatibility a barrier to easy exchange.

Strengths

○ Eases the burden of searching:
  – controls synonyms and near-synonyms and leads specific natural language concepts to the nearest preferred terms to broaden search
  – qualifies homographs
  – provides scope notes
  – displays broader, narrower and related terms
  – expresses concepts elusive in free text.

○ Overcomes syntax problems with compound terms and other devices.

○ At normal levels of indexing, avoids precision loss through over-exhaustivity (i.e. retrieval of minor concepts of peripheral interest).

○ An asset in numerical databases and multilingual systems.

Both natural and controlled language systems offer the same powerful search aids – truncation, word proximity, etc.

In Figure 1 the advantages and disadvantages of natural and controlled language are compared. Natural language has a number of advantages over controlled language but it also has weaknesses. Figure 1 indicates how controlled language may be used to compensate for the deficiencies of free text and *vice versa* in mixed controlled and natural language systems. The natural language gives currency and specificity to improve precision (the ability to exclude irrelevant information). Natural language's exhaustivity of coverage, where abstracts and full text are included, ensures good recall (the retrieval of relevant information in the database). On the other hand, the controlled language increases recall by synonym control and provision of an *aide-mémoire* to related terms. The controlled language may also improve precision by the use of compound terms, homograph control and devices such as 'links' and 'roles'. In some hybrid systems, the controlled language is simple and non-specific, acting primarily as a recall-improving device, but in other systems, the controlled language is fairly specific and sophisticated, as in the *INSPEC* database which uses a thesaurus and a classification system to complement the free-text terms and to improve recall and precision.

Natural language systems and the role of the controlled language are discussed in the following references: Fugmann, 1982; Johnston, 1982; Perez, 1982; Sievert and Boyce, 1983; Dubois, 1984 and 1987; Snow, 1985; Lancaster, 1986, Chapter 17 and 1989; Betts and Marrable, 1991; Fidel, 1991; Peters and Kurth, 1991; Cousins, 1992; and Rowley, 1994.

B1.2 The need for the thesaurus in the full-text era

With the explosion of full-text databases the thesaurus has new roles in indexing and searching.

Controlled vocabulary indexing may be used to enhance the performance of full text intelligent retrieval systems with their statistical and semantic information and linguistic techniques. (Milstead, 1997; Ward, 1999). Index terms can be weighted more heavily than the natural-language text, causing documents, which have been predetermined by human (or automatic) analysis to be relevant to the query, to be ranked more highly. The technology of thesaurus-based Machine Aided Indexing (MAI) (see F4) may be used to ensure indexing is less dependent on human input.

As for the role of the thesaurus in searching full-text systems, Milstead believes that in the future thesauri will be used more in retrieval than in input (Milstead, 1997). Thesauri have tended to be underused in database searches, due to their being frequently unavailable to searchers. This may change when the work of the thesaurus takes place increasingly behind the scenes, or when the user is able to interact with the thesaurus more easily. Where a thesaurus has not been used for indexing, a thesaurus designed specifically for searching may be available. This search thesaurus and its possible features are discussed in A1.3 above. The exact nature of the search thesaurus and how its features differ from those of the standard thesaurus remain to be fully clarified (Milstead, 1997). Some search engines and other knowledge management software suites have built-in corporate taxonomies or 'knowledge structures' that may be automatically generated or manually 'customized', as mentioned in A1.1.1 above. Starr describes a number of such tools that have features similar to a search thesaurus, such as clusters of equivalent terms, inter-term relationships, and hierarchies bearing resemblance to tree structures (Starr, 1999).

More research is needed to determine what modifications are most likely to make thesauri more useful in full-text systems, whether in indexing or searching. Changes may involve, among others, more subject-field specialization (Neilson, 1998), greater specificity, more rigorous categorization of relationships (see F1.3.2), classification of terms according to semantic type (see L3.2.2b), more definitions, better electronic displays and use of automatic, or semi-automatic, thesaurus construction techniques (see A1.1.1, F4).

B2. Information system considerations

If it is decided that a thesaurus is to be constructed, the information system and database should be examined next in more detail to find what thesaurus characteristics would best serve the system and improve its performance.

B2.1. Subject field

Consideration should be given first to the subject field of the system. The boundaries of the field should be defined. Core areas where depth treatment is essential should be identified, and also marginal areas where more superficial treatment will be sufficient. In the central area, which is likely to include specialized knowledge, a new thesaurus may have to be constructed, whereas in the peripheral areas existing thesauri or parts of these may be used.

Whereas discipline-based thesauri will be relatively homogeneous, mission-based thesauri, common in commercial firms, sometimes present problems of compatability with the need to reconcile terminologies arising from different areas of discourse.

B2.2. Type of literature/data

Nowadays, multimedia systems are becoming more common. Is the database to contain text-based documents; factual numerical data; or geographical material? If it contains non-textual material, a thesaurus linked with a classification or coding system might be the best choice. If the database is bibliographic, the type of literature which predominates should be considered. Is it mainly monograph literature, or do reports, journal articles, conference papers and other serial publications predominate? Books do not normally require the in-depth indexing of serials and this will have a bearing on the specificity of the thesaurus. (Where books do require in-depth indexing it is often sensible to treat sections or chapters as separate items.) If graphics are involved, they must be separately indexed. It can be useful to think of 'indexable items' and to treat each format appropriately.

B2.3. Quantity of literature/data

The size of the file and the rate of growth should be noted. The larger the quantity of documents/data to be indexed the greater the input costs. This may be an influencing factor in deciding to opt for a searching thesaurus rather than one used for indexing. On the other hand the quantities to be handled might weigh in a decision to design a thesaurus with precision devices to avoid the retrieval of irrelevant documents, admissible in a small file, but not tolerable in a large one. If the database is small and growing slowly, a detailed, extensive thesaurus could be an expensive luxury, unless the subject field covered is highly complex. In full-text systems, the amount of data processed and made available for retrieval is, obviously, much larger and as a result recall is likely to be higher and precision improved by iterative interrogation of the computer.

B2.4. Language considerations

Is the system bilingual or multilingual? If information is input and searched in more than one language a bilingual or multilingual thesaurus is needed, and the special construction problems this implies should be taken into consideration. It is worth remembering that English-English and American-English display many differences (see also D3.3 and I).

B2.5. System users

It is important to know who are the users of the system. Will the end-users operate the system or will they leave this to qualified intermediaries? If the system is end-user operated, the thesaurus should be user-friendly, having a minimum of complex devices, and using familiar uncomplicated terminology. The controlled language should be unobtrusive. As far as possible the natural language terms of the user should be mapped onto the nearest equivalent controlled terms to improve access and to allow for automatic translation of natural to controlled language in online searching.

B2.6. Questions, searches, profiles

What type of questions will be put to the system? Will they be general or detailed? If only broad subjects are treated, a specific vocabulary will be redundant, whereas if enquiries are for detailed information then the indexing terms must parallel this specificity. How many questions will be put to the system? Indexing may not be economic if searching is infrequent, and a thesaurus designed as a searching tool for a natural language system may be preferred. On the other hand, a sophisticated thesaurus for indexing and searching may be justified in a heavily used system, handling detailed questions, to improve the speed and quality of searches. A thesaurus will also be of great benefit in alerting systems, where profiles of the interests of individuals or groups are automatically matched against periodic input.

B2.7. Resources available

(a) Financial resources
This is a key factor, although often outside the control of the information system. The type and size of the organization, whether it is an international body, government establishment or an academic, institutional, commercial or industrial organization will have some influence on the finances available. Industrial organizations are particularly susceptible to financial fluctuations, but all information projects are liable to cut-backs. Where resources are limited or subsequently curtailed, economies may have to be made in the thesaurus project. This might take the form of adapting a thesaurus used by another organization, rather than developing a new one. If a new thesaurus has to be compiled, costs can be cut if the size is reduced, specificity moderated and structure simplified.

In theory, money spent on the design of the thesaurus will produce benefits in the ease of maintenance and in savings in search time. In practice, it can be seen that many organizations take a short term view, and some later regret it.

(b) Staff resources
If there is a shortage of staff to operate the system, the thesaurus should be designed to be easily maintained. This implies that it should be of moderate size and specificity. The structure of the thesaurus should be made as explicit as possible, and supported by introductory notes and explanations of such things as the symbols used, so that the end-user may search the system without help.

B2.8. Buying in resources

Mention is made below in B3.1 of buying, rather than compiling a thesaurus, and of adapting it to local needs. It is also common to hire a consultant to compile or adapt a thesaurus or to advise on design and implementation.

Procurement of text retrieval software is a more complex process; and care should be taken in devising a detailed specification whether this is to be sent direct to the supplier or through the organization's purchasing function. It is normal to draw up a list of mandatory requirements and another of desirable requirements, giving different weights to each. Nowadays, many software suppliers have elements of text retrieval in their packages and some claim to support a thesaurus. Sometimes what is meant is merely the ability to control synonyms and often the software does not support the sort of multi-relational thesaurus described in this Manual, one which is fully integrated with the retrieval facility.

B3. Choice of thesaurus

Once the information system parameters are established it is time to concentrate attention on the type of thesaurus which will best serve the system.

B3.1. New thesaurus versus adaptation

A check should first be made to establish whether a thesaurus already exists in the field to be covered. There is no current comprehensive bibliography of thesauri available, either in print or online. However, a check may be made in the current and back issues of the quarterly journal *Knowledge Organization*, published by the International Society for Knowledge Organization (ISKO), which includes a bibliography listing new classification schemes and thesauri (Knowledge Organization). Check also Aslib's *Current Awareness Abstracts, Section B. Indexing (cataloguing, classification and thesaurus construction)* (Current Awareness Abstracts). The clearing house at Toronto for English language thesauri (see J1.4) will accept queries regarding thesauri, but does not issue bibliographies. Aslib's Information Resource Centre holds a collection of thesauri, where published thesauri may be checked, but the collection is not complete. For a detailed bibliography of thesauri existing in 1992, many of which have appeared in later editions and are still in use, *Thesaurus Guide* (1992) might be checked. This bibliography, compiled for the Commission of the European Communities, included over 600 thesauri that had appeared in at least one of the languages of the European Union. The online version was available on the European Union's ECHO host service, but was withdrawn in early 1998.

A number of publicly available thesauri may be consulted on the Internet. Generally these are arranged with each page representing a single term, with hypertext links emulating the thesaural relationships, and some form of top-down access via a search function or alphabetic browsing. Thesauri available in this way may be identified by the use of a search engine, or from a list of online thesauri, found at websites, such as: American Society of Indexers – Thesauri online (http://www.asindexing.org/thesonet.shtml); BUBL Link/5:15 (http://bubl.ac.uk/link/types/thesauri.htm); Traugott

Koch–Controlled vocabularies, thesauri and classification systems available in the WWW (http://www.lub.lu.se/metadata/subject-help.html); Queensland University of Technology – Controlled vocabularies guide (http://www.fit.qut.edu.au/InfoSys/middle/cont_voc.html); Web thesaurus compendium (http://www.darmstadt.gmd.de/~lutes/thesauri.html); Willpower Information (http://www.willpower.demon.co.uk/thesbibl.htm#lists); and *word*HOARD (http://open.gov.uk/mdocassn/wrdhrd1.htm). The free of charge access is a notable benefit, especially when viewing a thesaurus to determine its potential for use as the thesaurus for a database in a particular subject area. It avoids the need to borrow or purchase the publication, or visit a library to assess it (see H1 for advantages and disadvantages of screen displays of thesauri).

The likely indexing languages should be examined to see if they may be (a) adopted *in toto*, with minimum alteration, or (b) adopted as an acceptable framework, within which certain areas must be modified or developed in greater detail.

If neither of these courses is appropriate (as suitable indexing languages are non-existent), it will be necessary to construct a purpose-built thesaurus with a system-oriented framework. Even so, existing thesauri should not be overlooked, since they may contain sections suitable for extraction, amendment and use in the new system.

These sections might be commonly applicable schedules dealing, for example, with materials, physical properties, or geographical divisions, or more specialized sections of marginal subject interest, which might be accepted into the new thesaurus with little alteration. It is usual to acknowledge all sources used in this way in the introduction to the thesaurus; and if a significant amount of material is to be used unedited it would be sensible to seek permission so as not to infringe copyright.

B3.2. Thesaurus and information retrieval system design elements

An indexing language consists not only of indexing terms or 'vocabulary', but also of certain 'indexing language devices', which were first analysed by the Cranfield Project (Cleverdon, 1966), and which, when varied, will influence the thesaurus performance. These devices should be carefully selected, bearing in mind the effect they may have on retrieval. Indexing language devices fall into two groups: those which tend to improve the retrieval of relevant documents – 'recall devices'; and those which tend to prevent the recall of irrelevant information – 'precision devices'. Some devices may improve both recall and precision, for example the display of structural relationships. Detailed consideration is given to these devices later in this manual (Sections D–G) but a summary is presented below.

B3.2.1. Recall devices include:

(a) Control of word form (number, grammatical form, word order and other variants)
This device prevents the loss of relevant information through the scatter of concepts under different forms of the same term (see D2–D4).

(b) Word fragment searching
This device is not an integral part of the thesaurus, but is used in online searching, whatever the type of indexing language, to achieve the same result as word form control, and in addition provides for improved recall by broadening the search to

include word stems and other fragments of words. For example, using right truncation 'hous*' will retrieve 'housing', 'houses', 'housebound', etc., and left truncation '*molecular' will retrieve 'intramolecular' and 'intermolecular' (see G2.2).

(c) Control of synonyms and quasi-synonyms
This device prevents the scattering of synonyms and quasi-synonyms across the database, by referring non-preferred synonyms to the preferred term (see F1.1).

(d) Specific to general entry terms
This device improves recall by leading the searcher from specific concepts, too detailed for the thesaurus, to the nearest indexing term available to represent them (see F1.1.3a).

(e) Structural relationships, hierarchical and non-hierarchical relationships
This device improves recall, widening a search by the introduction of closely related classes (see F1.2–F1.3). It may also improve precision, by suggesting narrower, more specific terms.

B3.2.2. Precision devices include:

(a) Specificity of the indexing language
The greater the detail and number of terms, the more precisely may the subject of the documents be described. Specificity controls the precision capabilities of the system and demands greater skill in indexing and searching (see E1).

(b) Coordination
A most powerful precision device. By increasing the number of terms in combination in indexing or in searching, the concepts required will be defined more accurately and unwanted information eliminated. Recall is improved by reversing the process and reducing the combination level (see G1).

(c) Compound terms – level of term pre-coordination
This is another form of coordination, but one built into the thesaurus, rather than being a feature of the operational system. Compound terms ensure that the subject of a document may be minutely identified, preventing the retrieval of non-relevant documents (see E2).

(d) Homographs and scope notes
These restrict and clarify the meaning of otherwise ambiguous terms, resulting in more precise terms for retrieval (see D5).

(e) Word distance indication
An online searching device to improve precision by specifying that words should be adjacent, or within the same sentence or paragraph (see G2.3).

(f) Structural relationships
These may lead the indexer or searcher from broad concepts to more specific terms, which will narrow the search and tend to exclude unwanted information.

(g) Links and roles
Devices which overcome false coordination and incorrect relationships, by labelling groups of associated terms or indicating the roles of terms (see G3–G4).

(h) Treatment and other aspect codes (see G5).

(i) Weighting
A device for differentiating between major and minor concepts (see G6).

B3.2.3.

Some devices, including specificity, hierarchies and synonym control, can be regarded as an integral part of the vocabulary. Other devices, such as coordination, or weighting, operate independently of the vocabulary and can be called 'auxiliary devices' (see Section G). Other thesaurus-independent devices include online word fragment searching and word distance indication.

In broad terms, there is an inverse relationship between recall and precision, which suggests that a gain in recall is accompanied by a loss in precision, and a gain in precision by a recall loss. When designing a thesaurus, it should be remembered that the introduction of a precision device, such as high specificity and multiword terms, will lower recall performance; whereas reducing vocabulary specificity, using single word terms or excluding auxiliary precision devices, will improve recall but impair precision.

The interaction between controlled and natural language has already been discussed (see B1). The reciprocal advantages of the combination of the two systems is another factor to bear in mind in thesaurus design. Natural language can compensate for lack of specificity in the controlled language, and improve precision; while controlled language can improve the recall through its control of synonyms and near-synonyms, and display of relationships. Also, the precision devices of controlled language, such as compound terms and homograph qualification, may offset the precision loss in exhaustive natural language systems.

A complex thesaurus, highly structured, with a systematic display, specific terminology and compound terms will be expensive to construct and to operate at the input stage, and will require effort to maintain. The cost of this effort should be balanced against the expected improvement in performance. On the other hand, thesauri that are cheap to produce and maintain, having broad terminology and minimum structure, may be more difficult, and therefore more expensive, to operate successfully at the search stage.

Section C: Standards for thesaurus construction and development

Thesaurus construction and development standards and guidelines are essential documents for thesaurus compilers. They should be read and absorbed before the work commences and always be available for reference during the operation.

Standards exist for both monolingual and multilingual thesauri. For monolingual thesauri the International Standard is ISO 2788 issued by the International Organization for Standardization. It was first published in 1974. A second edition was accepted in 1985 and published in 1986 (International, 1986).

In the 1986 edition of ISO 2788, the alphabetical approach represented by the American *Thesaurus of engineering and scientific terms (TEST)* of 1967, and the classificatory approach of European compilers are combined in the same Standard (See Lancaster, 1986 chapter 5). National standards for monolingual thesauri include the British Standard BS 5723 (British, 1987), the US Standard ANSI/NISO Z39.19 (National, 1994), the French Standard AFNOR NFZ 47–100 (Association, 1981), and the German Standard DIN 1463 (Deutsches, 1987–1993). The British Standard BS 5723 and ISO 2788 are identical.

There have been standards and guidelines for thesaurus construction from the early days of thesauri. Krooks and Lancaster have traced the development of principles of thesaurus construction and the evolution of the guidelines from 1959 to 1993 (Krooks and Lancaster, 1993). Williamson also traces the history of the thesaurus construction standards (Williamson, 1996a). Krooks and Lancaster find that the majority of basic problems of thesaurus construction had already been solved by 1967, and for this the credit is due to Eugene Wall. Another influential contributor to the development of the Standards is Derek Austin who, with Dale, wrote UNESCO's 'Guidelines for the establishment and development of monolingual thesauri' (UNESCO, 1981), which were incorporated into ISO 2788:1986 and BS 5723:1987. The US Standard ANSI/NISO Z39.19:1993 acknowledges its indebtedness to both these Standards. This latest US Standard is the first Standard to deal with screen display of thesauri and thesaurus management systems. The International Standard on multilingual thesauri is ISO 5964 accepted in 1985 (International, 1985). The British equivalent is British Standard BS 6723:1985 (British, 1985a).

The rules referred to in the sections which follow in this manual are based for monolingual thesauri on the latest edition of ISO 2788, its British equivalent, BS 5723, and US Standard ANSI/NISO Z39.190–1993. When reference is made to 'the Standards' it should be assumed that all three Standards agree on the recommendation. Where one Standard has a different rule, this will be made clear. The rules on multilingual thesauri in Section I are based on ISO 5964 and its British equivalent, BS 6723. The ISO, US and British Standards are ripe for revision, as they pre-date the emergence of the full-text systems and powerful search engines of the last decade (Milstead, 1997). Revised editions should include rules for the design of thesauri suitable for the new technology (see B1.2), for example, the search thesaurus (see A1.3). Williamson (1996a) and Spiteri (1997) would like to see the new editions cover more explicitly the role of facet analysis (see F2.3) in thesaurus construction.

Section D: Vocabulary control

Control of terminology in a thesaurus is achieved in various ways. First, the form of the term is controlled, whether this involves grammatical form, spelling, singular and plural form, abbreviations or compound form of the term. Second, a choice is made between two or more synonyms available to express the same concept. Third, a decision is to be made on whether to admit, and how to treat, certain types of terms, such as loan words, slang words, trade names and proper names. Fourth, the meaning of the term, which in a dictionary might be accompanied by illustrations of different usage, is deliberately restricted to that most effective for the purposes of a particular thesaurus. The restriction is indicated in a thesaurus by the addition of scope notes and definitions, and qualifying phrases in the case of homographs. All these methods of thesaurus control are dealt with in this section, except for compound terms which are considered in Section E. Synonyms and quasi-synonyms, although mentioned here under choice of term, are dealt with more fully in F1.1.

Vocabulary control recommendations in the International Standard ISO 2788 (International, 1986), British Standard BS 5723 (British, 1987), and US Standard ANSI/NISO Z39.19 (National, 1994) form the basis of the rules discussed in this section. It should be assumed that a rule is covered by all three Standards unless it is stated otherwise.

D1. Indexing terms – preferred and non-preferred

As defined by ISO 2788, and its equivalent BS 5723, an indexing term is 'the representation of a concept'. It can consist of more than one word, and is then known as a compound term. In a controlled language an indexing term may be either a preferred term or a non-preferred term. The preferred term is 'a term used consistently when indexing to represent a given concept'. It is sometimes known as a 'descriptor' or 'keyword'. A non-preferred term is the 'synonym or quasi-synonym of a preferred term'. It is not used in indexing, but provides a 'lead-in' or entry point from which the user may be directed by the instruction USE to the appropriate preferred term. The non-preferred term is also known as a 'non-descriptor'. The term 'descriptor' is used rather than 'preferred term' in the US Standard ANSI/NISO Z39.19.

D2. Indexing terms – general categories

The concepts represented by indexing terms belong to general categories. These include the fundamental categories used in the technique of facet analysis, described in F2.2 below. Three main categories and their sub-divisions are set out in ISO 2788, these being concrete entities, abstract concepts and proper nouns.

Examples:

Concrete entities

Things and their physical parts
PRIMATES
HEAD
BUILDINGS
FLOORS
ISLANDS

Materials
CEMENT
WOOD
ALUMINIUM
COATINGS
REFRIGERANTS

Abstract concepts

Actions and events
EVOLUTION
RESPIRATION
SKATING
MANAGEMENT
WARS
CEREMONIES

Abstract entities, and properties of things, materials and actions
LAW
THEORY
STRENGTH
EFFICIENCY

Disciplines and sciences
PHYSICS
METEOROLOGY
PSYCHOLOGY

Units of measurement
KILOGRAMS
METRES

Individual entities, or 'classes of one', expressed as proper nouns

NIGERIA
COMMISSION ON HUMAN RIGHTS
LAKE SUPERIOR

The ANSI Standard sets out a similar list without the major division between concrete entities and abstract concepts. The lists in the Standards are not intended to be exhaustive.

These categories have importance in deciding whether the singular or plural form is to be used and in determining the validity of hierarchical relationships, as well as in the analysis of subject fields.

D3. Indexing terms – form of term

An obvious step in vocabulary control is to regulate the form of admissible indexing terms. This section considers acceptable grammatical forms, singular and plural forms, variable spellings, transliteration, punctuation and capitalization, abbreviations and acronyms. Terms in compound form are treated in E2.

D3.1. Grammatical forms – Nouns, adjectives, adverbs, articles

D3.1.1. Nouns and noun phrases

Indexing terms usually consist of nouns and noun phrases. The most common form of noun phrase is the adjectival phrase.

Examples:

WOMEN WORKERS
BRITTLE FRACTURE
FLASH LAMPS
FLUVIAL SOILS
PRINT MEDIA
URBAN COMMUNITIES

The less common, but still admissible, form is the prepositional form

Example:

PHILOSOPHY OF EDUCATION

The ANSI Standard recommends that when possible, the noun phrase should exclude prepositions and that, for example, 'Educational philosophy' should be preferred to 'Philosophy of education'. Indexing terms in the form of prepositional noun phrases 'should be limited to concepts which cannot be expressed in any other way, or that have become idiomatic'.

Examples:

PROOF OF NATIONALITY
RIGHT OF ASSEMBLY
HEADS OF STATE
HEAT OF DISSOCIATION

D3.1.2. Adjectives

According to the Standards, adjectives are not generally acceptable as indexing terms, although some thesauri contain a limited number of broadly-applicable adjectives relating to time, conditions, size, shape, position and the like. The ANSI Standard does not recommend the use of adjectives in isolation, but it does accept that they may appear as separate preferred terms 'when designed to be pre-coordinated in indexing or post-coordinated in searching'.

Examples:

SIMULTANEOUS
MINIATURE
VARIABLE
AUXILIARY
PORTABLE
AXIAL
RECTANGULAR

In pre-coordinate indexing strings and in post-coordinate systems these adjectives may represent the adjectival components of compound terms when combined with the appropriate nouns.

Examples:

Miniature paintings
USE PAINTINGS and MINIATURE

Auxiliary workers
USE WORKERS and AUXILIARY

Portable typewriters
USE TYPEWRITERS and PORTABLE

Rectangular windows
USE WINDOWS and RECTANGULAR

This use of adjectives is not mentioned in ISO 2788 and BS 5723. It may be deduced, however, that it would not be favoured, as most of the compound terms that are factored by this use of adjectives are recommended by the Standard to be retained in compound form, being mainly entities and actions qualified by their properties (see E2). If it is necessary to include these concepts in the thesaurus, whether for use in isolation or as part of a factored compound term, a possible solution, although not mentioned in the Standards, might be to present them in the noun form.

Examples:

MINIATURE SIZE
PORTABLE DEVICES
AXIAL POSITION
TRIANGULAR SHAPE

The Standards, while recommending that the use of adjectives should be limited as far as possible, give an instance where they would be accepted. Adjectives may be used alone when a reference is made from a noun to an adjective that is the first word of several compound terms, especially if the adjectives and nouns differ widely in their spellings. For example, from the noun Netherlands to the adjective Dutch, or from the noun Kidney to the adjective Renal. *See also* references may also be made in the opposite direction, adjective to noun, as in Renal to Kidney. This applies in the case of both printed thesauri and on-screen displays.

D3.1.3. Adverbs

Adverbs such as 'very' and 'highly' are excluded from thesauri, unless they form part of a compound term.

Example:

VERY LARGE SCALE INTEGRATION

D3.1.4. Verbs

Verbs in the infinitive or participle form are also excluded. Nouns, and verbal nouns, including gerunds, represent them in the thesaurus.

Examples:

COMMUNICATION	(*not* COMMUNICATE)
ADMINISTRATION	(*not* ADMINISTER)
WALKING	(*not* WALK)
MACHINING	(*not* MACHINE)
DELIVERY	(*not* DELIVER)

D3.1.5. Initial articles

The use of initial articles is not mentioned in ISO 2788 and BS 5723, but it is covered in the ANSI Standard. The guidance in the Standard is that the use of initial articles should be avoided, if possible. The initial article should be deleted if the indexing term is clear without it. If not, a parenthetical qualifier should be used.

Examples:

THEATRE	*and not*	The theatre
STATE (political entity)	*and not*	The state

The initial article should be retained if it is an integral part of a proper name, and should be searchable. It should be included in the indexing term in direct order, but if not possible, in inverted order. Whether or not the article is included as an integral part of the name is dependent upon the language. The following examples would be acceptable in an English-language thesaurus.

LE MANS
EL SALVADOR
NARROWS, THE
REALLY USEFUL GROUP, THE

Where the article is included in direct order, a cross-reference from the element following the article should be made. For example, 'Mans use LE MANS'.

D3.2. Singular and plural forms

In languages where the distinction between singular and plural forms can be made, compilers are influenced by the traditions of their own language communities. Those working in the French and German languages, for example, tend to prefer the singular, with a limited number of exceptions, such as where the singular and plural forms have different meanings. In English-speaking communities, terms may be expressed in either the singular or the plural, determined by rules set out in the Standards, which are considered in this section.

When deciding upon the use of singular and plural forms in the English language, it is useful to divide terms into the two basic categories of concrete entities and abstract concepts, described in D2.

D3.2.1. Concrete entities

These include 'count nouns' and 'non-count nouns'.

Count nouns are defined as 'names of countable objects that are subject to the question "How many?" but not "How much?"' and are given as plurals.

Examples:

PLANETS
ESTUARIES
PLOUGHS
CHILDREN
AQUARIA

The rules are modified in the case of parts of the body. Plurals are used when more than one part occurs in a 'fully-formed organism', but if only one is present the singular is preferred.

Examples:

| EYES | *but* | MOUTH |
| ARMS | | RESPIRATORY SYSTEM |

The ANSI Standard suggests another possible but not mandatory exception to the plural count noun. In the case of museum catalogues, 'objects are typically given as unique items', and for this reason indexing terms should be given in the singular.

Examples:

WARDROBE
VASE

Non-count nouns are defined as 'names of materials or substances which are subject to the question "How much?" but not "How many?"', and are expressed as singulars.

Examples:

NICKEL
MICA
SNOW
FLOUR
LACE

This rule is more flexible, and consequently more ambiguous, than the 'count nouns' rule, since it allows exceptions in cases when 'the community of users served by the index regards a given substance or material as a class with more than one member. The class should then be expressed in the plural'.

Examples:

STEELS
FRUITS
CEMENTS

D3.2.2. Abstract concepts

Abstract concepts, comprising abstract entities and phenomena, properties, systems of belief, activities and disciplines are shown in the singular form.

Examples:

Abstract entities and phenomena

AUTHORITY
LOGIC
SOCIAL DISTANCE

Properties

PHOTOCONDUCTIVITY
HARDENABILITY
ECCENTRICITY
EMOTIONAL INSTABILITY

Systems of belief

SOCIALISM
HINDUISM

Actions

EXPLORATION
FUSION
PACKAGING
CONFLICT

Disciplines

BIOCHEMISTRY
ENGINEERING
ETHNOLOGY

As for non-count concrete entities, if an abstract concept is regarded as 'a class with more than one member', the term representing that class is expressed in the plural.

Examples:

INFORMATION STUDIES
BIOLOGICAL SCIENCES
IDEOLOGIES
EMOTIONS

D3.2.3. Unique entities

The ANSI Standard recommends that the names of unique entities, whether concrete or abstract, should be expressed in the singular.

Examples:

BIG BEN
RAINBOW'S END

D3.2.4. Co-existence of singulars and plurals

Occasionally, the singular and plural of the same word will have different meanings. When this occurs, both terms are entered in the thesaurus. If necessary, the distinction should be shown by adding a qualifying term or phrase to both terms.

Example:

COATINGS (material)   *or*   COATING (process)

The qualifier is an integral part of the indexing term, and is not a scope note.

Another solution, not mentioned in the Standards, is to change one of the terms into a compound term.

COATING (process)   COATING PROCESS

D3.2.5. Reference from non-preferred to preferred forms

Entry points are not normally given in the thesaurus from the non-preferred to the preferred singular and plural form. An exception is made when the difference in spelling separates the two forms of the term in the alphabetical sequence.

Example:

Foot
USE FEET

D3.3. Spelling

Spelling should conform to a recognized dictionary or glossary, and/or to the house style of the organization responsible for the thesaurus. In any case, the most acceptable spelling for the intended users of the thesaurus should be adopted. This rule extends to the choice between spellings made for cultural reasons, for example, between English-English and American-English. In thesauri originating in the United Kingdom, English-English should be used, consistently, with a note in the introduction stating this policy. Reference should be made from commonly-recognized variant spellings to the preferred forms. This rule applies also to references from American-English spellings to English-English in thesauri using English-English, when the thesaurus is likely to be used extensively by American-English language communities. However, it has been argued (Svenonius, 1986), that it may not be necessary to control spelling variations where these variations are systematic in nature and a program could be written which would automatically equate, for example 'fiber' and 'fibre', in searching. Examples of references between terms with different spellings are given in F1.1.2a.

D3.4. Transliteration, Romanization

To ensure consistency in transliterating or Romanizing terms from languages with different alphabets, the relevant ISO Standards, national standards or accepted library schemes should be consulted and followed as far as possible.

The ANSI Standard recommends that 'commonly-accepted spellings for terms written in non-Roman scripts, as found in authoritative reference sources, are preferable to systematic Romanization', that is applying a table to convert the characters from non-

Roman to Roman ones. A cross-reference should be given from the systematic Romanization to the established spelling.

Example:

CHEBYSHEV POLYNOMIALS
   UF Tchebyshev polynomials

Tchebyshev polynomials
   USE CHEBYSHEV POLYNOMIALS

It also recommends that, where the choice exists, a Romanization system that uses few or no diacritical marks should be selected.

D3.5. Punctuation, Capitalization

D3.5.1. Punctuation and non-alphabetic characters

ISO 2788 and BS 5723 do not have rules on punctuation and non-alphabetic characters, so that the house style of the organization responsible for the individual thesaurus may be the influencing factor in this area. It is, however, generally assumed that punctuation and non-alphabetic characters should be restricted. On the other hand, the ANSI Standard does include a section on this that covers parentheses, hyphens, apostrophes, diacritical marks and other symbols and punctuation marks. It recommends that established orthographic authorities should be used to determine when such characters are essential.

(a) Parentheses
Parentheses should be used only to enclose qualifiers (see D3.1.5, D3.2.4, D5.1) and for trademark indicators (see D4.3.1), or when they constitute part of a term.

Example:

N (2 FLUORENYL) ACETAMIDE

Although not mentioned in the Standards, parentheses may sometimes be used instead of a comma in the indirect entry of a compound term leading in to the direct form.

(b) Apostrophes
Unlike ISO 2788 and BS 5723, the ANSI Standard sets out firm guidelines on apostrophes indicating the possessive case. These should be retained in common nouns and proper names, whether in the singular or plural.

Examples:

CHILDREN'S HOSPITALS
FRENCHMAN'S CREEK

(c) Hyphens
The lack of rules on hyphens in the International and British Standards results in differences in practice, particularly in the treatment of prefixes in English language thesauri. However, the ANSI Standard does include rules on hyphens, and these are given below.

Hyphens in compound terms are avoided where possible.

Examples:

LONG TERM PLANNING
MEDIUM SIZE ENTERPRISES
PART TIME WORK
SELF EMPLOYMENT

The Standard does not specifically state that hyphens following prefixes should be removed, the space dropped, and the prefix be attached to the base word, although an example of the term 'Nonfiction' included in the Standard illustrates this rule. Other examples of hyphens removed to give attached prefixes are given below:

ANTISEMITISM
INSERVICE TRAINING
MULTIETHNIC SOCIETY
POSTGRADUATE COURSES
SEMISKILLED WORK

The Standard suggests that hyphens should be retained only when dropping them would lead to ambiguity, or when they occur as part of abbreviations, trade marks, chemical names or proper names. This includes another rule, not specifically mentioned but implied in the Standard, that hypens should be retained in letter-word and number-word combinations, or when a part of the compound term is not meaningful when used independently.

Examples:

N-TYPE STARS
5-HYDROXYINDOLE
P-BAND
X-RAY LASER WEAPONS
BERWICK-UPON-TWEED

Another useful rule, again not set out in the Standards, is that the hyphen should be retained to show a relationship between two or more independent concepts.

Examples:

CENTRE-PERIPHERY THEORY
NORTH-SOUTH COOPERATION
PARENT-TEACHER RELATIONSHIP
PROTON-NEUTRON INTERACTION

For rules for filing terms containing hyphens see H2.4.

(d) Diacritical marks
The Standard suggests that diacritical marks may be used if they are required for proper names or by the accepted standards of a discipline.

Examples:

MOSSBAÜER EFFECT
PACT OF SAN JOSÉ

(e) Other symbols and punctuation marks

The Standard recommends that symbols, such as the ampersand, and punctuation marks should be used only in trademarks and proper names because they create filing and searching problems.

Examples:

MARKS & SPENCER
CSMA/CD NETWORKS
RTL/2

D3.5.2. Capitalization

ISO 2788 and BS 5723 do not cover capitalization, but the ANSI Standard makes a recommendation on the capitalization of indexing terms, which does not appear to have been followed closely in English-language thesauri outside the United States.

It recommends that predominantly lower-case characters should be used in indexing terms. It recommends that 'capitals should be used only for the initial letter(s) of proper names, trade names, and for those components of taxonomic names, such as genus, which are conventionally capitalized; for all the letters of initialisms; or where featured in unusual positions in product or corporate names'. Since lowercase letters may also occur in unusual positions in proper names, 'using a combination of capitals and lowercase letters in thesauri indicates to the user the correct orthography of a term in natural language and serves to distinguish common nouns from similar proper names'.

Examples:

Dbase IV (Trademark)
PERT
CompuServe
information systems
Information System Corp.

D3.6. Abbreviations, initialisms, and acronyms

Abbreviations and acronyms may be used as indexing terms only when they have become so well known generally, or in a specialized field, that the abbreviated form is more familiar and the full form of the term is rarely used. LASER, for example, could be shown without its full form, 'Light amplification by stimulated emission of radiation' being given as an entry point. The full form of the term should be used when the abbreviated form is not widely used or generally understood.

Examples:

AIDS TO DAILY LIVING	ADL
HORMONE REPLACEMENT THERAPY	HRT
BRITISH SIGN LANGUAGE	BSL

The full form of the term should also be used if the abbreviation could represent two different indexing terms.

Example:

BBC/BRITISH BROADCASTING CORPORATION
BBC/BROWN BOVERI COMPANY

More examples of abbreviated and full form of terms are given in F1.1.2c.

D4. Indexing terms – choice of terms

In this section, various types of terms and choices between them are considered. These include loan words, neologisms, slang, trade names, scientific terms, place names and proper names. Further detail on choice between terms is given in F1.1. which deals with synonyms and quasi-synonyms.

D4.1. Loan words

Loan words, borrowed from other languages which have become well established in the borrowing language, should be admitted to the thesaurus.

Examples:

SUB JUDICE
ENTENTE CORDIALE
AQUA REGIA
FEMME FATALE

If a translation exists, but is not frequently used, it should be treated as a non-preferred term, and a reciprocal reference made between it and the loan word with the prefixed UF (use for) and USE.

Examples:

WELTSCHMERZ
    UF World weariness

World weariness
    USE WELTSCHMERZ

GLASNOST
    UF Openness in politics

Openness in politics
    USE GLASNOST

Should the translation or nearest equivalent term become more frequently used than the loan word, the loan word should be relegated to the status of a non-preferred term.

Example:

SOCIOCULTURAL ANIMATION
    UF Animation socioculturelle

Animation socioculturelle
    USE SOCIOCULTURAL ANIMATION

The ANSI Standard suggests rules for foreign-language terms, i.e., terms that have not become naturalized in the language of the thesaurus, which should be linked to terms in the preferred language in cases where the foreign terms are likely to be sought by users. The language chosen for the indexing term should be that which the user would be likely to expect, with a cross-reference from the equivalent term in the other language.

Example:

PENTECOST (*English*)
    UF Shavot (*Hebrew*)

Shavot
    USE PENTECOST

D4.2. Neologisms, slang terms and jargon

Neologisms, slang or jargon terms often cover new concepts originating within a particular speciality, subculture or social group. Such terms are generally not included in standard dictionaries. When no widely accepted alternative exists, the neologism, slang or jargon term should be accepted as a descriptor.

Examples:

DROP-INS
LATCHKEY CHILDREN
JOYRIDING
WHISTLEBLOWING
MONEY LAUNDERING

The ANSI Standard makes the additional suggestion that a neologism, slang or jargon term may be labelled 'provisional' and may be promoted to full indexing-term status when the term becomes accepted into the language.

A slang term that is an alternative to an existing and well-established term should be admitted as an entry term if it is so widely recognized that it might serve as the user's access point.

Examples:

BEFRIENDING
    UF Buddying

Buddying
    USE BEFRIENDING

Further examples of reference between slang and standard terms are given in F1.1.1c.

D4.3. Common names and trade names

The Standards recommend that where an equivalent common name exists, it should be used in preference to the trade name, because the common name is the more accurate representation of the concept.

The trade name should be admitted as a non-preferred term only if it is likely to be sought by the user. Examples of common and trade names are given in F1.1.1b.

The ANSI Standard recognises that both common names and trade names may be indexing terms in thesauri that cover generic products as well as specific brands. In this case trade names would be treated as narrower terms.

D4.3.1. Trademarks

The ANSI Standard, but not the ISO 2788 and BS 5723, suggests that as trademarks are recognized by law as proprietary, they should be identified as such in the thesaurus. One of four possible designations would be appropriate. These include: (Trademark), (TM), (Reg) or (R).

Example:

ANADIN (R)
OVALTINE (TM)

A trademark may be used as an indexing term without qualification only after its legal protection is lost.

Example:

ASPIRIN

D4.4. Popular names and scientific names

Where there is a choice between popular and scientific names, it is the advice of the Standards to choose the form most likely to be sought by the users of the thesaurus. In a thesaurus for a medical community the term RUBELLA might be used, whereas in a general or social-welfare thesaurus the popular form GERMAN MEASLES might be preferred. Reciprocal references should be made between the two forms of the term. Further examples of popular and scientific terms are given in F1.1.1a.

D4.5. Place names

Where there is a choice of more than one name for a country or geographical region within a single-language community, for reasons such as the following

(a) an 'official' and a 'popular' name are both in common use:

Example:

BURMA
MYANMAR

(b) the original (or anglicized) and the vernacular form co-exist:

Example:

IVORY COAST
CÔTE D'IVOIRE

the name that is most familiar to the users of the thesaurus should be designated as the preferred term. Other things being equal, preference should be given to the official rather than the popular name. Reciprocal references should be made between the preferred and non-preferred versions. The short form of the official name should be preferred. Where standard authorities exist, they should be consulted on the official forms (for example, the U.S. Board on Geographic Names).

Examples:

MYANMAR
   UF Burma

Burma
   USE MYANMAR

IVORY COAST
   UF Côte d'Ivoire

Côte d'Ivoire
   USE IVORY COAST

TANZANIA
   UF United Republic of Tanzania

United Republic of Tanzania
   USE TANZANIA

D4.6. Identifiers: proper names of institutions, persons, etc.

Although identifiers, that is proper names of persons, institutions, organizations, processes, types of equipment, laws, titles and places, are important access points for the retrieval of information, they are often excluded from the thesaurus, or their numbers are limited. Identifiers that are not included in the thesaurus may be held in a separate file, which controls the form of the proper name as for standard cataloguing practice but gives no structural relationships, or they may be left uncontrolled.

Frequency of need to access proper names is the usual reason for including identifiers in the main thesaurus; for example, in the case of a thesaurus on international relations, where country names are an integral part of the subject field. Other reasons for including proper names may be that the distinction between common terms and proper names is not distinct, or that it may be useful to link a class with its instances hierarchically, for example, 'Disablement benefits' with specific allowances, such as 'Mobility allowance'.

When proper names are included in a thesaurus, the form of the name should conform to the rules of a recognized code of cataloguing practice, such as the *Anglo-American cataloguing rules*. These names can sometimes vary, depending upon their origins, in which case ISO 2788 and BS 5723 recommend that the following rules be followed.

(a) Names of national and local institutions that conduct their business (including publishing) in one language should be entered in their untranslated forms. A reference from the translated form should be made if it exists.

Example:

CENTRO DE DOCUMENTACÂO CIENTIFICA
    UF Centre for Scientific Documentation (Lisbon)

Centre for Scientific Documentation (Lisbon)
    USE CENTRO DE DOCUMENTACÂO CIENTIFICA

(b) Names of international organizations, or local organizations that publish documents in more than one language, should be given in the form most familiar to the users of the thesaurus, with references from other forms if the thesaurus is likely to be used by members of other language communities.

Examples:

INTERNATIONAL FEDERATION FOR INFORMATION AND
    DOCUMENTATION
        UF Fédération International de l'Information et Documentation

Fédération International de l'Information et Documentation
    USE INTERNATIONAL FEDERATION FOR INFORMATION AND
        DOCUMENTATION

(c) Personal names should be given in their original forms, unless the local form of name, notably of historical figures who have achieved international recognition, is better known to the users of the thesaurus. In this case the local name is preferred and a reference made from the original form.

Example (in an English-language thesaurus):

HENRY OF NAVARRE
    UF Henri de Navarre

Henri de Navarre
    USE HENRY OF NAVARRE

D5. Indexing terms – restriction and clarification of meaning

D5.1. Homographs and homonyms

Homographs are words having the same spelling as another but differing in origin and meaning.

Example:

CELLS
which may refer to biological microsystems or electrical equipment.

Homographs may also have different pronunciations.

Example:

READING
which may refer to a communication process or to the town in England.

Homographs are sometimes referred to as polysemes, 'of many meanings', or as homonyms. Homonyms may be defined broadly as 'the same word used to denote different things', or more narrowly as 'words having the same sound but different meanings', that is, only one possible pronunciation (see CELLS above).

The usual method of removing ambiguities caused by homographs is to add qualifiers (printed within parentheses) after the terms, to distinguish the two or more different meanings.

Examples:

CELLS   (biology)
CELLS   (electric)

READING   (place)
READING   (process)

The qualifier becomes an integral part of the term. An alternative method, possible in some cases, is to represent one or both of the meanings by a compound term in the direct form.

Example:

CELLS or (BIOLOGICAL CELLS)
ELECTRIC CELLS

An entry point should be made from the word Cells in the compound term to the full term.

Examples:

Cells, electric
    USE ELECTRIC CELLS

Additional rules on methods of dealing with homographs are given in the ANSI Standard. These rules cover the form of the qualifier, which, ideally, should consist of one word. Qualifiers should be standardized within a given thesaurus as far as possible. For example, 'building' and 'construction', or 'biology' and 'bioscience' should not both be used as qualifiers.

The Standard also includes guidance on when qualifiers should be applied. Qualifiers should be added to entry terms as well as to the preferred terms, when this is necessary. A qualifier should be added to each homographic term, even when one is used in the primary sense of the domain and the second in a different sense. For example, 'reactors (nuclear)' should be the form of the term in an engineering thesaurus that also includes 'reactors (electric)'. A qualifier should be appended to a homographic term even when a descriptor is used in only one of its meanings within a thesaurus, for example, 'shafts (mines)' in a mining thesaurus. This facilitates cross-database searching and mapping of indexing terms in disparate subject fields.

The Standard also identifies instances when parenthetical qualifiers should not be used to represent compound concepts. For example, 'shafts (steel)' should not be used, as 'steel' here is used to indicate a type of shaft and not to disambiguate the word 'shaft'.

A compound term is preferred to the use of a parenthetical qualifier with a single term, if usage permits, i.e., if the compound term occurs in natural language.

Examples:

| WATER POLLUTION | *not* | POLLUTION (water) |
| MULTILATERAL TREATIES | *not* | TREATIES (multilateral) |

D5.2. Scope notes (SNs) and definitions

The symbol SN is used to represent scope notes, which sometimes include definitions. A scope note or definition is not regarded as forming part of the term to which it refers, as is the case with the qualifier attached to a homograph.

D5.2.1. Definitions

As a general rule, in the past, complete definitions, as found in a dictionary, have not been given in thesauri, but limited definitions, and even expanded definitions, have sometimes been needed to supplement the meaning conveyed by the thesaurus structure.

As the trend is now towards the blurring of the difference between thesauri and terminological databanks, the tendency appears to be towards the increase in the number of definitions in thesauri. Svenonius advocates the inclusion of as much definitional material as possible (Svenonius, 1997). More attention appears to be given to the form of definitions. For example, a model is suggested (Hudon, 1996) for preparing logical definitions for indexing and retrieval thesauri.

Research seems to show that definitions increase indexer consistency, but indexers using thesauri having definitions, but no associative relations, perform less well than with a standard thesaurus without definitions (Hudon, 1998).

Definitions tend to be necessary most frequently in social science and humanities thesauri, to clarify imprecise terminology, which occurs more often in these subject areas.

Examples:

CULTURAL MODELS
   SN Systems of relations providing specific arrangements for each particular culture and regulating for each individual member the behaviour he must have in order to function as a member of his group.

SEGREGATION
   SN Involuntary or voluntary concentration of particular groups (especially ethnic groups) in particular areas, or restriction of access of such groups to particular facilities or opportunities.

ASYLUM
   SN Protection granted by a State on its territory against the exercise of jurisdiction by the State of origin, based on the principle of non-refoulement and characterized by the enjoyment of internationally-recognized refugee rights, and generally accorded without limit of time.

The source of the definition may be added, in parentheses, at the end of the definition. A code may be used to represent the source, and full details of the source should be given in the thesaurus introduction.

D5.2.2. Scope notes

The scope note, as opposed to the definition, is used in the thesaurus in several ways.

(a) Indication of restrictions on meaning
It may be used to show restriction placed on the meaning of a preferred term.

Example:

INCOME
SN Income of individual organization or person.
Otherwise use 'National Income'.

(b) Indication of range of topics covered
It may be used to specify the range of topics covered by a concept for which only the generic term is included in the thesaurus. This occurs in marginal fields, or in thesauri covering a wide range of subjects at a limited depth.

Example:

MECHANICAL COMPONENTS
SN Includes manipulating parts, separating parts, linkages, inertial parts, seals and gaskets, bearings, fasteners, chains, machinery belts, etc.

(c) Instructions to indexers
The scope note may also serve to convey instruction to indexers on how indexing terms should be used, especially regarding the treatment of compound terms.

Example:

INTERIOR LIGHTING
SN For lighting of specific buildings or spaces, combine with appropriate terms, e.g. 'Shop lighting' use 'Shops' and 'Interior lighting'.

(d) Indication of 'dummy terms'
The scope note is also used to indicate 'dummy terms', that is terms needed to elucidate the structure of a systematic display (see H3), but which are themselves unsuitable for indexing. The term would be followed by a classmark in the alphabetical display.

Example:

EDUCATION OF SPECIFIC CATEGORIES OF STUDENTS   BV
SN Do not use as an indexing term.
NT Exceptional student education
NT Parent education
NT Women's education

(e) Term histories
The scope note may also provide term histories, indicating, for example, when a term was adopted, or when changes in the scope of a term took place:

Example:

TRANSIT TIME NOISE
SN Invalid term. After 1981 Random noise used.

The ANSI Standard recommends that this information should be recorded separately in a history note (HN). This would record date of entry, and track the history of modifications, recording previous forms with reasons for change. Where obsolete descriptors are retained but are not assigned in indexing, the date of replacement and reasons for it should be given.

(f) Reciprocal scope notes

The ANSI Standard recommends the use of reciprocal scope notes. When a reference is made to other preferred terms in a scope note, a reciprocal scope note should generally be provided for each preferred term mentioned,

Example:

DEPARTMENT FOR EDUCATION AND EMPLOYMENT
    SN Previously Department for Education. In July 1995 merged with the **Department of Employment** to become Department for Education and Employment.

DEPARTMENT OF EMPLOYMENT
    SN On July 1995 merged with the Department for Education to become the **Department for Education and Employment**.

Even where the scope of only one of the preferred terms requires clarification, it is useful to note in the term record for the second preferred term that it has been cited in a scope note of a different preferred term.

Example:

DIPLOMATIC PROTECTION
    SN The entitlement in international law for a State to protect its **Nationals** who have suffered injuries from another State from which they have been unable to obtain satisfaction.

NATIONALS
    X SN Diplomatic protection

The X preceding the scope note for 'Nationals' indicates that there is a reference in the scope note for 'Diplomatic protection' to the term 'Nationals'. This reciprocal reference will ensure that when a change is made to one of the preferred terms, or it is deleted, the effect on the other preferred term will be considered.

Section E: Specificity and compound terms

E1. Vocabulary specificity

The specificity of a retrieval language vocabulary depends on the ability of the indexing terms to express the subject in depth and in detail. Specificity has an important influence on the performance of the language, as it determines the accuracy with which concepts may be defined and consequently the facility to exclude unwanted documents.

In Figure 2 the specificity increases from indexing language A to indexing language D. In system A the concept 'Brown bread' will be indexed by the term 'Food', and in B by 'Bakery products', in system C by 'Bread' and in D by the identical term 'Brown bread'. If a lead-in is included in the entry vocabulary to the broader term under which the term is subsumed in A, B and C, there is an equal chance of recalling documents indexed on these topics in all four systems.

However, all four systems do not perform equally well in excluding unwanted material. In system A, 'Brown bread' will be recalled with all documents referring to 'Food'; in system B with all documents on 'Bakery products'; and in system C with documents on all types of 'Bread'. Only in system D will no irrelevant documents be recalled (except for those which may have been incorrectly indexed). With a good entry vocabulary, recall performance is not affected by specificity of the language, although precision is.

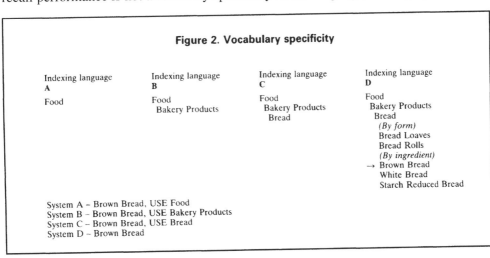

Figure 2. Vocabulary specificity

Indexing language A	Indexing language B	Indexing language C	Indexing language D
Food	Food Bakery Products	Food Bakery Products Bread	Food Bakery Products Bread *(By form)* Bread Loaves Bread Rolls *(By ingredient)* → Brown Bread White Bread Starch Reduced Bread

System A – Brown Bread, USE Food
System B – Brown Bread, USE Bakery Products
System C – Brown Bread, USE Bread
System D – Brown Bread

The disadvantage of a highly specific vocabulary is that the number of indexing terms is increased, (sometimes dramatically – consider a hierarchy where every term has five more specific terms and so on!) and it is consequently more expensive to compile, maintain, and operate. To construct a specific vocabulary, subject fields must be described accurately, which calls for greater knowledge of the terms, their meanings and relationships. The problems of term selection, organization and display are multiplied. Changes are needed more frequently in a specific vocabulary than in a system using only the more static broader concepts as indexing terms.

To reduce effort and expense, select a lower level of specificity, and recall will not be lost if lead-in entries are made from the specific concepts to the broader term or terms in combination used to represent them. As is illustrated in Figure 2 there are varying levels of specificity that may be chosen. In the same system different levels of specificity will be appropriate: a high level of specificity for areas central to the subject field and lower levels in the intermediate and marginal areas.

E2. Compound terms: levels of pre-coordination

According to the International Standard ISO 2788, 'it is a general rule that terms in a thesaurus should represent simple or unitary concepts as far as possible, and compound terms should be factored (i.e. split) into simple elements, except when this is likely to affect the users' understanding'. In practice, this is one of the most difficult rules to follow as in specialist fields unitary concepts may be defined differently and in respect of local needs.

In a thesaurus, 'complex subjects should be expressed by the combination of separate terms and these may be assigned as independent search keys in a post-coordinate system, or they may function as components of pre-coordinated index entries'.

Example:

The phrase
'Workload of dentists in Scotland'
factors into
WORKLOAD + DENTISTS + SCOTLAND

A difficult and constantly occurring problem in thesaurus construction is knowing when to factor compound terms into simpler terms, and when it may be better for system performance to retain the compound term (also known as the pre-coordinated term). A thesaurus having a majority of single terms is said to have a low pre-coordination level, and one with many two- or three-word compound terms is said to have a high pre-coordination level.

E2.1. Structure of compound terms

A compound term may be either an *adjectival phrase*, such as DRIED VEGETABLES or a *prepositional phrase*, such as PHILOSOPHY OF EDUCATION.

A compound term may be analysed into two parts: the focus and the difference.

• The focus

This is the noun component, also known as the genus term or the head, which, in the words of ISO 2788, identifies the broader class of things or events to which the term as a whole refers.

Examples

VEGETABLES
in the adjectival phrase DRIED VEGETABLES
PHILOSOPHY
in the prepositional phrase PHILOSOPHY OF EDUCATION

In a one-word term such as VEGETABLES or PHILOSOPHY the word *is* the focus.

- The difference

This is the part of the compound term, also known as the modifier or species term, which refers to a characteristic, or a logical difference, which when applied to a focus, narrows its connotation and so specifies one of its subclasses.

Examples:

DRIED
which specifies a subclass of vegetables in DRIED VEGETABLES
OF EDUCATION
which specifies a subclass of philosophy in PHILOSOPHY OF EDUCATION

E2.2. Order of words in compound terms

Natural language order (also known as direct form) should be used to enter compound terms in a thesaurus.

Examples:

DRIED VEGETABLES, not VEGETABLES, DRIED
PHILOSOPHY OF EDUCATION, not EDUCATION, PHILOSOPHY OF
(note the adjectival phrase Educational philosophy is acceptable)
WATER SOURCES, not SOURCES, WATER

Reciprocal entries should always be made from the indirect form of the prepositional phrase, but in the case of the adjectival phrase, only if the focal noun, for example 'sources' in 'Water sources', does not appear as an indexing term in the thesaurus (see also F1.1.2 b.).

Examples:

Education, philosophy of, USE PHILOSOPHY OF EDUCATION

Sources, water, USE WATER SOURCES

E2.3. Effect of compound terms on performance

The pre-coordination level of terms in a thesaurus is directly related to the specificity of the vocabulary. The more complex the indexing terms, the more specific the vocabulary and the greater the total number of terms. One of the factors that affect the pre-coordination level is the generality of the subject field. In a thesaurus covering a limited field, terms may be used without qualification to represent concepts that may be ambiguous in a wider context. For example, in a thesaurus devoted to 'education', the single terms 'buildings', 'testing' may be unequivocal, whereas in a general thesaurus having specific terms for other applications of these concepts, such as 'public buildings', 'mechanical testing', the compound terms 'educational buildings' and 'educational testing' would be needed to distinguish the educational from these other aspects.

E2.3.1. Advantages of compound terms

Compound terms are more exact and specific than single terms used in combination to represent the same concept. They are able to prevent false drops and to ensure good precision.

For instance, a document on 'Fuels selection and water storage capacity in central heating systems' might be correctly indexed by the single terms FUELS, SELECTION, WATER and STORAGE. It would be retrieved as an irrelevant document in a search for the concept 'Fuel storage' using in combination the single terms FUELS and STORAGE, but would be excluded by a search using the compound term FUEL STORAGE.

Another advantage of using compound terms is that the thesaurus displays information about the term (synonyms, broader, narrower and related terms, for example) that is lost if the compound term is factored, unless a special effort is made to show thesaural relationships against the non-preferred term (see 'Syntactical factoring' in E2.4.2(a)).

E2.3.2. Disadvantages of compound terms

A thesaurus with many highly pre-coordinated terms is more expensive to compile and maintain than one having a low pre-coordination level, because of its greater size and complexity. It also adds to indexing problems, as it is necessary to ensure that all the relevant specific, pre-coordinated terms have been assigned to the document. Use of compound terms can also lead to recall loss. This is more of a problem in manual systems, where a search for a part of a compound term rather than the whole term may not retrieve the document. For instance, a search for information on 'Boiler maintenance' using the terms BOILERS and MAINTENANCE would not retrieve documents indexed STEAM BOILERS and ENGINEERING MAINTENANCE, unless the indexer has 'posted up' to the generic terms by indexing the document also under BOILERS and MAINTENANCE. In online searching, the document would be retrieved, as the constituent terms in compound terms may be retrieved independently if the controlled terms are searched using the free-text facility. That is, a search on BOILERS and MAINTENANCE would retrieve the term BOILERS in STEAM BOILERS and MAINTENANCE in ENGINEERING MAINTENANCE.

E.2.3.3. Advantages of factored terms

Factored (also sometimes known as synthesized) terms give a better recall performance than compound terms in manual systems and allow for a smaller and less complex vocabulary. To be most effective the thesaurus should include a substantial entry vocabulary of lead-in terms from the compound form of the factored terms to the factored components.

E2.3.4. Disadvantages of factored terms

Factored terms give a poorer precision performance than compound terms because of their lack of specificity. Recall too may be lost if the entry vocabulary is not adequate.

Without a good entry vocabulary, indexers and searchers may use a different combination of terms to represent a concept, resulting in recall failure.

Another disadvantage is the loss of information in thesaural relationships (i.e., synonyms, broader, narrower and related terms) when the compound term is factored.

E2.4. Rules for the treatment of compound terms

The first Standard to contain detailed procedures for dealing consistently with compound terms was the 1979 edition of British Standard BS 5723, which was drafted by Derek Austin, designer of the *PRECIS indexing system.* A paper on the evolution of guidelines for thesaurus construction (Krooks and Lancaster, 1993) notes that Austin and Dale drew heavily upon the rules in the 1979 British Standard when writing the 1981 revised edition of UNESCO's '*Guidelines for the establishment and development of monolingual thesauri*' (UNESCO, 1981). The rules are repeated in ISO 2788: 1987 and in BS 5723: 1986. In the 1993 edition of the US Standard ANSI/NISO Z39.19, the rules for the treatment of compound terms are substantially the same as in the International and British Standards, with one or two exceptions, noted below.

E2.4.1. Retention of compound terms

The Standards suggest that compound terms should be retained in the following circumstances (see also E.2.4.2(c) Exceptions to the factoring rules).

(a) The compound term has become so familiar in common use, or in the field covered by the thesaurus, that its expression as separate elements would hinder comprehension.

Examples of terms in common use or familiar in certain special fields:

Breaking Factoring Rule 1 (see page 44 below)

WOMENS' RIGHTS
PIPE FITTINGS
GROUP STRUCTURE

Breaking Factoring Rule 2 (see page 45 below)

PATIENT CARE
CHILD MINDING
WASTE DISPOSAL

(b) Compound terms should be retained when factoring would lead to a loss of meaning, or ambiguity.

Example:

GROUP + DISCUSSION
could be either
GROUP DISCUSSION or DISCUSSION GROUP

so the term is retained in the compound form although it breaks Factoring Rule 3 in the ISO 2788 and BS 5723 (see E.2.4.2(b) page 45).

(c) Proper names and terms containing proper names.

Examples:

SALVATION ARMY
LAKE DISTRICT
MARKOV PROCESSES
OEDIPUS COMPLEX

(d) Terms in which the difference has lost its original meaning, so that the meaning of the compound term as a whole is not the sum of the meaning of its parts.

Examples:

CABINET MAKING
MUNICIPAL ENGINEERING

(e) Terms in which one component of the term is not relevant to the scope of the thesaurus or is too vague to exist as an independent term. This rule appears in ANSI/NISO Z39.19 but not in ISO 2788 and BS 5723.

Examples:

PULL TOYS
SPEECH DAYS
COMPOSITE DRAWINGS
FIRST AID

(f) Terms containing a difference that suggests a resemblance, as in a metaphor, to an unrelated thing or event.

Examples:

TWILIGHT AREAS
BLACK ECONOMY

(g) Terms which cannot be re-expressed without the use of an extra noun (or nouns) that are present in the compound term only by implication. This rule does not appear in ANSI/NISO Z39.19.

Examples:

INTEREST HOLIDAYS
i.e. HOLIDAYS for PEOPLE with special INTERESTS

LANGUAGE LABORATORIES
i.e. Education facilities providing AUDIOVISUAL AIDS for the TEACHING of LANGUAGES.

(h) Terms in which the difference is not a valid species of the focus. The noun in these cases is described as syncategorematic, as it cannot stand alone as an indicator of the class of concepts to which the whole of the term refers.

Examples:

PINK ELEPHANTS
Not a species of elephant

RUBBER BONES
Not a species of bone

E2.4.2. Factoring of compound terms

E2.4.2.(a) Factoring techniques

There are two techniques for factoring compound terms – semantic factoring and syntactical factoring.

- Semantic factoring

This technique is applied to single as well as to compound terms. It is defined in ISO 2788 as follows: 'A term which expresses a complex notion is re-expressed in the form of simpler or definitional elements, each of which can also occur in other combinations to represent a range of different concepts'.

Example:

CARDIAC FAILURE
could be re-expressed by a combination of four terms
HEART + OUTPUT + BELOW + NORMAL

Semantic factoring leads to precision loss, and is not recommended by ISO 2788, except for fringe subject areas.

- Syntactical factoring

This technique is applied to compound terms that are 'amenable to morphological analysis into separate components, each of which can be accepted as an indexing term in its own right'.

Example:

COTTON SPINNING
factors into the two terms
COTTON + SPINNING

If the factored compound term is likely to be sought as a lead-in point, the term as a whole should be entered in the thesaurus as a non-preferred term, and a reference should be made to the components of the term used in combination.

Example:

Cotton spinning
    USE COTTON + SPINNING

Reciprocal entries should be made from each term used in combination.

Example:

COTTON
    + SPINNING
    UF Cotton spinning

SPINNING
    + COTTON
    UF Cotton spinning

An alternative method of layout is found in *Thesaurus of engineering and scientific terms (TEST)* and other thesauri modelled on it.

Example:

Cotton spinning
    USE COTTON AND SPINNING

COTTON
    UF †Cotton spinning

SPINNING
    UF †Cotton spinning

Figure 11 from *TEST* (see H2.1) includes an example of a factored term displayed in this style. The entry:

COOLING FINS.
    UF †Finned tubes

shows 'Cooling fins' is one of the two terms used in combination to represent the compound term 'Finned tubes'. The other term, not shown in Figure 11, is 'Tubes'. The main entry for the concept is:

Finned tubes
    USE COOLING FINS AND TUBES

Definitions and thesaural relationships of factored compound terms (synthesized terms) are usually omitted, but it is possible to retain this information while indicating that the term is to be factored.

Example:

Day care of young people
    USE DAY CARE + YOUNG PEOPLE
    BT   DAY CARE
    NT   LATCHKEY PROVISION
    RT   ALTERNATIVE EDUCATION
           INTERMEDIATE TREATMENT
           YOUNG PEOPLE

E2.4.2.(b) Factoring rules

The Standards set out recommendations for syntactical factoring, based upon general criteria. It is stressed that these recommendations are not regarded as mandatory instructions to be rigidly applied in all circumstances. Exceptions are permitted in particular situations. These are discussed in E2.4.2.(c) below.

• Factoring Rule 1

The first rule recommends that 'a compound term should be factored if the focus refers to a property or part (including materials) and the difference represents the whole or a possessor of that property or part'.

Examples:

BICYCLE WHEELS
where BICYCLE is the containing whole and WHEELS is the part, factor:
BICYCLES + WHEELS

HOSPITAL FLOORS
where HOSPITAL is the containing whole and FLOORS is the part, factor:
HOSPITALS + FLOORS

INSTRUMENT RELIABILITY
where INSTRUMENT is the possessor of the property and RELIABILITY is the property, factor:
INSTRUMENTS + RELIABILITY

The rule does allow, however, that 'the name of the thing may be modified by its parts or property'.

Examples:

SPARE WHEELS
EMERGENCY HOSPITALS
PRECISION INSTRUMENTS

- Factoring Rule 2

The second rule recommends that 'the name of a transitive action should not be modified by the name of the patient on which the action is performed'.

Examples:

GLASS CUTTING
where CUTTING is the transitive action and GLASS is the patient of the action, factor:
GLASS + CUTTING

BEARING LUBRICATION
where LUBRICATION is the transitive action and BEARING is the patient of the action, factor:
BEARINGS + LUBRICATION

PILOT TRAINING
where TRAINING is the transitive action and PILOT is the patient of the action, factor:
PILOT + TRAINING

Conversely, the rule allows that 'the name of a thing or material may be modified by the name of the action carried out upon it'.

Examples:

CUT GLASS
LUBRICATED BEARINGS
TRAINED PILOTS

- Factoring Rule 3

The third rule recommends that 'the name of an intransitive action should not be modified by the name of the performer of the action'.

Examples:

BOILER EXPLOSIONS
where EXPLOSIONS is the intransitive action and BOILER is the performer of the action, factor:
BOILERS + EXPLOSIONS

BEAM OSCILLATION
where OSCILLATION is the intransitive action and BEAM is the performer of the action, factor:
BEAMS + OSCILLATION

DOCTOR EMIGRATION
where EMIGRATION is the intransitive action and DOCTOR is the performer of the action, factor:
DOCTORS + EMIGRATION

On the other hand, the rule allows that 'the name of the thing may be modified by the name of the intransitive action in which it is or was engaged'.

Example:

CORRODED BOILERS
OSCILLATING BEAMS
EMIGRATING DOCTORS

An additional rule, not included in the Standards but suggested by Lancaster's *'Vocabulary control'*, chapter 8 (Lancaster, 1986) is that a compound term representing two different principles of division should always be factored.

Example:

UNDERWATER CINE CAMERAS
factors into
UNDERWATER CAMERAS + CINE CAMERAS

The differencing rules in the *Precis manual* (Austin, 1984) also reject as 'lead-terms' those compound terms which include 'a focus modified by more than one difference at the same level'.

Example (PRECIS manual, p. 52):

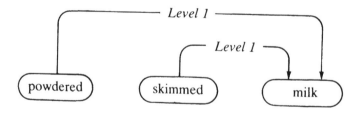

Compound lead-terms in the index:

POWDERED MILK
SKIMMED MILK
but not POWDERED SKIMMED MILK

However, if the differences are not at the same level, the full compound term can appear in the index.

Example (PRECIS manual, p. 53):

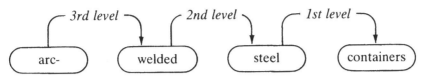

where 'Arc' and 'Welded' refer to 'Steel' and not to 'Containers'.

Compound lead-terms in the index:

ARC-WELDED STEEL CONTAINERS
WELDED STEEL CONTAINERS
STEEL CONTAINERS

E2.4.2.(c) Exceptions to the factoring rules

The Standards allow for the factoring rules to be overridden when certain conditions obtain in a particular information system, so relieving the compiler from constraints that might hinder the ability of the thesaurus to meet the requirements of that system.

The factoring rules may be set aside 'when indexing in a special field requires special treatment'. This means that the nature of the terminology in a given field may call for special criteria to regulate the treatment of compound terms. An example of such special treatment is found in the *Art and architecture thesaurus* (see E.2.4.3 below).

The US Standard suggests that compound terms should be retained when a printed index is used in an information system, if the printed index consists of standalone terms rather than rotated terms in coordinated strings. In such an index the term HOUSING MANAGEMENT is more specific and helpful to the user than the separate, broader headings of HOUSING and MANAGEMENT, although the compound term breaks the second factoring rule.

Another instance, not mentioned in the Standards, when the factoring rules may be ignored, is in the 'master language' of an integrated thesaurus or switching language, which needs to be as specific and pre-coordinated as the most detailed language in the system, in order to operate efficiently (see L2.1.1).

E2.4.3. The Art and Architecture Thesaurus compound term rules

This section discusses Appendix C from the *Guide to indexing and cataloguing with the Art and architecture thesaurus* (Petersen and Barnett, 1995) which gives the *AAT* Compound term rules, and is listed below as Appendix A. The rules are an example of how the Standard rules may be modified to meet the needs of a specialist field.

The *AAT* compilers have clearly given much thought to the problem of compound terms. The rules for the retention of compound terms are divided into two main categories. The first rule, specific to the *AAT*, states that compound terms should be retained if they contain one or more components which are not *AAT* descriptors and are not appropriate to add. Subdivisions of this rule include advice to retain compound terms containing proper nouns, which is common to all the Standards, but covers other rules not in the Standards, for example, the retention of a compound term that includes relational parts of speech, as in 'Chest with drawers' (Rule 1.2). The second retention rule recommends the retention of compound terms when the meaning of the expression cannot be accurately reconstructed from the constituent independent parts. Most often this is because the difference or the focus term changes its meaning in the compound expression. Subdivisions of this rule include two rules that feature in the Standards, but also three rules that do not. An example of the latter is the rule that states that compound terms are to be retained when the difference defines a specific shape or type of the focus term, as in 'Window seats', or 'Basket capitals' (rule 2.3).

The factoring rules have only one recommendation in common with the Standards. This is Rule 4.1: 'When the focus term refers to a property or part, and the modifier (i.e. difference) represents the whole or possessor of that property or part', as in 'Airport lounges', which should be expressed as 'Airport' + 'Lounges'. However, Rule 4.3: 'When the modifier is the location or context of the focus term', as in 'Furniture marks', expressed as 'Furniture' + 'Marks', appears to be closely related to Rule 4.1. The other rules advise factoring where the Standards would recommend retention, but where factoring is appropriate in the specialized field of art and architecture. For example, factoring is recommended if the difference is a style or period, as in 'Impressionist painter', expressed as 'Impressionist' + 'Painter' or when the difference describes a characteristic of the focus term, as in 'Stone floors' or 'Painted chairs', expressed as 'Stone' + 'Floors' and 'Painted' + 'Chairs', or when the difference specifies the scope or content of the focus term, as in 'Textile museums', expressed as 'Textile' + 'Museums'.

Section F: Structure and relationships

An intrinsic feature of a thesaurus is its ability to distinguish and display the structural relationships between the terms it contains. This section deals with the structure and inter-term relationships of the thesaurus and the classification techniques needed to determine these. The associated topic of display of structure and relationships is treated in Section H.

There are two broad types of relationships within a thesaurus. The first is at the micro level and concerns the semantic links between individual terms. The second is at the macro level and is concerned with how the terms and their inter-relationships relate to the overall structure of the subject field.

It is difficult to discover the first type of relationship, the micro level inter-term relationship, without first establishing the structure of the thesaurus at the macro level. It is consequently important to develop a display showing the basic structure of the thesaurus, even if this is not retained after the inter-term relationships have been established.

To determine the structure of the subject field, and the inter-term relationships, classification techniques are used. These include classification in its broadest sense, 'arranging in classes according to a method', and classification with more specific meanings in information work, such as systematic classification, an intellectual operation in which a sequence of classes is brought together and organized by a coding system, or notation.

Classification techniques, including facet analysis, are described in some detail in section F2. Automatic classification, which uses statistical and linguistic techniques to find groupings of terms, is discussed in F4.

F1. Basic thesaural relationships

The thesaurus construction standards stipulate the use of three basic inter-term relationships. These are the equivalence relationship (F1.1), the hierarchical relationship (F1.2) and the associative relationship (F1.3). Critical analysis of these relationships has been made in papers by Willets (1975), Maniez (1988) and Dextre Clarke (2000). Dextre Clarke makes the point that the Standard rules on thesaurus relationships are not always meticulously applied. Such inconsistencies, both between and within thesauri, may be attributable 'not to carelessness, but to pragmatic and subjective decisions about what will serve human users best' (Dextre Clarke, 2000).

F1.1. Equivalence relationships

As defined by the Standards, this is 'the relationship between preferred and non-preferred terms where two or more terms are regarded, for indexing purposes, as referring to the same concept'. In other words, they form an equivalent set. The preferred term is the one chosen to represent the concept in indexing, while the non-preferred term (or terms) is the one not selected. The non-preferred terms form an 'entry vocabulary' directing the user from terms not selected to those that are. The following conventions are used to express the reciprocal relationship.

UF
(Use for)
written as a prefix to the non-preferred term

USE
(or U)
written as a prefix to the preferred term

Example:

PERMITTIVITY
  UF Dielectric constant

Dielectric constant
  USE PERMITTIVITY

In the alphabetical display of a printed thesaurus (see H2), it is usual to distinguish typographically between the preferred and non-preferred terms.

The equivalence relationships includes synonyms, lexical variants, quasi-synonyms, and factored and unfactored forms of compound terms.

F1.1.1. Synonyms

The Standards define synonyms as 'terms whose meanings can be regarded as the same in a wide range of contexts, so that they are virtually interchangeable'. In general linguistics, synonyms are not common, but they do occur more frequently in scientific terminology. This is due to the proliferation of trade names and popular names and other variations depending on local usage and opinion or on etymological root. In all fields, not only scientific, there are more synonyms in controlled language than in natural language, because the meanings of terms are intentionally limited in controlled language.

There are several types of synonyms. Those listed below are typical of true synonyms likely to occur in thesaurus-building.

(a) Popular names and scientific names

Examples:

FLIP-FLOPS/BISTABLE MULTIVIBRATORS
SPIDERS/ARACHNIDA
MERCY KILLING/EUTHANASIA

(b) Common nouns or scientific names, and trade names

Examples:

AMODIAQUININE/CAMOQUIN
POLYMETHYL METHACRYLATE/PERSPEX

(c) Standard names and slang

Examples:

HIGH FIDELITY EQUIPMENT/HI-FI EQUIPMENT
SUPPLEMENTARY EARNINGS/PERKS

(d) Terms of different linguistic origin

Examples:

DOMICILIARY CARE/HOME CARE
ALIENS/FOREIGNERS
GEOMAGNETISM/TERRESTRIAL MAGNETISM
CAECITIS/TYPHLITIS

(e) Terms originating from different cultures sharing a common language

Examples:

AERIALS/ANTENNA
POSTAL SERVICES/MAIL SERVICES
RAILWAYS/RAILROADS
PAVEMENTS/SIDEWALKS

(f) Competing names for emerging concepts

Examples

TELEWORKING/DISTANCE WORKING
INDIVIDUAL DEVELOPMENT PLANNING/ACTION PLANNING

(g) Current or favoured term versus outdated or deprecated term

Examples

DISHWASHERS/WASHING-UP MACHINES
JOB CENTRES/EMPLOYMENT EXCHANGES
CHILDREN'S HOMES/ORPHANAGES
HOVERCRAFT/AIR CUSHION VEHICLES/GROUND EFFECT MACHINES

F1.1.2. Lexical variants

In ANSI/NISO Z39.19, a distinction is made between synonyms which are different terms for the same concepts, and lexical variants which are different word forms for the same expression, such as spelling, grammatical variation, irregular plurals, direct versus indirect order and abbreviated formats (see also D3).

(a) Variant spellings – including stem variants and irregular plurals

Examples:

GIPSIES/GYPSIES
MOSLEMS/MUSLIMS
MOUSE/MICE
FIBRE OPTICS/FIBER OPTICS
HAEMODYNAMICS/HEMODYNAMICS

The last two are examples of differences between standard English and North American spelling.

(b) The direct and indirect form

Example:

ELECTRIC POWER PLANTS/POWER PLANTS, ELECTRIC

Entry under indirect form is required only where the focus of the compound term (POWER PLANTS in the example) is not an indexing term.

In some thesauri both direct and indirect forms of compound terms are made accessible, not by entry terms in the main alphabetical display, but by means of a separate permuted index (see H2.3).

It has been suggested (Svenonius, 1986) that entry under the indirect form is unnecessary where the two syntactic variants may be described by an algorithm either built into the system or easily constructed by a user at the time of each search.

(c) Abbreviations and full names.

Examples:

ECG/ELECTROCARDIOGRAPHY
INDOR/INTERNATIONAL DOUBLE RESONANCE
TQM/TOTAL QUALITY MANAGEMENT

(see also D3.6)

The selection of preferred terms from among possible synonyms should always be influenced by the needs of the users of the thesaurus. These will vary, depending on such factors as whether subjects are treated at a general or detailed level, or from the popular or specialist or scientific viewpoint. Whichever alternatives are adopted, they should be applied consistently throughout the thesaurus. Every effort should also be made to find all appropriate non-preferred synonyms for the preferred terms, in order to enrich the entry vocabulary and with it the usefulness of the thesaurus as a recall improvement device.

F1.1.3. Quasi-synonyms

Quasi-synonyms, also known as near-synonyms, are defined as terms whose meanings are generally regarded as different in ordinary usage, but they are treated as though they are synonyms for indexing purposes. Quasi-synonyms include terms having a significant overlap.

Examples:

URBAN AREAS/CITIES
CAR PARKS/PARKING SPACES
SPEECH IMPAIRED PEOPLE/STAMMERERS
GIFTED PEOPLE/GENIUSES

The acceptability of sets of terms as quasi-synonyms will be affected by the subject field covered by the thesaurus. For example, in a specialist thesaurus on 'Occupational health', the terms 'industrial injury' and 'occupational injury' might not be treated as synonymous, whereas in a more general thesaurus on 'Health sciences' they might be accepted as quasi-synonyms. The quasi-synonym device should be avoided as a means of reducing the size of the vocabulary by grouping together terms that ought to be treated as independent indexing terms, except in marginal subject areas.

Quasi-synonyms may also cover antonyms: terms that represent different viewpoints of the same property continuum.

Examples:

DRYNESS/WETNESS
HEIGHT/DEPTH
EQUALITY/INEQUALITY
LITERACY/ILLITERACY

If it is likely that a search on 'Literacy', for example, will always involve the examination of documents discussing both 'Literacy' and its antonym, 'Illiteracy', the terms should be treated as quasi-synonyms. On the other hand, if a useful distinction can be made between two opposite terms, they should both be used as indexing terms and references made between them, otherwise precision may be lost.

Some search thesauri (i.e., those used only to support searching, see A1.3 above) aim to increase recall by listing as many alternative terms as possible. In these cases it is not necessary to select a preferred term from a group of terms representing a concept. Some software packages now come complete with electronic glossaries for this purpose, while others provide what are called automatic synonym rings. In this latter case, the searcher may key in any term from a ring, thereby automatically invoking all other members of the ring. If the members of the ring are displayed, then the searcher may have the opportunity to override the action if unhappy with the inclusion of quasi-synonyms in the ring.

F1.1.3a. Upward posting

This is a technique, also known as generic posting, that treats narrower terms as if they are equivalent to, rather than a species of, their broader terms. The effect is to reduce the size of the vocabulary, but at the same time to retain access via the specific terms to the broader terms used to represent them.

Examples:

THERMODYNAMIC PROPERTIES
    UF   Enthalpy
           Entropy

    Free energy
    Heat of adsorption
    etc.
  Enthalpy
    USE THERMODYNAMIC PROPERTIES
  Entropy
    USE THERMODYNAMIC PROPERTIES
  etc.

  SOCIAL CLASS
    UF Elite
        Middle class
        Upper class
        Working class

  Elite
    USE SOCIAL CLASS

  Middle class
    USE SOCIAL CLASS

  etc.

This device may be applied in peripheral subject areas of the thesaurus, or in thesauri covering a wide range of subjects at a fairly low level of specificity, or in a large thesaurus where the numbers of preferred terms may be reduced by posting natural-language terms to the nearest preferred broader term(s) in the systematic display.

Terms treated in this way as equivalent terms may be promoted later to the status of preferred indexing terms, if the frequency of occurrence of the terms in indexing and searching justifies it.

F1.1.4. Factored and unfactored forms of compound terms

Cross-references should be made from a compound term to the elements used in combination to express it.

(see also D3.1.2, E2.4.2(a) and H2.1)

Examples:

  MILK HYGIENE/MILK and HYGIENE
  PRISONERS' FAMILIES/PRISONERS and FAMILIES

F1.2. The hierarchical relationship

This relationship shows 'levels of superordination and subordination. The superordinate term represents a class or whole, and the subordinate terms refer to its members or parts'. This relationship is used in locating broader and narrower concepts in a logically progressive sequence. It is a basic feature of the thesaurus, distinguishing it from unstructured term lists, and an important factor in the improvement of recall and also of precision performance. An additional function is to clarify the scope of a term.

The relationship is reciprocal and is set out in a thesaurus using the following conventions.

> BT (i.e. broader term)
> written as a prefix to the superordinate term

> NT (i.e. narrower term)
> written as a prefix to the subordinate term

Example:

PRIVATE ENTERPRISES
> BT Enterprises

ENTERPRISES
> NT Private enterprises

The hierarchical relationship includes the generic relationship, the hierarchical whole-part relationship, the instance relationship and the polyhierarchical relationship. Terms are hierarchically related only if both are members of the same fundamental category, that is, they both represent *entities*, *activities*, *agents* or *properties*, etc. (see D2 and F2).

In the example below, 'Curators' and 'Museum techniques' are *agents* and *actions* respectively and do not belong to the same fundamental category, i.e., *entities*, as the superordinate term 'Museums', and are therefore not NTs to it. They are, in fact, associated terms, discussed in the next section (F1.3.).

Example:

	Fundamental categories
MUSEUMS	Entity
Archaeological museums	Type of entity
Ethnographic museums	Type of entity
Curators	Agents
Museum techniques	Action
Scientific museums	Type of entity
Theatrical museums	Type of entity

It is important to remember that not all terms indented under a term in a faceted systematic display (see F2, H4.3) will be hierarchically related to the one at the level above. They may be associatively related, and if so should be treated as such (see F1.3). Bean has analyzed the relationships in the 'tree structures' in *MeSH* and found that a significant proportion are not hierarchical but associative (Bean, 1998).

Where many levels of hierarchy are possible, it may be decided to omit or include certain levels, depending on the interests of the users of the thesaurus. Dextre Clarke illustrates this by showing two very different hierarchies for 'Cattle' in the *Emtree Thesaurus* and the *CAB thesaurus* (Dextre Clarke, 2000).

The display of hierarchies is considered in Section H and also in F2 and J7.2.1. Alphabetical displays usually show only one level of hierarchy under the superordinate term, but multiple level display is possible (see H2.2). In alphabetical displays it is usual to mix, in one sequence, subordinate terms characterized by different principles of division, whereas in systematic displays it is possible to achieve helpful subgroupings of homogeneous terms at the same hierarchical level. The subgroups are preceded by facet indicators (named 'node labels' in the Standards). Facet indicators in hierarchical displays are illustrated more fully in F2.3.1, H4.3*, J7.2.1, J7.3.

Example:

Systematic display	**Alphabetical display**
PAINTS	PAINTS
(By composition) ← Facet indicator	NT Cement paints
Oil paints	Oil paints
Water paints	Primers
Cement paints	Top coats
	Undercoats
(By use) ← Facet indicator	Water paints
Primers	
Undercoats	
Top coats	

F1.2.1. The generic relationship

The Standards define this relationship as the one which 'identifies the link between a class or category and its members or species'. It has the mathematical property of inheritance, whereby what is true of a given class is also true of all the classes subsumed under it. The relation is also known as the inclusion relationship. It has long been used in biological taxonomies, as in the first example below, but it is also applied between concepts in every subject field.

Examples:

VERTEBRATA
   NT   Amphibia
         Aves
         Mammalia
         Pisces
         Reptilia

GASTROINTESTINAL AGENTS
   NT   Antidiarrhoeals
         Antiulcer agents
         Bile acids
         Cathartics
         Digestants

INTERNAL COMBUSTION ENGINES
   NT   Compression ignition engines
         Dual-fuel engines
         Gas engines
         Petrol engines
         Spark ignition engines

ONE-PARENT FAMILIES
    NT   Fatherless families
         Motherless families

The generic relationship applies to types of actions, properties and agents, as well as to types of things (entities).

Examples:

HEAT TREATMENT
    NT   Annealing
         Decarburization
         Hardening
         Tempering

THINKING
    NT   Contemplation
         Divergent thinking
         Lateral thinking
         Reasoning

VALUE
    NT   Cultural value
         Economic value
         Moral value
         Social value

TEACHERS
    NT   Adult educators
         School teachers
         Special education teachers
         Student teachers

The relationship is correct if both the genus and the species are of the same fundamental category, as explained in F1.2 above. A further test is suggested in the Standards. This is the 'all-and-some' test for validity, as shown in the following diagram.

The diagram indicates that some members of the class of 'Rodents' are 'Squirrels', while all 'Squirrels' by definition, and regardless of context, are 'Rodents'.

If, however, 'Squirrels' is subordinated to a class such as 'Pests', the diagram shows that this is not invariably a true generic relationship, since some 'Pests' are 'Squirrels', and only some 'Squirrels' are 'Pests'.

It is better to allocate 'Squirrels' to the 'Rodent' category, rather than to the inconstant 'Pests' category, except perhaps in a thesaurus on 'Pest Control'.

The Standards suggest that the generic relationship may be identified by the abbreviations NTG (narrow term generic) and BTG (broad term generic) or their equivalent in other languages.

Example:

CONVEYORS
   NTG   Belt conveyors

BELT CONVEYORS
   BTG   Conveyors

This special code would seem to be unnecessary to distinguish the generic from the hierarchical whole-part relationship, described below, as coding only the latter provides sufficient distinction.

F1.2.2. The hierarchical whole-part relationship

The whole-part relationship, except perhaps in a thesaurus in a narrow subject field, is regarded as an associative relationship. There are, however, a few circumstances where 'the name of the part implies the name of the possessing whole in any context'. The terms may then be regarded as a whole–part hierarchy. These are four instances admitted in the Standards.

(a) Systems and organs of the body

Example:

EAR
   EXTERNAL EAR
   LABYRINTH
      SEMICIRCULAR CANALS
      VESTIBULAR APPARATUS
   MIDDLE EAR

(b) Geographical location

Example:

ENGLAND
   EAST ANGLIA
      ESSEX
         COLCHESTER DISTRICT

(c) Discipline or field of study

Example:

GEOLOGY
  ECONOMIC GEOLOGY
  ENGINEERING GEOLOGY
  PHYSICAL GEOLOGY
    PETROLOGY

(d) Hierarchical social structure

Example:

METHODIST CHURCH ORGANIZATION
  METHODIST DISTRICT
    METHODIST CIRCUIT

The option is given in the Standard of using the following abbreviations, or their equivalents in other languages, to indicate the whole–part relationship:

BTP Broader term (partitive)
NTP Narrower term (partitive)

Example:

COLCHESTER DISTRICT
  BTP Essex

ESSEX
  NTP Colchester District

F1.2.3. The instance relationship

This is the relationship between 'a general category of things and events, expressed by a common noun, and an individual instance of that category, the instance then forming a class of one which is represented by a proper name'. These proper names are identifiers, a class of term which is often excluded from the main part of the thesaurus, and is held in a separate file. However, when the identifier forms part of the thesaurus, the relationship between the identifier and its broader term is the instance relationship.

Example:

SEAS
  NT Baltic Sea
      Caspian Sea
      Mediterranean Sea

since the 'Baltic Sea', 'Caspian Sea', etc., are not types, but instances of seas.

In the ANSI Standard it is suggested that the instance relationship may be indicated specifically by the following abbreviations:

BTI   Broader term (instance)
NTI   Narrower term (instance)

Example:

FRENCH CATHEDRALS
    NTI   Chartres Cathedral
    NTI   Rheims Cathedral
    NTI   Rouen Cathedral

CHARTRES
    BTI   French cathedrals

F1.2.4. Polyhierarchical relationships

It is not unusual for terms to occur, equally correctly, under more than one category. The relationship between the term and its two or more superordinate terms is said to be polyhierarchical. This phenomenon may apply to both the generic and hierarchical whole–part terms.

Examples:

(a) Generic
NURSES   HEALTH ADMINISTRATORS
    NT Nurse administrators   NT Nurse administrators

                        NURSE ADMINISTRATORS
                            BT Health administrators
                               Nurses

(b) Whole–part
EAST AFRICA   SOUTHERN AFRICA
    NT Zambia   NT Zambia

                        ZAMBIA
                            BT East Africa
                               Southern Africa

(c) Whole–part/generic
EAR   NERVES
    NT Acoustic nerve   NT Acoustic nerve

                        ACOUSTIC NERVE
                            BT Ear
                               Nerves

(Ear = whole–part; Nerves = generic relationship)

If some of the generic relationships possessed by the term are not 'true' generic relationships (see F1.2.1.), they may still be considered polyhierarchical and be treated as in the examples above.

F1.3. The associative relationship

The third basic relationship is less easy to define than the previous two. Put simply, the associative relationship is found between terms that are closely related conceptually but not hierarchically and are not members of an equivalence set. In other words, the terms are associated, but in a way other than described in the two previous paragraphs.

The Standards state that associatively related terms (known as related terms) may be admitted if 'they are mentally associated to such an extent that the link between them should be made explicit in the thesaurus, on the grounds that it would reveal alternative terms which might be used for indexing and retrieval'. The relation is reciprocal, and is distinguished by the abbreviation 'RT' (related term).

Example:

TEACHING
    RT   Teaching aids

TEACHING AIDS
    RT   Teaching

There is always the risk that thesaurus compilers may overload the thesaurus with valueless relationships, which may impair precision performance without much improving recall. To overcome this tendency, the Standard recommends that 'one of the terms should be strongly implied, according to the frames of reference shared by the users of the index, whenever the other is employed as an indexing term'. The Standard goes on to suggest that where terms are closely related 'it will frequently be found that one of the terms is a necessary component in any definition or explanation of the other'. For example, the term 'Teaching' is needed to define the term 'Teaching aids', but not vice versa. The Standard does not go so far as to recommend that relationships are invalid if this definition test is failed. Subjective relationships are more likely to occur in specialized fields for a particular type of clientele. For example, a link between the terms 'Divorce' and 'Legal aid' might appear in a thesaurus in the field of community information if research on terms appearing in enquiries put to community information agencies showed a strong co-occurrence between these terms. In a thesaurus with a different clientele, such a relationship might not be justified.

Molholt has drawn attention to the weaknesses of associatively-related inter-term links in many thesauri (Molholt, 1996). There is a lack of rules on defining and constructing related terms and this causes inconsistency and 'idiosyncratic application and incomplete pathways through information systems'. It is not possible to build meaningful RTs where the vocabulary is an alphabetical list of terms without much structure. A thesaurus with a controlled hierarchical structure within well-defined facets, such as the *Art and architecture thesaurus* (*AAT*) (F2.3.2, H4.3.2), offers a well-understood and highly stable basis for the application of associatively-related links. For instance, where categories of terms are already well-defined it is possible to make RTs to the broadest term in a category, rather than to one or more of the terms within it.

In the construction of faceted thesauri, structured by subject field rather than broad facets, it is usual to recognise associatively-related terms during the initial process of analyzing the subject field (see F1.3.4, F2.3.1, J7.2.1) rather than at a later stage. Williamson has described the ease with which associatively related thesaurus terms may be recognised from the layout of the faceted schedules of the universal *Bliss classification* (*BC2*) (Williamson, 1996).

A rather different method of finding associatively related terms is by automatic, statistical means, described in F4.

There are two types of associative relationship, those that belong to the same, and those that belong to different, categories.

F1.3.1. Terms belonging to the same category

It is not necessary, as a general rule, to relate terms belonging to the same class or genus, i.e., sibling terms. The relationship may be seen by scanning the systematic display, if one exists, or by checking the relevant broader term in the alphabetical display, which will list all the sibling terms at the same level as the sought term.

Example:

Term sought: Radial bearings

RADIAL BEARINGS JCK
   BT   Bearings
   RT   Plain bearings
         Rolling bearings } not necessary

Find related siblings by checking JCK or BT = BEARINGS.

Systematic display	*Alphabetical display*
JC Bearings	BEARINGS JC
JCC Plain bearings	NT Plain bearings
JCC.D Sliding bearings	Radial bearings ←
JCF Rolling bearings	Roller bearings
JCF.B Ball bearings	
→ JCK Radial bearings	

The Standards suggest that exceptions should be made to this rule when the sibling terms have overlapping meanings and are sometimes used loosely and almost interchangeably, even though each of the terms is amenable to an exact definition, and consequently they do not form an equivalent set. The Standard gives as an example, 'ships' and 'boats', which are both species of the genus 'vessels'.

Pairs of siblings may also be related if they have some particularly strong link between them, which does not occur between other members of the same species. This may be a derivational or familial relationship (i.e., one of the concepts is derived from the other). These will also require RT relationships. Examples include the relationship between 'donkeys', 'horses' and 'mules', which are all narrower terms of 'equines', but 'mules' and 'donkeys' only would need an RT link as they share a derivative relationship.

F1.3.2. Terms belonging to different categories

Much effort, in the past, has gone into classifying associative relationships into various categories. In 1965 Perreault published a classified list of 120 relationships, including those proposed by a number of philosophers and classification specialists, ranging from Aristotle to Ranganathan, De Grolier, Farradane and Mills (Perreault, 1965), but such detailed categories have not been regarded as mandatory in the Standards, and have been applied only rarely in practice. Svenonius points out that the lack of finer categorizing is in part due to the fact that 'often two terms are helpfully related in ways difficult to verbalize' (Svenonius, 1987). Milstead believes that more complex categories of associatively-related terms would pose difficulty for indexers applying these to the text and for searchers requesting the precise relationship (Milstead, 1995).

However, recently, there has been an increase of research into relationships, particularly in connection with the *Unified medical language system* (*UMLS*) where 49 non-hierarchical relationships have been distinguished in its *Semantic network* (see L3.2.2.b). Also in the biomedical field, Bean has reported on research to determine which non-hierarchical relationships in medical controlled vocabularies could be characterized, organized and structured (Bean, 1996). The research investigated whether there was a consistent operating logic in the pattern of relationships and whether the selection of relationships might be automated using, among other techniques, morphological analysis of medical terminology. In a new approach to the development of multilingual thesauri, Schmitz-Esser (1999) proposes distinguishing 13 relationship categories, 10 of which are new sub-categories of the associative relationship. More generally, Green is involved in research into the development of an inventory of relationships, or a relational thesaurus, to provide terminological control over relationships, in the same way as a conventional thesaurus controls concepts (Green, 1996).

The Standards give examples of some of the most frequently mentioned types of related terms, although there is no attempt to include these as mandatory. These are given below with some others encountered in practice.

(a) The whole–part associative relationship
Apart from the four instances of hierarchical whole–part relationships listed above (F1.2.2.), the whole–part relationship is associative, as this is a link between terms in different fundamental categories. This relationship is fairly easy to recognize, particularly when concrete objects are involved.

Examples:

NUCLEAR REACTORS
   RT Pressure vessels

OPERATING THEATRES
   RT Surgical equipment

BUILDINGS
   RT Doors

The Standards allow that in a highly specialized thesaurus the whole–part relationship may be treated as hierarchical if the 'name of the whole is implied by the name of the part'. For instance, in a thesaurus in the field of 'Fan Engineering', the term 'Blades' might be shown as NT and not RT to 'Fans', because in this limited field, other applications of the term 'Blades' would not occur. However, when the whole–part relationship is not exclusive to a pair of terms, i.e., the part can belong to multiple wholes, as in the case of, for example, 'braking systems', which may be part of a 'motor vehicle', 'bicycle' or 'train', the associative relationship should be preferred. In general, there is less likelihood of inconsistency in the determination of whole–part relationships, if the hierarchical whole–part relationship is reserved for the four categories given above in F1.2.2.

(b) A discipline or field of study and the objects or phenomena studied

Examples:

SEISMOLOGY
   RT Earthquakes

ONCOLOGY
   RT Neoplasms

MECHANICAL ENGINEERING
   RT Prime movers

ETHNOGRAPHY
   RT Primitive societies

(c) An operation or process and the agent or instrument

Examples:

VELOCITY MEASUREMENT
   RT Speedometers

TURNING
   RT Lathes

MOTOR RACING
   RT Racing cars

HAIRDRESSING
   RT Hair driers

(d) An occupation and the person in that occupation

Examples:

ACCOUNTANCY
   RT Accountants

SOCIAL WORK
   RT Social workers

BRICKLAYING
   RT Bricklayers

SPORT
   RT Professional sportsmen

(e) An action and the product of the action

Examples:

SCIENTIFIC RESEARCH
   RT Scientific inventions

ROADMAKING
   RT Roads

VIOLENCE
   RT Violence victims

PUBLISHING
  RT Music scores

(f) An action and its patient

Examples:

DRIVING
  RT Road vehicles

DATA ANALYSIS
  RT Data

TEACHING
  RT Students

ART THERAPY
  RT Psychiatric patients

(g) Concepts related to their properties

Examples:

SURFACES
  RT Surface properties

STEEL ALLOYS
  RT Corrosion resistance

WOMEN
  RT Femininity

(h) Concepts related to their origins

Examples:

WATER
  RT Water wells

INFORMATION
  RT Information sources

(i) Concepts linked by causal dependence

Examples:

FRICTION
  RT Wear

INJURY
  RT Accidents

(j) A thing or action and its counter-agent

Examples:

PESTS
  RT Pesticides

CORROSION
  RT Corrosion inhibitors

CRIME
  RT Crime prevention devices

(k) A raw material and its product

Examples:

AGGREGATES
  RT Concretes

HIDES
  RT Leather

(l) An action and a property associated with it

Examples:

PRECISION MEASUREMENT
  RT Accuracy

COMMUNICATION
  RT Communication skills

(m) A concept and its opposite (antonym not treated as quasi-synonym)

Examples:

SINGLE PEOPLE
  RT Married people

TOLERANCE
  RT Prejudice

Although it is useful to be aware of the above varieties of related terms, and of others not mentioned here, the compiler need establish only that the relationship falls into the broad category of related term. This may be done by applying the validation tests set out in F1.2. (If these show that the terms are not hierarchically related they must be related terms.) On the whole, it is easier to judge the correct relationship between terms in the pure sciences and technology than in the social sciences and humanities. The existing broad categorization of related terms, and their somewhat inconsistent application, will possibly remain acceptable so long as thesauri are used mainly to guide human users in term selection. However, the increasing automated use of thesauri is likely to create 'a demand for thesauri with relationships that are sub-categorized and more consistently applied' (Dextre Clarke, 2000).

Compilers should look out for a common error in manually produced thesauri, when both BT and RT relationships occur between the same pair of terms. The mistake arises when the compiler makes a different decision about the relationship when handling the second term than was made, some time earlier, when handling the first term. This is usually due to the relevant reciprocal entry either not having been generated or becoming mislaid.

F1.3.3. Related terms in the alphabetical display

Related terms in the alphabetical display are usually arranged in one alphabetical sequence, following the RT code. The ANSI Standard suggests another possible layout which would 'bring closely related concepts together in the alphabetical array under a given descriptor' by dividing related terms 'into categories that do not form part of a logical display'. These related terms should be identified by a facet indicator, or node label. In the example below (*Equipment*) functions as a facet indicator.

Example:

FIREFIGHTING
  RT
    (*Equipment*)
    Breaching equipment
    Fire hoses
    Ladders

For other sections concerned with facet indicators in thesaurus display, see sections F1.2, F1.3.4, F2*, H4.3, J7.2.1 and J7.3.

F1.3.4. Related terms in the systematic display

Systematic displays that are organized to give an overview of a subject field or discipline (F2.3.1) and are not organized according to basic facets (F2.3.2) will inevitably include some terms from different fundamental categories (F2.1) that are not generically related, so that hierarchically and associatively-related terms appear mixed in the same schedule. These relationships are shown in the schedules in two ways, either indented under superordinate related terms, as if they were species or members of a hierarchy, or listed as a cross-reference under the reciprocally-related term.

(a) Indenting under superordinate related term

Example

LF		**Fire**
		(*Risks*)
LFD	(*RT*)	Fire risks
LFD.F		Flammable atmospheres
		(*Safety measures*)
LFH	(*RT*)	Fire safety
		(*Firefighting measures*)
LFP	(*RT*)	Firefighting
		(*Equipment*)
LFP.C	(*RT*)	Firefighting equipment
LFP.CC		Fire hoses

In the above example, all the terms indented one level below the term 'Fire' are associatively and not hierarchically related to it. They are coded RT accordingly, so that the correct relationship will be shown between the terms in the alphabetical display. That is:

FIRE
  RT Fire risks
  RT Fire safety
  RT Firefighting

The RT may be omitted from the printed display or replaced by a '-' or other symbol.

It is important not to confuse schedule subordination with hierarchical subordination in the systematic display.

(b) Cross-references between related terms in different classes and hierarchies

In the example below, the term 'Fire insurance', shown indented as an RT under 'Fire', has its main place in a different subject field, i.e., under 'Insurance'. Reciprocal references are made between the related terms in the two fields, each cross-reference being preceded by the abbreviation RT (or sometimes *RT). (Systematic displays are covered in more detail in sections F2.3, H4.3, J7.2.1, and J7.3.)

Example:

LF		**Fire**
		RT Fire insurance TVH
		(Risks)
LFD	*(RT)*	Fire risks
...		
TV		**Insurance**
		...
TVH		Fire insurance
		RT Fire LF

F2. Classification and facet analysis

Classification is an essential tool when finding structure and relationships during thesaurus construction. The effectiveness of a thesaurus is likely to be reduced if relationships between terms in an alphabetical list are determined without resort to classification. Stella Dextre Clarke refers to two large alphabetically-arranged thesauri in the agricultural field that required constant amendment after publication, due to the lack of a basic structure (Dextre Clarke, 1995). The building of a common classified structure between the two thesauri was the means found to improve and reconcile them (see L3.2.1), and to facilitate translation and the creation of multilingual editions (Dextre Clarke, 1997).

The most commonly-used form of systematic classification in thesaurus construction is faceted classification. This is a type of analytico-synthetic classification. It is synthetic in that it provides for the combination of terms to represent detailed topics that are not specifically enumerated in the schedules, and analytical because it is structured in such a way that the classmarks represent simple concepts, organized into clearly-defined categories during a rigorous process known as facet analysis.

F2.1. Thesauri and use of facet analysis

A faceted classification is similar in structure to a thesaurus and is unlike enumerative classification systems, which deal in complex terms and phrases that have only a limited facility for combining with one another. The affinity between faceted classification schemes and thesauri means that faceted classification is useful in thesaurus construction in several ways. First, it provides a tool for the analysis of subject fields and for determining the relationships between concepts therein (see also J7). Second, the resulting faceted classification may be used as the systematic display in the published or online thesaurus (see H4.3). Third, facets may be added to terms in existing vocabularies, to further define their meaning and role. There are a number of thesauri that use facet analysis as a construction technique, and several that contain facet displays. The layout of some of these displays is discussed in H4.3.

F2.1.1. The Bliss classification, and other universal schemes, as thesaurus sources

Faceted classification schemes in special subject areas are a useful source of terminology and structure. In addition, there is a second edition of the *Bliss classification (BC2)*, which is a fount of detailed terminology, analyzed and organized within subject fields by facet techniques.

The first edition of the *Bliss classification* appeared between 1940 and 1953, the result of a lifetime of study by its compiler, H.E. Bliss. It was notable for its carefully-planned main classes, alternative places, short notation and some synthetic qualities (Thomas 1997–1998). The second edition, edited by Jack Mills and Vanda Broughton, and supported by the Bliss Classification Association, is in course of development (Mills and Broughton, 1977–). The original shell of the system remains with minimum change, and within each class the schedules are designed on facet principles. In the Introductory volume and elsewhere, Jack Mills has described the underlying philosophy. The plan is to produce *BC2* in separate parts for individual main classes, each with its own introduction, schedules and index. By 1999, volumes for 12 main classes had been published, and volumes for several others were nearing completion.

The Bliss Classification Association (http://www.sid.cam.ac.uk/bca/bcahome.htm) encourages this use of the scheme as a source of terms and structure for special classification schemes or thesauri, so long as due acknowledgement is made in any publication which results. For thesaurus purposes, the detail in the schedule has to be edited to introduce more precision into word form control and into recognizing and labelling the hierarchical, polyhierarchical and associative relationships present. See articles by Aitchison on the use of *Bliss* as a thesaurus resource (Aitchison, 1986, 1995). *BC2* has also been used as the facet framework in an experiment to restructure the schedules of the *Universal decimal classification (UDC)* into a fully-faceted classification system with accompanying thesaurus (McIlwaine and Williamson, 1994; Williamson, 1996).

The Dewey decimal classification is also adopting a higher degree of faceting (Miksa, 1998). For example, in the 21st edition, it is possible to build the compound concept 'anatomy of the nerves of the heart of deer' using no less than three unambiguous facet indicators in the notation. At the same time the *Library of Congress subject headings* is moving closer to the ANSI Standard for thesauri, both in conventions used and structural guidelines.

F2.2. Fundamental facets

The distinctive feature of a faceted classification is the division of terms into categories, or facets, using only one characteristic (or principle) of division at a time, to produce homogeneous, mutually-exclusive groups. Another feature is the recognition of a limited number of fundamental categories or facets, which may be represented in any concept and underlie all subject fields. For example, the concept 'paintings' may be classified as a member of the fundamental facet *entities*, while 'painting' may be regarded as a member of the fundamental facet *action* and 'paints' as a manifestation of the fundamental facet *materials*.

Fundamental facets were first named by J. Kaiser, but it was S.R. Ranganathan, the originator of analytico-synthetic classification, who developed and popularized facet analysis and applied it in his *Colon classification* (Ranganathan, 1987). He listed five fundamental categories: *personality, matter, energy, space,* and *time* (PMEST). *Space, time* and *matter* are self-explanatory. *Energy* is a category representing activities, processes and problems. *Personality* is difficult to define, but represents the key facet, which may include things, kinds of things, or actions and kinds of actions, depending on the bias of the subject field. Over several years of research and application in different disciplines and subject fields, fundamental facets are now usually considered to consist, among others, of those listed below. A few examples of terms that fall within these categories are also given.

Entities/things/objects

(*By characteristics*)
Abstract entities
  e.g. Ideas, Disciplines

Naturally occurring entities
  e.g. Radiation, Clouds, Rivers

Living entities, Organisms
  e.g. Bacteria, Viruses, Mammals

Artefacts (man-made)
  e.g. Manufactured goods, Art objects

Attributes: properties/qualities, states/conditions
  e.g. Temperature, Colour, Reliability, Size

Materials/substances, constituent substances
  e.g. Minerals, Wood, Leather, Plastics, Fabrics, Drugs

Parts/components
  e.g. Tyres, Rudders, Body parts, Ceilings, Floors

Whole entities/Complex entities
  e.g. Motor vehicles, Ships, Buildings, Schools

(*By function*)
Agents (Performers of action – inanimate and animate)
  Individuals, personnel, organizations
    e.g. Artists, Seamen, Doctors, Professional associations

  Equipment/apparatus
    e.g. Machine tools, Computers, Respirators, Dish washers

Patients (Recipients of action – inanimate and animate)
  e.g. Victims, Benefit recipients, Polluted water

End-products
  e.g. Food products, Residues, Research results

Actions/activities

Processes/functions (internal processes, intransitive actions)
  e.g. Development, Diseases, Thinking, Walking

Operations (external, transitive actions)
  e.g. Machining, Teaching, Healing, Management

Space/place/location/environment

Time

In addition, Kinds or Types; Systems and Assemblies; Applications and Purposes of the above categories.

As well as being used to organize terms during the construction of a thesaurus or classification scheme, fundamental facets have also been added to controlled vocabularies to further define the terms contained. For example, fundamental facets are used as concept categories or types in the *Semantic network* of the *Unified medical language system* (see L3.2.2). The categories are applied to the concepts in the *Metathesaurus*, to aid in the disambiguation of terms and to act as role indicators during searching. Figure 3 shows that the top terms of the categories are 'Entity' and 'Event'. 'Entity' is split into 'Conceptual entity': including 'Idea' or 'Concept', 'Language', etc.; and 'Physical object': including 'Organism' (animal, plant, etc.), 'Substance', 'Manufactured object' and 'Anatomical structure'. 'Event' is divided into 'Activity': including, 'Behaviour', 'Daily or Recreational activity', 'Occupational activity' and 'Machine activity'; and 'Phenomenon or Process': covering 'Anthropogenic phenomenon or process', 'Injury or Poisoning' and 'Natural phenomenon or process', including 'Biologic function'.

Fundamental facets are also used as role operators in the *PRECIS* system, to determine the order of terms in a pre-coordinate indexing system (Austin, 1984). Again, in another application, fundamental facets may be used as role indicators in databases subject to false drops. For example, the difference between the role of the term 'tomatoes' as a living plant and as a marketable product could be distinguished by adding at the indexing stage the fundamental facet role indicators, *organism* or *end product*, to the term, as appropriate. (For further discussion on roles and links, see G3 and G4.)

Figure 3. Fundamental facets in the UMLS Semantic Network

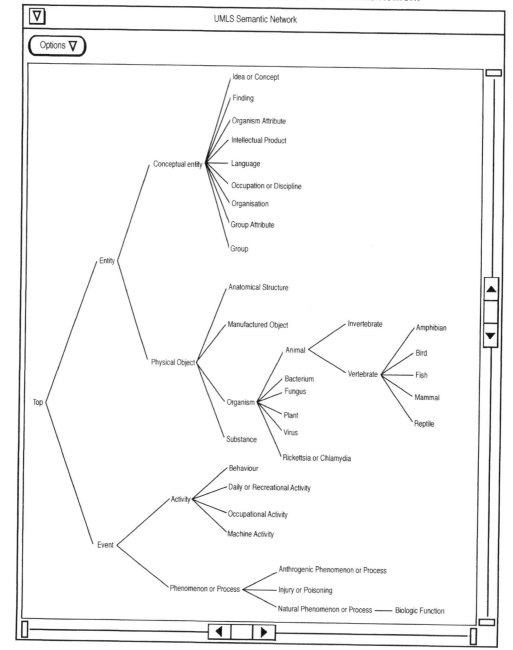

F2.3. Structuring by facet analysis

F2.3.1. Thesauri structured by subject fields and disciplines

When structuring the area of knowledge covered by a thesaurus, it is usual first to group the terms into subject fields or disciplines before applying facet analysis. Within each subject field concepts are initially divided into main facets, representing some aspect of the fundamental facets. For example, in the field of 'clothing technology', the main facets might include *end-products, parts, properties, operations* and *agents* (*human and machine*). The main facets are further analyzed and appropriate terms allocated to each. These terms are then sorted into subfacets (also known as arrays) and their hierarchies.

The 'Clothing technology' schedule in Figure 4 shows that the *end-product* facet, 'Clothing', may be divided by *type*; according to *process used*: 'Knitwear'; by *property*: 'Lightweight clothing'; by *purpose*: 'Outerwear', 'Nightwear'; by *user*: 'Baby clothing', 'Womens clothing'. The *parts* facet might contain 'Collars', 'Sleeves', 'Linings', etc., and the *materials facet* 'Textile fabrics', 'Leather' and other substances. The *operations* facet might cover manufacturing processes, such as 'Patternmaking', 'Cutting', 'Sewing', and special skills such as 'Tailoring'. The *agents* facet might be represented by 'Clothing technology equipment' and human agents, 'Clothing personnel', those involved in the clothing industry.

The subfacets may be divided by a second round of concepts representing fundamental *facets*, and these may be divided by a third round, and so on. For example 'Womens clothing' may be divided by *type* according to *purpose*, 'Maternity wear', while a further round might distinguish a *'property'*, 'Maternity wear sizes'. This operation of 'judging the correct relationship that each term has to the general class and assigning it accordingly' is what facet analysis entails. As each facet and subfacet is identified, it is preceded by a facet indicator (also known as node label), which labels the facet by its characteristics of division. Facet indicators are shown in parentheses and in italics in Figure 4.

F2.3.2. Thesauri with fundamental facets as main division

Although the area of knowledge covered by a thesaurus is usually divided first by subject fields or disciplines, an alternative is to divide first by fundamental facets. The *Construction industry thesaurus* was an early example of this approach (Construction, 1976). *The Art and architecture thesaurus* (*AAT*) is a more recent example (Art, 1994). In this thesaurus the hierarchies are grouped within seven fundamental facets. These facets, subfacets, and the hierarchies within them are shown below.

> *ASSOCIATED CONCEPTS FACET*
> 　Associated Concepts
> *PHYSICAL ATTRIBUTES FACET*
> 　Attributes and Properties, Conditions and Effects
> 　Design Elements, Color
> *STYLES AND PERIODS FACET*
> 　Styles and Periods
> *AGENTS FACET*
> 　People, Organizations
> *ACTIVITIES FACET*
> 　Disciplines, Functions, Events,
> 　Physical Activities, Processes and Techniques
> *MATERIALS FACET*
> 　Materials
> *OBJECTS FACET*
> 　Object Groupings and Systems,
> 　Object Genres, Components

Figure 4. Faceted classification

M	CLOTHING TECHNOLOGY
	(Personnel)
MC	Clothing technology personnel
MCE	Clothing technology managers
MCP	Clothing workers
MCP.D	Sewing machinists
	(Equipment)
ME	Clothing technology equipment
MEH	Sewing machines
	(Operations)
MG	Clothing manufacturing processes
MGH	Patternmaking
MGJ	Cutting
MGL	Sewing
MGT	Tailoring
MGV	Dressmaking
	(Materials)
MI	Clothing materials
MIK	Woollen fabrics
MIR	Leather
MIV	Fur
	(Parts)
MKL	Collars
MKP	Sleeves
MKQ	Cuffs
MKV	Linings
	(End-products)
MM	Clothing
	(By process used)
MNP	Knitwear
	(By property)
MOR	Lightweight clothing
	(By material)
MPI.K	Woollen clothing
MPI.V	Fur clothing
	(By purpose)
MQQ	Outerwear
MQQ.C	Coats
MQQ.H	Dresses
MQQ.N	Suits
MQR	Hosiery
MQS	Headwear
MQT	Footwear
MQU	Underwear
MSN	Nightwear
MST	Sportswear
MTU	Uniforms
	(By user)
MVC	Baby clothing
MVE	Childrens clothing
MVM	Womens clothing
MVM.P	Maternity wear
MVR	Mens clothing

Built Environment
    Settlements and Landscapes,
    Built Complexes and Districts, Single Built Works,
    Open Spaces and Site Elements

Furnishings and Equipment
    Furnishings, Costume, Tools and Equipment,
    Weapons and Ammunition, Measuring Devices,
    Containers, Sound Devices, Recreational Artifacts,
    Transportation Vehicles

Visual and Verbal Communication
    Visual Works, Exchange Media, Information Forms

The hierarchies are further divided according to characteristics of division, indicated by guide terms (i.e. facet indicators or node labels) (see H4.3.2. and Figure 22a).

Terms in the hierarchies within each facet are all of the same fundamental facet. This ensures that all the inter-term relationships are generic or whole-part hierarchical (BT/ NT) and not associative. Associative relationships (RT) between the terms in the different hierarchies are added after the hierarchies are completed and are shown only in the accompanying alphabetical display.

F2.3.3. Order of facets in a faceted display

The filing order, or the arrangement of facets within a subject field, is preferably in the order of increasing specificity, complexity and concreteness. Put in other ways, the schedules show an evolutionary order, or place 'means before ends'. In a faceted thesaurus solely for post-coordinate use, the order of the facets is not crucial, but in pre-coordinated system applications, where the filing order affects the citation order, it has significance. The citation order is the order in which the concepts in the faceted schedule are cited in a compound classmark or string of terms in a pre-coordinated index. In the 'Clothing technology' schedule in Figure 4 the citation order would be the reverse of the filing order.

Filing order	*Citation order*
Agents	End-products
Operations	Parts
Materials	Materials
Parts	Operations
End-products	Agents

A compound subject, for example, 'Clothing workers engaged in patternmaking for womens clothing', would be expressed by citing classmarks (or their equivalent terms) in the following order.

End product	*Operation*	*Agent*
MVM	MGH	MCP
Womens clothing	Pattern making	Clothing workers

In the compound classmark, or string of terms, only the preferred or first cited classmark or term is accessible in the lead position. To ensure that each concept comes to the lead position, it is necessary to make three strings, in each of which a different term or classmark is at the head.

Although the order of terms in a faceted classification used in a thesaurus post-coordinately is less significant than for one used pre-coordinately, it is still helpful for the compiler and the user if a consistent pattern may be discerned, at least in similar subject fields. The 'general to specific' order is the most likely to be generally acceptable. A possible arrangement for the facets of a subject field or discipline, and one in which the influence of *BC2* may be discerned, might be as follows.

> Common subdivisions
> > Document form
> > Time. Historical aspects
> > Space. Place subdivisions
> > Research, education, communication, and information in the subject; administrative and legal aspects.
> Influence of/relations with other fields
> Principles and theory
> Agents
> > Persons and organizations
> > Facilities and equipment
> Actions
> > Processes
> > Operations
> Properties
> Materials
> Parts
> Whole entities
> Systems of entities

This order need not be strictly adhered to, and may be modified to suit special situations. For instance, 'Administration' in 'Health care' may need to be treated as a major operations facet and be moved from its place under common subdivisions. It is nevertheless useful to the compiler to have as a reference point an agreed underlying order.

The order of concepts within subfacets may follow the same pattern as within the main facets, where this is helpful. For instance, in Figure 4 the subfacets under 'Clothing' are arranged according to type, in the same standard order as the main facets, 'By process used' preceding 'By property' and 'By material'.

A rather different order of facets is found in Dahlberg's *Systematifier* (Dahlberg, 1978). This is a formula for the organization of subject fields, developed by Dahlberg after the analysis of the content of several hundreds of fields. The recommended order of facets is:

1. Theories, principles
2. Objects, entities (kinds and parts)
3. Activities (states, processes and operations)

4, 5, 6. Special attributes of 2 and 3
7. Influencing concepts, or concepts from outside fields
8. Application of methods in 3 to other fields
9. Distribution of knowledge in 1–8 through education and information

Faceted schedules that show a consistent 'general before special' order, as in the example in Figure 4, allow all later concepts to be qualified by those that occur earlier in the schedules. If this is done consistently, terms will be placed specifically with the concepts they qualify. For example, 'Sewing machines' is 'brought down' to appear under 'Sewing' at MGL.E and not earlier in the schedule under 'Clothing technology equipment' at MEH, and 'Sewing machinists' is 'brought down' to appear under 'Sewing machines' at MGL.ECP rather than earlier in the schedule at 'Clothing workers' MCP.D. When used as the systematic display of a thesaurus, a reference must be made from the earlier location in the schedule for the term to its specific place later (see H4.3.3), or the term may be entered in both places (see H4.3.4).

Example:

MCP   Clothing workers
           *NT Sewing machinists MGL.ECP
ME   Clothing technology equipment
           *NT Sewing machines MGL.E
MG   Clothing manufacturing processes
           ...
MGL   Sewing

           (*Equipment*)
MGL.E   Sewing machines
           *BT Clothing technology equipment ME

           (*Operators*)
MGL.ECP   Sewing machinists
           *BT Clothing workers MCP

(Note: the *classmarks* MGL.E, MGL.ECP are built up retroactively by 'bringing down' the E and CP from ME and MCP, see F3.3.)

In a faceted thesaurus display it would be equally valid to leave 'Sewing machines' under 'Clothing technology equipment', and 'Sewing machinists' under 'Clothing workers', and to show the associative relationship between 'Sewing machines' and 'Sewing', and 'Sewing machinists' and 'Sewing machines' by RT references (see F1.3.4).

Example:

MCP   Clothing workers
MCP.D   Sewing machinists
                 *RT Sewing machines   MEH
ME   Clothing technology equipment
MEH   Sewing machines
                 *RT Sewing MGL
                 *RT Sewing machinists   MCP.D

```
MG          Clothing manufacturing processes
MGL             Sewing
                    *RT Sewing machines      MEH
```

How facet analysis is used in building a small thesaurus is illustrated in the section J7 of Construction techniques below.

F2.3.4 Facet analysis references

For further reading on faceted classification, see items in the bibliography:

Aitchison, 1992; Austin, 1976; Batty, 1981; Buchanan, 1979, chapters 5, 6; Classification Research Group, 1955; Croghan, 1971; Ellis and Vasconcelos, 1999; Foskett, A.C., 1996, chapters 6, 8, 2000; Foskett, D.J., 1974; Hunter, 1988, pp. 7–33; Maltby, 1968; Mills and Broughton, 1977, Introductory volume; Ranganathan, 1987; Rowley, 1992, pp. 187–8, 190; Spiteri, 1997; Vickery, 1960, 1975, 1992.

F3. Notation

The main function of the notation, a set of symbols added to the classification system, is to represent the concepts and give each one a filing value in a self-evident order. Symbols commonly used in notation are Arabic numerals and the Roman alphabet (small letters and capitals), which have a widely recognized filing order. Other symbols are used, such as hyphens, colons and oblique signs, with an imposed arbitrary order, as they lack an obvious value.

F3.1. Expressive notation

A possible secondary function of notation is to express the hierarchy of the classes, showing subordinate classes (subclasses) and coordinate classes (equal classes). A notation that attempts to show hierarchy is known as an expressive or hierarchical notation and one that does not is a non-expressive or ordinal notation. An expressive notation may be used in online searches to retrieve all documents classified by notation more specific than the cut-off point of a truncated class mark. For instance, all documents classified 831.5+, 'Fire fighting' and its subdivisions, in the example Expressive notation (i) below.

In practice, although it is possible to maintain a notation that shows every step of the hierarchy, the principle will break down when the subclasses of any genus out-number the characters available in the notation. This may be as few as 10 in a conventional decimal notation, although 26 in an alphabetical notation of capital letters only. Expressive notations are also 'inhospitable'. This means they do not easily allow the interpolation of new concepts, because of the rigidity of the structure. In the example below, Expressive notation (i), it is not possible to insert a new concept at the same hierarchical level between 'Fire' at 831 and 'Explosions' at 832. Lack of hospitality is more pronounced in ten-place decimal notations than in alphabetical notations. However, where a lengthy class mark may be tolerated, numerical notations exist that are expressive, hospitable and can be used for online 'exploded' class mark searches, as found in *MeSH* (*Medical subject headings*) and other thesauri.

These use blocks of up to 3-digit numbers, used as integers, not decimals, separated by full stops which that up to 1000 places at each hierarchical level. The example below, Expressive notation (ii), shows that using this type of notation to express 'Carbon dioxide fire extinguishers' could produce a classmark as long as

830.500.650.450.260.40

to cover the five hierarchical steps separating it from its generic term 'Hazards'.

Example:

Expressive notation (i)

83	Hazards
831	Fire
831.5	Fire fighting
831.53	Fire fighting equipment
831.532	Fire extinguishers
831.532.5	Carbon dioxide fire extinguishers
832	Explosions

Expressive notation (ii)

830	Hazards
830.560	Fire
830.650.650	Fire fighting
830.500.650.450	Fire fighting equipment
830.500.650.450.260	Fire extinguishers
830.500.650.450.260.40	Carbon dioxide fire extinguishers
830.620	Explosions

A possible solution to overcome the problem of a lengthy expressive notation is to employ a short, non-expressive notation for the printed or online display, and to use the fully expressive notation for searching the database. This approach has been adopted for the *Unified agricultural thesaurus* (Dextre Clarke, 1996) among others.

F3.2. Ordinal and semi-ordinal notation

An alternative to an expressive notation is the non-hierarchical, ordinal or semi-ordinal notation, which ensures a generally shorter classmark, because the notation can more easily be evenly distributed throughout the scheme, and allows new concepts to be inserted in the correct place, when required. For instance, HNY might be used in the example below to represent the hazard 'Dangerous environments' inserted between 'Fire' and 'Explosions'.

Example:

Ordinal notation

HK	Hazards
HL	Fire
HM	Firefighting
HN	Firefighting equipment
HNB	Fire extinguishers

HNE	Carbon dioxide fire extinguishers
HNY	Dangerous environments
HO	Explosions

When an ordinal notation is used, the indenting of the text of the classification is the sole indicator of hierarchical levels, unless the notation is itself indented, as is done in the *Thesaurus of consumer affairs* (Askew, 1979).

Example:

D100	Production
.D105	Production methods
..D107	Automation

Another advantage of the ordinal notation is that it is possible to give a brief class mark to important concepts that are in a subordinate position in a hierarchy. The following examples are taken from the *British catalogue of music classification* (Coates, 1960) and from *BC2* (Mills and Broughton, 1977-).

Examples:

PW	Keyboard instruments
Q	Piano
R	Organ
TSZ.T	Financial administration
TT	Accountancy

Most ordinal notations do show an element of hierarchy and are in fact semi-ordinal. This usually appears in the lower levels of division. The *ROOT thesaurus* (British Standards, 1985), for example, has a notation that is ordinal when representing the broader subclasses and expressive for narrower terms. The structure of the broader classes is shown by indicating the range of classmarks used to cover the hierarchical step.

Example:

KB/KO	Electrical engineering
KE/KJ	Electrical equipment
KF	Electric machines
KFT	Electric motors
KFT.C	Alternating current motors
KFT.CD	Synchronous motors

This type of notation gives a medium-length class mark, while showing to some extent the structure of the scheme. This expressiveness gives way to the ordinal approach when the number of subclasses exceeds the characters available or the exact reflection of the hierarchical steps would prevent the insertion of a new concept at the correct place.

F3.3. Synthetic and retroactive notation

Hospitality, which allows the system to grow and absorb new concepts, is another essential quality of a notation. The insertion of new concepts within arrays is easily achieved if an ordinal notation is used, as has been seen. Another way of achieving hospitality is by using synthesis in notation, which allows the combining of symbols representing concepts in one facet or array with those of others. Such synthesized class marks should only be used in a thesaurus when the equivalent terms would not be factored, according to the rules (see E2.4.2). Some thesauri have common terms in auxiliary schedules which may be used throughout the scheme to build new concepts.

Example:

Synthesis using Common Terms		**Enumeration**	
AT	Information	P	Architecture
ATM	Information services	PB	Architectural information
		PBM	Architectural information services
P	Architecture		
PAT	Architectural information		
PAT.M	Architectural information services		

The use of the synthetic device makes the scheme, in part, self-updating. On the other hand, a synthesized class number is usually longer than an enumerated one, as is the case in the example above.

A device known as retroactive notation is used in some faceted classifications to shorten the synthesized class marks. Any notation following at some later point in an array or subdivision of a field may be assigned the subnotation of some earlier subdivision, so as to indicate its own subdivision. In this way, compound concepts are built up 'backwards' – hence 'retroactive'. The schedules have to be designed so that the more general concepts appear in the earlier part of the schedules to qualify the more specific concepts later in the sequence. The class marks are short because the facet indicator from the earlier notation is dropped when this is added to the later, as is illustrated in Figure 4 above, and also in the example on page 77 of F2.3.3. above. The following examples are from *BC2* (Mills and Broughton, 1977), which has a retroactive notation throughout.

Example:

QL	Children
	...
QLV	Old people
	...
QM	Handicapped people
	...
QMP	Mentally handicapped people
QMP L	Mentally handicapped children
QMP LV	Mentally handicapped old people

Retroactive notation should not be used to synthesize compound terms that would be better factored for thesaurus purposes.

Example:

QD   Social work

...

QL   Children

...

QLD   Social work with children

QLD produces an unacceptable compound term, breaking the second factoring rule (see E2.4.2.b) that a transitive action is not qualified by the patient of the action.

F3.4.

The choice and allocation of the notation should be, it is again emphasized, a secondary process to the major one of arranging the concepts of the classification, and is usually deferred until after the classification is completed. On the other hand, a poorly designed notation can reduce the value of the best constructed scheme.

F4. Automatic approaches to thesaurus construction

Automatic thesaurus construction is one component of the wider field of automatic information retrieval which also encompasses automatic indexing, automatic abstracting and automatic document classification. In all these operations, statistical techniques or computational linguistics replace human intellectual processes. There are two early reviews of the whole field (Stevens, 1980; Sparck Jones, 1974). Lancaster devoted a chapter to a review of automatic thesaurus construction in his *Vocabulary control* (Lancaster, 1986, chapter 21), and Crouch gives a more recent review of the subject (Crouch, 1990).

Automatic extraction indexing, that is the automatic selection of words and phrases to represent the content of the documents, has been shown to be a viable indexing aid for an operational situation. The application of this technique in the selection of candidate terms for conventionally-compiled thesauri is mentioned later (J5.2.2).

Another indexing aid which shows real promise is automatic assignment indexing, or Machine Aided Indexing (MAI). Using this technique, classification codes and indexing terms from a humanly-compiled vocabulary or thesaurus are assigned to a document if they match, above some statistical threshold, the automatically-extracted words and phrases (Aitchison T.M. and Harding, 1983). Advances in this technology are allowing the use of powerful text analysis software to suggest candidate terms for indexing, without having to rely on the costly development of a rule-base, which was previously necessary. A substantial number of already-indexed documents are used to train the text analysis software, which then assigns candidate index terms to the documents for indexer review (or, without indexer review), to produce automatic indexing (Milstead, 1997).

The use of automatic techniques in the construction of thesauri is still not widely applied in the operational situation, although research with experimental systems continues. In the automatic generation of thesauri, relationships between indexing terms are identified mainly statistically rather than semantically. The computer is programmed to form clusters of related terms on the basis of co-occurrence of words derived from a corpus of text.

Automatically-constructed thesauri are of two types, those that are created as an 'internal' or 'global' thesaurus from the processed text before searching, and are used to index both documents and queries, as illustrated in the work of Salton (Salton, 1975, 1983, 1989); Crouch (Crouch, 1990); and Chen (Chen and Lynch, 1992, Chen et al, 1995, 1997); and those that do not require calculation of association prior to the search, sometimes referred to as 'local' thesauri. In this latter approach, developed by Doszkocs (Doszkocs, 1978; Doszkocs and Rapp, 1979), the source of the thesaurus is found in the words associated with the documents retrieved on processing the query against the database. Terms are considered for thesaurus clustering only if they occur in the retrieved set more frequently than in the database as a whole.

In the automatic generation of an 'internal' or 'global' thesaurus, co-occurrence analysis is carried out on the terms or documents in the system to form thesaurus classes, using term weighting based on the Vector Space Model, devised by Salton, and a clustering algorithm.

The Vector Space Model determines the frequency (or weight) of a term in a document (i.e., the number of times the term appears in a document). Terms that appear frequently in a document indicate that a term is highly relevant to a document, and should be given a heavier weight. The inverse document frequency is the total number of documents in which the term appears. Terms that appear in fewer documents in the whole database (the more specific terms) are given higher weights. The combined weight of a term is then computed by multiplying term frequency by inverse term frequency. This reflects the importance of the term within the document, but also within the document collection. The co-occurrence analysis is carried out using an appropriate clustering algorithm to form thesaurus classes, made up of clusters of low-frequency terms. The resulting classes may be fairly heterogeneous.

The purpose of both forms of automatically-generated thesauri is to improve retrieval performance by substituting the appropriate cluster of terms for one of its members. The heterogeneous nature of the clusters makes it more likely that recall rather than precision will be enhanced. The results of tests have shown improved retrieval performance of up to 15% (Crouch, 1990; Chen et al, 1995).

Svenonius has discussed the development of algorithms for constructing related-term relationships, using co-occurrence data. This might be the co-occurrence of terms in text to be searched, when it is assumed that terms that occur frequently in the text are likely to be related. Alternatively, the construction of related-term relationships can be based on co-occurrence data found in transaction-log analyses. The fact that terms have been associated in search strategies in the past increases the probability that they will be associated in future searches. Relationships determined in this way ensure strict adherence to the rule in the Standards that related terms should only be established if they are likely to be used in retrieval (Svenonius, 1986, 1987). For automated categorization as used in corporate taxonomies, see A1.1.1.

Section G: Auxiliary retrieval devices

Auxiliary retrieval devices are those varied tools which generally exist independently of the thesaurus vocabulary itself. It should be noted, however, that some of these, particularly role indicators, are often described as a part of the thesaurus proper; indeed it may be difficult to decide, and may be a matter of opinion, whether devices of this sort form a part of a thesaurus or not. They should, nonetheless, be distinguished from devices such as specificity and use of compound terms, which are unarguably an integral part of the vocabulary, and which are described elsewhere in this book.

G1. Post-coordination and pre-coordination

Coordination of terms in indexing and searching is a powerful device in retrieval. Precision is improved by increasing the number of terms combined in a search, and recall is improved by reducing the number. By combining A and B, greater specificity and precision is achieved than if A or B is treated alone.

In a post-coordinate system (usually a computer database, but historically including systems based on earlier forms of mechanised documentation, such as punched card and optical coincidence systems), the indexing terms allocated to the document are not combined with one another but remain independent. At the searching stage, a request for an combination of these terms can be met. As Lancaster puts it (Lancaster, 1986, Chapter 2), a 'multidimensionality of relationship' amongst the terms is retained. For example, the phrase 'Testing the sound level of audiology rooms in hospitals' consists of four concepts: 'Audiology rooms', 'Sound level', 'Testing' and 'Hospitals'. If all four terms are asked for in combination, the highest level of coordination, and therefore of precision, is achieved. Documents that do not include testing, for example, or that are concerned with audiology rooms not in the hospital environment are excluded. There is always the danger of recall loss with high pre-coordination. Some excluded documents might have been relevant, but the indexer in one document might have omitted the term 'Hospital', and in another might have used the term 'Examination' rather than 'Testing'. By reducing the coordination level to the three terms 'Audiology rooms' 'Sound level' and 'Testing', the first document is retrieved, and by reducing the level to two ('Audiology rooms' and 'Sound level'), the second omitted relevant document is also recalled.

In pre-coordinate systems, such as printed indexes or library subject catalogue entries, terms are combined by the indexer, and are not free to respond to every combination of terms required by the searcher. The terms are combined in a linear 'string', so that the searcher has not only to match the terms used, but also the order within the 'string'. For example, the document on 'Testing the sound levels of audiology rooms in hospitals' might be indexed in the term order 'Audiology rooms': 'Sound levels': 'Testing':

'Hospitals'. A broad search on 'Audiology rooms' would retrieve the document, and all other documents with the term in the lead position, but searches on the other terms in the string would not retrieve the document, unless the terms in the string were rotated to bring each term into the lead position. If the search is to be made more precise by increasing the coordination level, the chances of matching the order of the terms in the indexing decreases with the number of terms in combination in the search. A search with terms in the order 'Audiology rooms': 'Hospital': 'Sound levels': 'Testing' would not retrieve the document mentioned above, for example, which is indexed by the same terms but combined differently. This limitation is partially overcome by restricted rotation of terms in the subordinate positions in the 'string'. Full permutation of the terms would increase unacceptably the size of the printed index.

G2. Post-coordinate searching devices

There are a number of devices which are an essential part of post-coordinate search strategies. All of these may be used with controlled as well as natural language systems. Although these devices are entirely independent of the vocabulary, their application alongside the terminology in searching justifies a mention of them here in this manual. Weighting as a searching device is discussed under G6 below.

They are to be found in bibliographic retrieval systems, CD-ROM products, online databases and (to a more limited extent) in Internet search engines.

G2.1. Logical operators

Post-coordinate systems provide a means of combining search topics into logical groups with the Boolean operators: *OR, AND,* and *NOT.*

The *OR* operator produces retrieval of records having any or all of the *OR* terms. For example, the logical statement:

AUDIOLOGY ROOMS *OR* SOUND LEVEL

will retrieve documents that have one or more of these terms. The use of the *OR* operator broadens the search, reduces the coordination level and tends to increase recall.

The *AND* operator causes the retrieval of records where two or more terms or sets of terms co-occur in the same record. For example, the logical statement:

AUDIOLOGY ROOMS *AND* SOUND LEVEL

will retrieve only those records containing both terms. The *AND* operator narrows the search, increases the coordination level and improves precision.

The *NOT* operator prevents the retrieval of records indexed by a specific term. For example, the logical statement:

AUDIOLOGY ROOMS *NOT* SOUND LEVEL

will exclude those documents that have the term 'Sound level'.

The *NOT* operator should be used with care, as it is easy to eliminate relevant documents as well as the irrelevant. The *NOT* operator is particularly useful in non-subject searching (for example, language and form of document) to further refine a search. For example:

NOT GERMAN LANGUAGE
NOT THESIS

It is important to remember that the order of use of different operators will have a profound effect on the search; and different software packages may work in slightly different ways. For example the search statement A *AND* B *OR* C may be interpreted as either (A *AND* B) *OR* C or A *AND* (B *OR* C).

G2.2. Word fragment searching

A search may be broadened by searching on word fragments. This device is particularly useful when searching in natural language, but it is also applicable with controlled language.

Word fragment searching may use *right truncation*. For instance, all terms beginning with the stem AUDIO?

Or it may use *left truncation*. For example, all words ending with the stem ?OLOGY.

Or it may use *infix truncation*, which retrieves words for which the beginning and end are specified but the middle is not. For example, P?DIATRICS will retrieve 'pediatrics' and 'paediatrics'.

Or the search may be made for a word fragment from any part of the term. For example, ?ELECTRIC? will retrieve 'piezoelectric', 'electricity', 'electrical conductivity', etc., (the last case will depend, of course, on the computer having been instructed to treat 'electrical conductivity' as a compound term).

Truncation, while increasing recall, may retrieve many non-relevant items: the shorter the stem, the greater the possibility of ambiguity. In natural language searching, especially in science and technology databases, a type of thesaurus entry may be built up at the search stage by grouping word fragments, which will retrieve related terms. Lancaster (Lancaster, 1986, Chapter 17) shows how 'the ability to search on the suffixes "biotics or illin or mycin or cycline or myxin" goes a long way toward equivalency with a conventional thesaurus entry "antibiotics" that leads to a list of narrower antibiotic terms'.

Some software packages, particularly those used in full-text retrieval systems, incorporate automatic stemming algorithms. These automatically operate right hand truncation, and have enough machine intelligence to recognize irregular constructions, and to take appropriate action.

G2.3. Word distance device

This device allows for retrieving terms which appear within a specified distance from each other. The range of proximity specifications includes adjacent words.

Example:

AUDIOLOGY (W) ROOMS   The terms are to be adjacent in the order given.

It also includes words within the range of one or more words.

Example:

AUDIOLOGY (nW) ROOMS   The terms are to appear within up to n intervening words in the order given.

Other possibilities are that the terms are to appear in any order and in any subfield of the same field.

This device improves precision and reduces false drops. Compound terms in controlled language perform a precision improvement role similar to that of the adjacent term device.

Some software packages offer what they call 'phrase searching'. This is simply a facility which recognizes that the two or more terms keyed in are adjacent and in the order in which they are presented.

G3. Links

This device, used in post-coordinate systems to avoid false drops, is applied at both the indexing and searching stages. Links are used to show which terms are related in the same document, so that inappropriate combinations of terms are not retrieved. For example, a document number 1000 on 'welding of copper pipes and heat treatment of steel structures' would be indexed:

WELDING	1000A
COPPER	1000A
PIPES	1000A
HEAT TREATMENT	1000B
STEEL	1000B
STRUCTURES	1000B

where the letters A and B indicate which terms are associated, thus ensuring that the document is not retrieved in a search for 'welding of steel'.

Links are powerful devices, but can be detrimental to recall. The linkage may eliminate true as well as false combinations. For example, when links are used with different hierarchical levels:

LEAD	COATINGS	for	COPPER	PIPES
1000A	1000A		1000B	1000B

the false combination 'copper coatings for lead pipes' is avoided, but the legitimate 'coatings for pipes' is also excluded. The use of compound terms, for example, 'lead coatings' and 'copper pipes' serves the same purpose as links in the avoidance of false drops. The *API EnCompass thesaurus (API)* is an example of a thesaurus employing links. Links add to indexing costs and need to be used with caution.

G4. Roles

The role indicator is a signal attached to the index term at the indexing stage to indicate the sense and use of the term in a particular context. It may be shown that a term is functioning as a 'raw material', 'end product' or 'component', or that it is 'passively receiving an operation' or functioning as an 'agent' or 'tool'.

The role indicator is most useful in avoiding recall of terms with incorrect function, particularly in chemical or nuclear processes. For instance, roles may be added to 'Nuclear particles' to distinguish between their functions as 'Projectiles' and as 'Products' in nuclear reactions:

Document	**Index terms**
Gamma neutron reaction (γn)	Reaction. Gamma (2). Neutron (3)
Neutron gamma reaction (nγ)	Reaction. Neutron (2). Gamma (3)

Roles: (2) Projectile, (3) Product

A set of role indicators produced by the Engineers Joint Council (EJC) is shown in Figure 5. Compilers of retrieval languages may develop their own roles, for example, the *API EnCompass thesaurus (API)*, although the EJC table provides a useful checklist. The example given below illustrates the use of EJC-type roles in a practical situation.

Example:

Document: 'Testing of the electric strength of oil impregnated cable paper by means of switching surges'

Roles

8	(Primary topic)	Testing
9	(Passively receiving an operation)	Oil impregnated paper
9	(Passively receiving an operation)	Electric strength
10	(Means to accomplish operation)	Switching surges

The use of roles here, for example, would effectively prevent the recall of this document in response to a search in which switching surges are considered the major topic.

Another, more recent, example of roles is the set of 38 codes introduced in 1996 by Chemical Abstracts Service (Figure 6), such as 'Byproduct', 'Agricultural use', and 'Pollutant'. These role indicators are themselves assigned to one or more of seven sections, or 'supercodes', such as 'Biological study', 'Preparation', and 'Uses', with a small number of 'specific roles', such as 'Properties', remaining outside this categorization. Chemical Abstracts describes these roles as being included in their thesaurus, and denotes them as precision tools, offering advantages such as:

- quick way to find information on reported uses of a substance or substance class
- concise searching with one term for a complex concept
- an easy way to search for the precise role of a substance in indexed records

Since this set of roles is restricted to indicating the significance of chemical substances, and makes no sense independently of substance identification, their use is necessarily restricted to qualification of index terms for specific or generic substances.

Figure 5. EJC role indicators

0 Adjectives Bibliographic Terms

Authors, Both Personal and Corporate
Types of Documents
Journals – – Names, Month, Year, Volume Number, Issue Number (As Five Separate Terms)
Language of Original Document (If Foreign)
All Adjectives

1 Input or Raw Material

Reactant
Base Metal Being Alloyed
Components, Constituents, Or Ingredients Being Combined
Materials Being Shaped or formed
Materials of Construction
Components Being Assembled

2 Output Or Product

Products and Byproducts
Alloys Produced by Designated Name
Mixture or Formulation Produced
Forms or Shapes Being Made
Structures Built or Erected
Devices Resulting From Assembling

3 Undesirables

Contaminants
Impurities
Pollutants
Poisons
Adulterants
Undesirable Components
{ In Inputs
In Outputs
In Media or Environments
In Materials Used
In Materials Passively Receiving Actions }

4 Indicated Uses

To Be Used For – –
To Be Used As – –
For Use With – –
For Later Use In – –
To Be Used On – –
For Later Use As – –

5 Materials "In Which"

In A – – Solvent
In A – – Medium
In – –As a Vehicle
In An Atmosphere Of – –
In – – As a Carrier Gas
In – –As The Dispersion Means

6 That which Affects
7 That which is Affected

Examples
(A) The Document Discusses The Effect of (6) – – – – – On (7) – – – – –
(B) How (6) – – – – – Influences (7) – – – – – is Discussed.
(C) The Document Discusses How (7) – – – – – is Affected by (6)
(D) How (7) – – – – – Depends on (6) – – – – – is Considered.

8 Primary Topics Of Discussion

– – Is Discussed
– – Is Reported
– – Is Described
– – Is Considered
The Topic of Discussion Is – –
The Subject of Consideration Is – –

9 Passive Recipients Possessive (Possessors) Location (Place And Time)

Passive Recipients – Terms for both concrete and abstract concepts which receive operations or processes but which are unchanged by the action

Possessive (Possessors) – Objects of the preposition "of", meaning possession, and other possessive forms.

Location (Place and Time) – – Objects of the prepositions "in", "on", or "at", and other forms meaning location of place or in time; also objects of preposition, "within".

10 Means Used

Using – –
By Means Of – –
By – –
With – – (Meaning "Using")
In or On – – (Meaning "Using")
Through – – (Meaning "Using")

Figure 6
List of CAS Roles

Super roles have 4-letter codes. Specific roles have 3-letter codes. An asterisk (*) means that the specific role is upposted to more than one super role.

ANST Analytical Study
ANT Analyte
AMX Analytical Matrix
ARG Analytical Reagent Use*
ARU Analytical Role, Unclassified

BIOL Biological Study
ADV Adverse Effect Including
     Toxicity
AGR Agricultural Use*
BMF Bioindustrial Manufacture*
BAC Biological Activity or Effector,
     Except Adverse
BOC Biological Occurrence
BPR Biological Process*
BUU Biological Use, Unclassified
BSU Biological Study, Unclassified
BPN Biosynthetic Preparation*
FFD Food or Feed Use*
MFM Metabolic Formation*
THU Therapeutic Use*

FORM Formation, Nonpreparative
FMU Formation, Unclassified
GFM Geological or Astronomical
     Formation
MFM Metabolic Formation*

OCCU Occurrence
BOC Biological Occurrence*
GOC Geological or Astronomical
     Occurrence
OCU Occurrence, Unclassified
POl Pollutant

PREP Preparation
BMF Bioindustrial Manufacture*
BPN Biosynthetic Preparation*
BYP Byproduct
IMF Industrial Manufacture
PUR Purification or Recovery
PNU Preparation, Unclassified
SPN Synthetic Preparation

PROC Process
BPR Biological Process*
GPR Geological or Astronomical
     Process
PEP Physical, Engineering, or
     Chemical Process
REM Removal or Disposal

USES Uses
AGR Agricultural Use*
ARG Analytical Reagent Use*
BUU Biological Use, Unclassified*
CAT Catalyst Use
DEV Device Component Use
FFD Food or Feed Use*
MOA Modifier or Additive Use
NUU Nonbiological Use,
     Unclassified
POF Polymer in Formulation
TEM Technical or Engineered
     Material Use
THU Therapeutic Use*

The following are specific roles that are not upposted to any super roles:

MSC Miscellaneous
PRP Properties
RCT Reactant

Another, similar, example is the series of subheadings used in databases indexed with the *MeSH* medical thesaurus, such as 'Therapeutic use', 'Drug treatment' and 'Adverse effect'. These are similarly restricted in their application to particular types of term. Clearly, only a disease can have a 'Drug treatment', and only a drug can have an 'Adverse effect'.

As with links, roles are precision devices which, except in certain subject areas, are likely to be detrimental to recall. The reasons for this are clear: it is difficult for indexers to apply the roles consistently.

It is even more difficult for the searcher to match the use of a role by the indexer. For instance, in the example above on page 89 the searcher might consider 'Electric strength' as the main topic and code it 8. 'Oil impregnated cable paper' could be coded as role 5 'Environment', or as role 1 'Input' or 'Raw material'.

But it is not only the ambiguity of the roles that complicates searching, it is also the fact that the searcher is in ignorance of the inter-relationship of terms in the indexing, when roles may be affected by the existence of unknown terms not featured in the terms of the questions.

Roles can be simulated to some extent by use of pre-coordinated terms. For example, the use of compound terms:

Gamma projectiles
Gamma product

is just as effective as using 'Gamma' (Role 2) and 'Gamma' (Role 3) to differentiate between the function of the particle as projectile and the particle as product, within a nuclear reaction.

Since roles are likely to curtail recall, and are at the same time expensive to operate at both the search and indexing stage of an information retrieval system, they are not cost-effective except in some specialized subject fields, generally in scientific, technical and biomedical areas. Fugmann, for example, describes the relational indicators that form part of a very detailed set of syntactical tools used in the ICD chemical information system (Fugmann, 1988). The *API EnCompass thesaurus* (*API*) uses roles as well as links, which are described in an article by Hack (Hack, 1984).

G5. Treatment and other aspect codes

The precision performance may be improved by searching on terms, subheadings or equivalent codes added in a separate field at the time of indexing, which specify the treatment and other aspects of the document. For example, the treatment may be 'Practical', 'Experimental', 'Theoretical', or be concerned with 'New developments'. Similarly, it is possible to specify such aspects as the intended audience for the document, the language or physical form, or the subject bias of the document, such as 'diagnosis' or 'side effects' in a medical database; though this latter should be distinguished from the use of roles qualifying a particular term, as discussed above.

G6. Weighting

In weighting systems, values are allocated to indexing terms or search terms according to their importance in particular documents or search programs. Weighting acts as a precision device and also as an output ranking device.

Figure 7 shows an early system of weights worked out by Maron and others (Maron et al., 1959).

Figure 7. Weights (Maron)

Weight	Description	When used
8/8	Major subject	The term is highly specific and covers an entire major subject of the document.
7/8	Major subject	The term is specific and covers most of a major subject of the document.
6/8	More generic subject	The term is too broad and covers a major subject.
5/8	Other important terms	Terms that would be used in a binary indexing system but not a major subject.
4/8	Less generic subject	The term relates to, but is too narrow to cover, a major subject.
3/8	Minor subject	Includes such terms as relate to results of experiments, intermediate methods, possible uses, etc.
2/8	Other subjects	Other relevant tags.
1/8	Barely relevant	Subjects classifier would not want to use, but feels that some users might consider relevant.

A less complex weighting system was used by the second Cranfield Project (Cleverdon, 1966):

9/10   for concepts in the main theme of the document
7/8   For concepts in a major subsidiary theme
5/6   For concepts in a minor subsidiary theme

Pre-coordinate weights are those added to the document at the indexing stage. For example, using weights, a document 'Low temperature silicon epitaxy' might be indexed as follows:

9.   Low temperature
9.   Silicon
10. Epitaxial growth
8.   Substrates
7.   Films
8.   Vapour deposition
8.   Crystal growth
6.   Mercury vapour lamps

In this document mercury vapour lamps are used to illuminate the substrates during deposition; therefore 'Mercury vapour lamps' is a minor concept. It would not be retrieved in response to a search for 'Mercury vapour lamps' as a major concept, weighted more than 6. If all documents on 'Mercury vapour lamps' were required, the weights could be ignored. Term weights in individual documents may also be derived statistically, from within-document frequencies (Croft, 1983).

In post-coordinate weighting, values are assigned to the search terms, reflecting their relative importance to the query. A document score is calculated from the sum of the weights of the matching terms. The output is then ranked in order of the document score. This procedure may be varied, for example, by weighting groups of terms and ranking the output according to the document score calculated on the sum of the matching-group weights. Weighting of search terms may also be a guide when adjusting search strategies. For instance, when reducing the coordination level, terms with lower weights may be excluded first, in the expectation that this will give optimum recall improvement.

Weighting has been widely applied in experimental information retrieval systems, but has, until recently, found little application in operational systems. Databases such as *Medline* and *Biosis* make use of a simple form of weighting, indicating concepts indexed by thesaurus terms as being MAJOR or MINOR aspects of the whole. Some Internet search engines make use of complex weighing algorithms, based on statistical analysis of term frequency, to rank output, but this is wholly automatic, and not associated with thesaurus use (see also F4 for weighting used in automatic generation of indexing languages).

Section H: Thesaurus displays

Methods of displaying thesauri, on paper and on the computer screen, are very varied, and may be categorized in different ways. In this section four types of display are distinguished:

- alphabetical displays showing scope notes, and equivalence, hierarchical and associative relationships for each term
- hierarchical displays generated from the alphabetical display
- systematic and hierarchical displays, showing the overall structure of the thesaurus and all levels of hierarchy
- graphic displays of varying sorts

All thesauri will have an alphabetical display, which may or may not be associated with the other forms of display.

Rotated and permuted display, giving access to each individual word in each term, which the ANSI/NISO Z39.19 Standard regards as a separate kind of display, is included here within alphabetical displays.

The treatment of displays in multilingual thesauri are considered in a separate section (H6), at the end of this chapter.

H1. Screen displays

The ANSI Standard is the only Standard providing guidelines on both printed and screen displays. It points out that the screen display is harder for the searcher to browse and to remember the context. As well as being more tiring to view than the printed display, the size of the screen 'page' can make it 'difficult to grasp information that is perfectly comprehensible in the printed page'.

On the other hand, if hypertext is available to provide easy switching between terms in different displays (see K4.2.3), this can speed up the locating of terms and moving between them, which, with a large and bulky printed thesaurus, can be a slow and cumbersome process. Another advantage of a thesaurus in electronic form is that implementations that facilitate searching by all the words in a compound term provide a service equivalent to that of a permuted index (see H2.3), which is not always available in a printed thesaurus.

Figure 8 shows an example of a screen display from the *Zoological record online thesaurus* on the Dialog system. The entry shows the term 'Sedation', including scope notes, and broader, narrower and related terms. Thesauri are also available over the Internet (see B3.1), for example the *NASA thesaurus* (NASA) (see Figure 9).

Figure 8. Screen Display – Alphabetical thesaurus Zoological Record Online®

Ref	Items	Type	RT	Index-term
R1	24		9	*SEDATION-
R2	0	S		Used only when technique itself is
R3	0	S		discussed/evaluated.
R4	46	B	45	TECHNIQUES-
R5	0	N	7	ANAESTHESIA-
R6	0	N	6	DARTING-
R7	0	N	4	IMMOBILIZATION-
R8	0	N	6	TRANQUILIZATION-
R9	4	R	10	HANDLING-TECHNIQUES
R10	1	R	6	PHYSICAL-RESTRAINING-TECHNIQUES

In the thesaurus entry, the term entered is listed first. If scope notes are included, they are listed next, indicated by S under Type. Broader terms are listed under Type as B (for examples, TECHNIQUES-), narrower terms as N (DARTING-), and related terms as R (HANDLING-TECHNIQUES). At this point, users can select the appropriate term and search or explode the term. To explode, use the term, including hyphens, followed by an exclamation mark (!). This will search the term and all narrower terms listed under it.

Figure 9. Screen Display – Alphabetical thesaurus NASA

GALACTIC CLUSTERS

Narrower Terms:

LOCAL GROUP (ASTRONOMY)
VIRGO GALACTIC CLUSTER

Broader Terms:

CELESTIAL BODIES
GALAXIES

Related Terms:

AGGLOMERATION
CLUSTERS
COOLING FLOWS (ASTROPHYSICS)
DISK GALAXIES
ELLIPTICAL GALAXIES
METALLICITY
MISSING MASS (ASTROPHYSICS)
STAR CLUSTERS
STAR DISTRIBUTION
STELLAR SYSTEMS

Scope Note:

(RESTRICTED TO CLUSTERS OF GALAXIES; EXCLUDES OPEN CLUSTERS)

An advantage of a screen display is that it may give full details of an individual term record, as illustrated by the example in Figure 10, showing entries from a thesaurus using the *Lexico* software. The term record includes, in addition to scope notes and standard relationships, details of the record type, record approval status, cataloguer's notes, date created and latest update data. It is likely that the current interest in visualization will affect the way in which thesauri may be accessed online. For an interesting discussion of visualization see Song (2000).

Figure 10. Screen display term record
Thesaurus using the Lexico software system

```
┌─────────────────────────────────────────────────────────────────────┐
│ ■  LEXICO/2 - TGM - II                                      ▣  ▣      │
├─────────────────────────────────────────────────────────────────────┤
│ Application Edit Print Refresh Options Exit Help                      │
├─────────────────────────────────────────────────────────────────────┤
│    Contents of Record by: TERM                              ▣  ▣      │
├─────────────────────────────────────────────────────────────────────┤
│ Switches Copy Print Format                                            │
├─────────────────────────────────────────────────────────────────────┤
```

Term	Bible cards	
Record Type	Main Term	
Approval Status	y	
Approval Status Date	26-Aug-93	
Public Note	Cards with a scriptural picture or quotation, or both. Sometimes issued in sets and often used as rewards of merit in Sunday schools.	
Cataloger's Note	MARC field 655.	
Used For	Scripture cards	
	Sunday school cards	
Broader Term	Devotional images	
Related Term	Collecting cards	
	Rewards of merit	
Date Created	10-Nov-92	
Latest Update	26-Aug-93	
Term	Billboard posters	
Record Type	Main Term	
Approval Status	y	
Approval Status Date	20-Aug-93	
Public Note	Large multi-sheet posters; intended for posting on billboards, fences or similar surfaces.	
Cataloger's Note	MARC field 655	
Broader Term	Posters	

H2. Alphabetical display

This kind of display is ubiquitous, whether in paper or electronic form, and is usually the most acceptable to end users. Alphabetical displays in multilingual thesauri are considered in H6.

H2.1. Layout and reference structure

The conventional form of the alphabetical display became established in 1967 on the publication of the *Thesaurus of engineering and scientific terms* (*TEST*) (Thesaurus, 1967) (see Figure 11).

Figure 11. Conventional alphabetical display
Thesaurus of Engineering and Scientific Terms.

—Food services
Cooking devices 0608
  UF Electrical cooking devices
      French fryers
      Pressure cookers
      Toasters
      Waffle irons
  RT Kitchen equipment and supplies
      Kitchens
Cooking liquors (pulping) 1112
  NT Spent sulfite liquors
      Sulfite cooking liquors
      White liquors
  RT—Chemical pumping
      Semichemical pulping
      —Spent liquors (pulping)
Cook off 2102
  RT Propellant storage
      —solid rocket propellants
Coolant pumps 1311
  BT Pumps
  RT—Air conditioning equipment
      Cooling systems
      —Refrigerating machinery
Coolants 1301 1107
  RT Air conditioning
      Air Cooling
      —Brines
      —Coolers
      —Cooling
      Cooling systems
      Cutting fluids
      Dry ice ®
      Gas cooling
      —Liquid cooling
      Liquid metal coolants
      Nuclear reactor coolants
      —Nuclear reactors
      Refrigerants
      Water cooling
Coolers 1301
  UF Aftercoolers
      Intercoolers
      Precoolers
  NT Air coolers
      Beverage coolers
      Milk coolers
      Oil coolers
      Unit coolers
      Water coolers
  RT—Air conditioners
      —Air conditioning equipment
      —Compressors
      Coolants
      —Cooling
      Cooling systems
      Dehumidifiers
      Freezers
      Ice refrigeration
      —Refrigerating
      —Refrigerating machinery
      —Refrigerators
Cool flames 2102
  BT Flames
  RT—Combustion
Cooling 1301 2013
  UF Chilling
      Heat dissipation
  NT Adiabatic demagnetization
      Air cooling
      —Evaporative cooling
      Expansion cooling
      Film cooling
      —Liquid cooling
      Radiant cooling
      Sublimation cooling
      Sweat cooling
      Thermoelectric cooling

Water cooling
  RT Ablation
      Air conditioning
      Cold treatment
      —Condensing
      Contraction
      Coolants
      —Coolers
      —Cooling coils
      Cooling curves
      Cooling load
      Cooling rate
      Cooling systems
      Cooling towers
      Desuperheating
      Environmental engineering
      —Fans
      Flooding
      —Freezing
      —Heating
      Heat loss
      Heat radiators
      —Heat transfer
      Hilsch tubes
      Jackets
      —Melting
      —Quenching (cooling)
      Racalescence
      —Refrigerating
      Supercooling
      —Temperature
      Temperature control
      Temperature distribution
      Thermal cycling tests
      Thermal shock
      Thermal stresses
      —Ventilation
      Venting
      Wetting
Cooling coils 1301
  NT Direct expansion cooling coils
  RT—Air conditioning equipment
      —Condensers (liquefiers)
      Condenser tubes
      —Cooling
      Cooling systems
      Evaporators
      Expansion valves
      Gas expanders
      —Refrigeration machinery
Cooling curves 1301
  BT Charts
      Graphs (charts)
  RT—Cooling
      Cooling rate
      Phase diagrams
      —Thermal analysis
Cooling fans 1301
  BT Fans
Cooling fins 1301
  UF †Finned tubes
      Fins (coolers)
  BT Fins
  RT Cooling systems
      Engine blocks
      Engine cylinders
      Heat exchangers
      Heat radiators
Cooling load 1301
  RT Air conditioning
      —Cooling
      Enthalpy
      Fluid infiltration
      Heating load
      Heat storage
      —Heat transfer
      Heat transmission
      —Loads (forces)

—Thermal insulation
Cooling rate 1301
  BT Rates (per time)
  RT Air conditioning
      —Cooling
      Cooling curves
      Cooling systems
      —Freezing
      —Precipitation heat treatment
      —Refrigerating
      Thermal shock
      Thermal stresses
Cooling systems 1301
  UF Water cooling systems
  RT Absorbers (equipment)
      Absorption refrigeration
      Air circulation
      —Air conditioners
      Air conditioning
      —Air conditioning equipment
      Air cooling
      Beverage coolers
      Blowers
      —Compressors
      —Condensers (liquefiers)
      Coolant pumps
      Coolants
      —Coolers
      —Cooling
      —Cooling coils
      Cooling fins
      Cooling rate
      Cooling towers
      Dehumidification
      Ducts
      Engine blocks
      —Evaporative cooling
      Evaporators
      —Exhaust systems
      —Fans
      Gas expanders
      Heat exchangers
      Heat pumps
      Heat radiators
      Heat sinks
      Humidity control
      —Intake systems
      —Liquid cooling
      Lubrication systems
      Mechanical refrigeration
      Piping systems
      —Porous metals
      Refrigerants
      —Refrigerating
      —Refrigerating machinery
      Registers (air circulation)
      Steam jet apparatus
      Steam jet refrigeration
      Temperature control
      Thermoelectric refrigeration
      —Transpiration
      Transport refrigeration
      Unit coolers
      —Ventilation
      Vents
      Water coolers
      Water cooling
Cooling towers 1301 0701 1309
  UF Water cooling towers
  RT—Air conditioning equipment
      Columns (process engineering)
      —Cooling
      Cooling systems
      —Evaporative cooling
      —Refrigerating machinery
      Water conservation
      Water coolers

Subject Category Index numbers follow main terms; (—) = See main entry for narrower terms; † = Consult main entry;

Preferred and non-preferred indexing terms are listed in one sequence in the following order.

PREFERRED TERM
    SN Scope notes or definitions
    UF References to equivalent non-preferred terms
    BT References to broader terms
    NT References to narrower terms
    RT References to related terms

Non-preferred term
  USE PREFERRED TERM

Non-preferred term
  USE PREFERRED TERM 1
    and PREFERRED TERM 2

Example:

Preferred term entry

  DEPRIVED FAMILIES
    SN Socially disadvantaged and underprivileged
    UF Underprivileged families
    BT Families
    NT Homeless families
        One parent families
    RT Deprivation

Non-preferred term entry

  Underprivileged families
    USE DEPRIVED FAMILIES

Non-preferred term entry to terms to be used in combination to represent the concept (see also 'Syntactical factoring' in E2.4.2(a))

  One parent family welfare
    USE ONE PARENT FAMILIES
    and (or +) SOCIAL WELFARE

with access points under the constituent preferred terms

  ONE PARENT FAMILIES
    and (or +) SOCIAL WELFARE
    UF One parent family welfare

  SOCIAL WELFARE
    and (or +) ONE PARENT FAMILIES
    UF One parent family welfare

For the layout used to display factored terms in the *Thesaurus of engineering and scientific terms (TEST)*, see E2.4.2(a) and 'Cooling fins' in Figure 11.

The ANSI Standard refers to the layout as 'Conventional flat thesaurus'.

International symbols may replace the standard SN, UF, BT/NT/RT abbreviations illustrated above. For example:

Preferred term
= Equivalent terms, non-preferred terms
< Broader terms
> Narrower terms
− Related terms

Non-preferred term
→ Preferred term

A slightly modified version of these is used in the British Standards Institution *ROOT thesaurus* (British, 1985b) (See Figure 23).

H2.2. Multilevel hierarchies

The conventional alphabetical thesaurus does not show the full hierarchy of broader and narrower terms at the entry point for the indexing term. The information given is at only one hierarchical step above and below the term.

Some thesauri, for example the *CAB thesaurus* (CAB, 1995) shown in Figure 12 and the European Community's *Food: multilingual thesaurus* (Commission, 1979) give broader and narrower terms to more than one level in the main alphabetical display, for example:

DEPRIVED FAMILIES
    UF   Underprivileged families
    BT1   Families
      BT2   Social institutions
    NT1   Homeless families
    NT1   One parent families
      NT2   Fatherless families
    RT   Deprivation

Other thesauri show multilevel hierarchies inherent within the structure of the alphabetical thesaurus by computer-derived hierarchical displays, which are printed in a sequence separated from the main alphabetical section (see H3).

A disadvantage of multilevel hierarchies in the alphabetical display is the redundancy involved in repeating the printing of lengthy hierarchies from different entry points. It is for this reason that the *CAB thesaurus* has abandoned this style of alphabetical display in future editions.

H2.3. Permuted index

In some thesauri a separate index may be prepared to bring to the front the second and third words in compound terms. This index is especially useful in making accessible constituent terms which are not indexing terms and therefore do not occur anywhere else in the thesaurus. The permuted index is usually in the form of a KWIC or KWOC index. Figure 13 shows an extract from the permuted index, in KWOC form, included in the *International thesaurus of refugee terminology* (Aitchison, 1996).

Figure 12. Multilevel alphabetical thesaurus
CAB thesaurus

AIR POLLUTANTS *cont.*
- rt   air pollution
- rt   pollution

AIR POLLUTION
- uf   *atmospheric pollution*
- BT1   pollution
- rt   air
- rt   air pollutants
- rt   air quality
- rt   factory fumes
- rt   fallout
- rt   greenhouse effect
- rt   nitrogen oxides
- rt   scrubbers

AIR QUALITY
- BT1   quality
- rt   air
- rt   air cleaners
- rt   air conditioning
- rt   air filters
- rt   air pollution

air resistance
- USE   **drag**

AIR SACS
- BT1   respiratory system
- BT2   body parts
- NT1   pneumatophores
- rt   air
- rt   respiratory gases

air, saturated
- USE   **aerated steam**

AIR SPORA
- BT1   air microbiology
- BT2   microbiology
- BT3   biology
- rt   air

AIR TEMPERATURE
- BT1   temperature
- rt   air
- rt   convection
- rt   environmental temperature
- rt   greenhouse effect
- rt   solar radiation
- rt   terrestrial radiation

AIR TRANSPORT
- uf   *air freight*
- uf   *aviation*
- uf   *transport, air*
- BT1   transport
- rt   aerial methods
- rt   agricultural aviation
- rt   air
- rt   aircraft
- rt   airports

AIRA
- BT1   poaceae
- NT1   aira caryophyllea
- NT1   aira multiculmis
- NT1   aira praecox

AIRA CARYOPHYLLEA
- BT1   aira
- BT2   poaceae
- BT1   pasture plants

AIRA MULTICULMIS
- BT1   aira
- BT2   poaceae
- BT1   pasture plants

AIRA PRAECOX
- BT1   aira
- BT2   poaceae

AIRBORNE INFECTION
- BT1   infection
- BT2   disease transmission
- BT3   transmission

AIRCRAFT
- NT1   balloons
- NT1   helicopters
- NT1   microlight aircraft
- rt   aerial sowing
- rt   aerial surveys
- rt   aerodynamic properties
- rt   aerodynamics
- rt   agricultural aviation
- rt   air
- rt   air transport
- rt   airports
- rt   bird strikes
- rt   hovercraft
- rt   propellers
- rt   vehicles

airfields
- USE   **airports**

AIRPORT MALARIA
- BT1   malaria
- BT2   human diseases
- BT3   diseases
- BT2   mosquito-borne diseases
- BT3   vector-borne diseases
- BT4   diseases
- BT2   protozoal diseases
- BT3   parasitoses
- BT4   diseases

AIRPORTS
- uf   *airfields*
- rt   air transport
- rt   aircraft

AIRTIGHT STORAGE
- uf   *storage, airtight*
- BT1   storage
- rt   leakage

AIZOACEAE
- uf   *mesembryaceae*
- NT1   carpobrotus
- NT2   carpobrotus edulis
- NT1   cephalophyllum
- NT2   cephalophyllum loreum
- NT1   conophytum
- NT1   delosperma
- NT2   delosperma alba
- NT1   dorotheanthus
- NT2   dorotheanthus bellidiformis
- NT1   drosanthemum
- NT2   drosanthemum hispidum
- NT1   faucaria
- NT2   faucaria bosscheana
- NT1   fenestraria
- NT1   galenia
- NT2   galenia pubescens

AIZOACEAE *cont.*
- NT1   gisekia
- NT2   gisekia pharmacoides
- NT1   lampranthus
- NT2   lampranthus productus
- NT1   lithops
- NT2   lithops bromfieldii
- NT2   lithops divergens
- NT2   lithops fulviceps
- NT2   lithops marmorata
- NT1   malephora
- NT2   malephora croceus
- NT2   malephora luteolus
- NT1   mesembryanthemum
- NT2   mesembryanthemum crystallinum
- NT1   nelia
- NT2   nelia meyeri
- NT1   pleiospilos
- NT2   pleiospilos nobilis
- NT1   sesuvium
- NT2   sesuvium portulacastrum
- NT1   trianthema
- NT2   trianthema decandra
- NT2   trianthema portulacastrum
- NT2   trianthema triquetra
- rt   caryophyllales

AJELLOMYCES
- uf   *emmonsiella*
- BT1   gymnoascales
- BT2   ascomycotina
- BT3   eumycota
- BT4   fungi
- NT1   ajellomyces capsulatus
- NT1   ajellomyces dermatitidis
- rt   blastomyces

AJELLOMYCES CAPSULATUS
- uf   *emmonsiella capsulata*
- BT1   ajellomyces
- BT2   gymnoascales
- BT3   ascomycotina
- BT4   eumycota
- BT5   fungi
- rt   histoplasma capsulatum

AJELLOMYCES DERMATITIDIS
- BT1   ajellomyces
- BT2   gymnoascales
- BT3   ascomycotina
- BT4   eumycota
- BT5   fungi
- rt   blastomyces dermatitidis

AJMAN
- BT1   united arab emirates
- BT2   persian gulf states
- BT3   west asia
- BT4   asia

AJUGA
- BT1   lamiaceae
- NT1   ajuga chamaepitys
- NT1   ajuga iva
- NT1   ajuga reptans

AJUGA CHAMAEPITYS
- BT1   ajuga
- BT2   lamiaceae
- BT1   antibacterial plants
- BT1   antifungal plants
- BT1   insecticidal plants

Figure 13. Permuted Index
International thesaurus of refugee terminology

REFUGEES
Child refugees 3RT
Convention refugees BCO.G
De facto refugees BCO.K
Disabled refugees 3RX
Environmental refugees 3O
Historical groups of refugees 3RB
Mandate refugees BCO.M
OAU Convention refugees BCO.I
Refugees 3R
Refugees in orbit 3RK
Refugees in transit 3RL
Refugees sur place 3RN
Refugees without asylum country 3RP
Rural refugees 3RD
Safety of refugees BYP
Stateless refugees 3RR
Statutory refugees BCO.E
Teaching materials on refugees NLG.R
Urban refugees 3RE
Women refugees 3RW

REGIONAL
Nationalities and regional groups 5
Regional organizations DP
Regional refugee instruments BCI.V
Regional treaties IRM.G

REGISTRATION
Registration of immigrants IOR.A

REGULATION
Regulation of status JGI.ILE

REHABILITATION
Medical rehabilitation OPH

REINTEGRATION
Reintegration COE

REJECTED
Rejected asylum seekers 3PD

REJECTION
Rejection at border BKS

RELATED
Refugee-related declarations BCI.T

RELATIONS
Community relations JUI
Foreign relations GYH
Interethnic relations 4AA.R
International relations GY
Labour relations LOI
Public relations VJC
Refugee/local community relations CRT.CE

RELATIONSHIPS
Social relationships JLP

RELIEF
Emergency relief CAP
Emergency relief operations CAP.O
Emergency relief organizations CAP.B
Emergency relief programmes CAP.D
Emergency relief supplies CAP.S
Public relief MJK.Y

RELIGION
Freedom of religion HHE.B

RELIGIOUS
Religious conflict FEH
Religious discrimination HVR
Religious groups 6
Religious institutions KRO
Religious leaders KRB
Religious persecution BPM
Religious practice KRK

RELOCATION
Forced relocation JGN.F

REMAIN
Exceptional leave to remain IOK.EME

REMITTANCES
Remittances LJQ.E

RENEWABLE
Renewable energy resources TNK

REPATRIATION
Involuntary repatriation COQ
Repatriation CO
Voluntary repatriation COH
Voluntary repatriation programmes COH.G

REPORTS
Annual reports VMG.EGA
Project reports VMG.EGP
Reports VMG.EG

REPRESENTATION
Legal representation IJD.C

REPRESSION
Repression GIN

REPUBLIC
Central African Republic Y5120
Czech Republic Y8018.2
Democratic People's Republic of Korea Y7121
Dominican Republic Y6129
German Democratic Republic Y8024
Lao People's Democratic Republic Y7533
Mongolia, People's Republic Y7138
Republic GT9
Republic of Korea Y7144
Republic of Palau Y9022
Saharan Arab Democratic Republic Z5551
Slovak Republic Y8044.5
Syrian Arab Republic Y7348
United Republic of Tanzania Y5264
Yemen Arab Republic Y7356
Yemen Democratic Republic Y7357

On occasion, entries from a permuted index may be interfiled with the main alphabetical display. This layout is found in the *UNESCO thesaurus* (UNESCO, 1995). Where a computer-generated permuted index does not exist, it may be useful to add to the main alphabetical sequence lead-in terms from words in compound terms, which do not exist as preferred terms in the thesaurus. For example:

Induction, electrostatic
    use ELECTROSTATIC INDUCTION

where the term 'Induction' is not an indexing term (see also E2.2 and F1.1.2.b).

H2.4. Alphabetization

There are two main human systems of alphabetization: letter-by-letter or word-by-word. Once the decision has been made to accept either of these systems, the rules should be clearly stated in the introduction to the thesaurus.

(a) Letter-by-letter arrangement
In this system all spaces between words are ignored, as well as all characters other than left parenthesis, numbers and letters. Items are filed according to the sequence:

Left parenthesis
Numerals in ascending value
Letters A–Z

The system brings together words which may be spelled as one word, two words, or hyphenated:

Metalworking
Metal working
Metal-working

but, on the other hand, related terms may be separated in the sequence, as are the terms for 'Lead compounds' generally and specific 'Lead compounds' in the following example:

Lead compounds
Leadership
Leading edges
Lead oxide
Lead selenide

(b) Word-by-word arrangement
In this system, favoured by the British Standard on alphabetical arrangement, each word is considered in turn and a given complete word will precede any term beginning with the same sequence of letters as part of the word. Word-by-word arrangement leads to the grouping of related terms, but this does not happen consistently because the arbitrary separation or joining of words affects the sequence. The two systems of alphabetization are compared below:

Word-by-word	*Letter-by-letter*
Black Arts	Black Arts
Black Book	Blackberry
Black Earth	Black Book

Blackberry	Blackburn
Blackburn	Black Earth

Hyphens are usually treated as spaces in alphabetization.

H2.5. Different alphabetical displays for end-users and indexers

An alphabetical display may, on occasion, have different degrees of detail and forms of annotation, according to whether it is envisaged for use by end users or by indexers/searchers. A good example is *Medical subject headings (MeSH)* (Medical) which has a version for end users less detailed than the 'annotated alphabetic list' shown in Figure 20b.

H3. Hierarchies generated from the alphabetical display

These are hierarchical displays generated by computer from the one-level broader/narrower term data existing in the alphabetical thesaurus. They complement the alphabetical thesaurus by displaying preferred terms in the context of their full hierarchy (see also H2.2).

H3.1. Top term arrangement

In this type of hierarchical display, developed for the *INSPEC thesaurus* (INSPEC, Figure 14), the top terms (TTs) of the hierarchy are listed in a separate alphabetical sequence, each followed by the full sequence of subordinate terms. Indexing terms are located within these hierarchies via entries in the alphabetical display showing the top term of the hierarchy to which the term belongs.

Example in the style of the INSPEC thesaurus:

> *Alphabetical section*
> One parent families
>   BT Deprived families
>   NT Fatherless families
>   TT Social institutions
>
> *Computer-generated hierarchies*
> Social institutions
>   ...
>   Families
>   .Deprived families
>   ..Homeless families
> →..One parent families
>   ...Fatherless families

Figure 14. Hierarchies generated from the alphabetic display
INSPEC thesaurus

Hierarchies

telecontrol
. telerobotics

temperature
. atmospheric temperature
. boiling point
. Debye temperature
. ferroelectric Curie temperature
. magnetic transition temperature
. . Curie temperature
. . Morin temperature
. . Neel temperature
. melting point
. plasma temperature
. superconducting transition
  temperature

test equipment
→ . automatic test equipment
. battery testers

testing
. aerospace testing
. . aircraft testing
. antenna testing
→ . automatic testing
. . automatic test software
. boundary scan testing
. built-in self test
. cable testing
. . power cable testing
. computer testing
. conformance testing
. electron beam testing
. electron device testing
. . electron tube testing
. . semiconductor device testing
. . superconducting device testing
. electronic equipment testing
. . circuit testing
. . . integrated circuit testing
. . . printed circuit testing
. . computer equipment testing
. . telecommunication equipment
   testing
. environmental testing
. . environmental stress screening
. impulse testing
. insulation testing
. . insulator testing
. life testing
. logic testing

Top term entry to hierarchies

automatic teller machines
BT EFTS
TT computer applications
    data handling
    finance
RT bank data processing
    banking
    computer networks
    point of sale systems
CC C5540; C7120; D2020E
DI   January 1985
PT EFTS

→**automatic test equipment**
UF computerised test equipment
BT computerised instrumentation
    test equipment
TT computer applications
    instrumentation
→   test equipment
RT automatic test software
    automatic testing
    logic analysers
    portable instruments
    quality control
    reliability
    testing
CC B7210B; C3200; C3380; C7410H
DI   January 1969

automatic test software
includes software for computerised
instrumentation
BT automatic testing
    computer software
    electrical engineering computing
TT computer applications
    computer software
    engineering
    testing
RT automatic test equipment
    computerised instrumentation
    electronic engineering computing
CC B7210B; C7410H
DI   January 1995
PT automatic test equipment
    automatic testing

→**automatic testing**
UF ATPG
    self testing
NT automatic test software
BT testing
→TT testing
RT automatic optical inspection
    automatic test equipment
    boundary scan testing
    built-in self test
    design for testability
    quality control
    reliability
CC B7210B; C3380; C7410H
DI   January 1969

automation
NT branch automation
    factory

Figure 15. Hierarchies generated from the alphabetical display
Thesaurus of ERIC descriptors
Two-way hierarchical term display

```
::: MEASURES (INDIVIDUALS)
:: TESTS
: OBJECTIVE TESTS
MULTIPLE CHOICE TESTS

: DISABILITIES
MULTIPLE DISABILITIES
. DEAF BLIND

: EMPLOYMENT
MULTIPLE EMPLOYMENT

::::: METHODS
:::: EVALUATION METHODS
::: DATA ANALYSIS
:: STATISTICAL ANALYSIS
: REGRESSION (STATISTICS)
MULTIPLE REGRESSION ANALYSIS

::: LIBERAL ARTS
:: MATHEMATICS
: ARITHMETIC
MULTIPLICATION

::: FACILITIES
:: EDUCATIONAL FACILITIES
: CLASSROOMS
MULTIPURPOSE CLASSROOMS

: LEARNING
MULTISENSORY LEARNING

:: METHODS
: RESEARCH METHODOLOGY
MULTITRAIT MULTIMETHOD
   TECHNIQUES

:: INSTITUTIONS
: SCHOOLS
MULTIUNIT SCHOOLS

:::: METHODS
::: EVALUATION METHODS
:: DATA ANALYSIS
: STATISTICAL ANALYSIS
MULTIVARIATE ANALYSIS
. CLUSTER ANALYSIS
. DISCRIMINANT ANALYSIS
. FACTOR ANALYSIS
.. OBLIQUE ROTATION
.. ORTHOGONAL ROTATION
. MULTIDIMENSIONAL SCALING
. PATH ANALYSIS

:: GEOGRAPHIC REGIONS
: URBAN AREAS
: COMMUNITY
MUNICIPALITIES
. BOOMTOWNS
. SMALL TOWNS

:: INDIVIDUAL CHARACTERISTICS
: PHYSICAL CHARACTERISTICS
MUSCULAR STRENGTH

: MUSCULOSKELETAL SYSTEM
MUSCULAR SYSTEM

MUSCULOSKELETAL SYSTEM
. MUSCULAR SYSTEM
. SKELETAL SYSTEM
```

```
: FACILITIES
MUSEUMS

::: LIBERAL ARTS
:: HUMANITIES
: FINE ARTS
MUSIC
. APPLIED MUSIC
. HARMONY (MUSIC)
. JAZZ
. MELODY
. ORIENTAL MUSIC
. ROCK MUSIC
. VOCAL MUSIC
.. CHORAL MUSIC
.. SONGS
... ART SONG
... BALLADS
... HYMNS

: ACTIVITIES
MUSIC ACTIVITIES
. CONCERTS
. INSTRUMENTATION AND
     ORCHESTRATION
. SINGING

MUSICAL COMPOSITION

: EQUIPMENT
MUSICAL INSTRUMENTS

:: EDUCATION
: AESTHETIC EDUCATION
MUSIC APPRECIATION

: EDUCATION
MUSIC EDUCATION
. KODALY METHOD
. ORFF METHOD
. SUZUKI METHOD

: FACILITIES
MUSIC FACILITIES

:: GROUPS
: ARTISTS
MUSICIANS

:: LITERACY
:: LANGUAGE ARTS
: READING
MUSIC READING

:::: GROUPS
::: PERSONNEL
:: PROFESSIONAL PERSONNEL
: TEACHERS
MUSIC TEACHERS

: METHODS
MUSIC TECHNIQUES

: THEORIES
MUSIC THEORY

: THERAPY
MUSIC THERAPY

MUTUAL INTELLIGIBILITY
```

```
:::: LIBERAL ARTS
::: SCIENCES
:: NATURAL SCIENCES
: BIOLOGICAL SCIENCES
MYCOLOGY

::: DISABILITIES
:: VISUAL IMPAIRMENTS
: AMETROPIA
MYOPIA

MYSTICISM

MYTHIC CRITICISM (1969 1980)

MYTHOLOGY

NARCOTICS
. COCAINE
.. CRACK
. HEROIN
. MARIJUANA
. SEDATIVES

: LITERARY DEVICES
NARRATION

::: MEASURES (INDIVIDUALS)
:: TESTS
: ACHIEVEMENT TESTS
NATIONAL COMPETENCY TESTS

: CURRICULUM
NATIONAL CURRICULUM
. BRITISH NATIONAL CURRICULUM

: NATIONAL SECURITY
NATIONAL DEFENSE

NATIONALISM
. PATRIOTISM

:::: INSTITUTIONS
:::: INFORMATION SOURCES
::: LIBRARIES
:: SPECIAL LIBRARIES
: GOVERNMENT LIBRARIES
NATIONAL LIBRARIES

::: DATA
:: STATISTICAL DATA
: NORMS
NATIONAL NORMS

:: GROUPS
: ORGANIZATIONS (GROUPS)
NATIONAL ORGANIZATIONS

: PROGRAMS
NATIONAL PROGRAMS

NATIONAL SECURITY
. NATIONAL DEFENSE

::: METHODS
:: EVALUATION METHODS
: SURVEYS
NATIONAL SURVEYS

:: INSTRUCTION
: HUMANITIES INSTRUCTION
```

H3.2. Two-way hierarchies

Another way of showing multilevel hierarchies is found in the two-way hierarchical term display of the *Thesaurus of ERIC descriptors* (Thesaurus, 1995) illustrated in Figure 15, where the broader and narrower terms of the indexing term are given above and below the preferred term in indented positions.

Example:

:Social institutions	(Broader term 1)
Families	(Preferred term)
.Deprived families	(Narrower term level 1)
..Homeless families	(Narrower term level 2)
..One parent families	(Narrower term level 2)
...Fatherless families	(Narrower term level 3)

The preferred terms are arranged in alphabetical sequence.

H4. Systematic displays and hierarchies

A systematic display (also known as a classified or subject display or hierarchy) 'arranges categories or hierarchies of terms according to their meanings and logical inter-relationships'.

A systematic thesaurus must always have two parts:

- The systematic section
- The alphabetical section (either an index or a full thesaurus which directs the user to the appropriate parts of the systematic section)

Thesauri differ in the emphasis each puts on the two sections. The systematic section may be an auxiliary if the main part of the thesaurus is alphabetical; or it may be the main part of the thesaurus, carrying all definitional and relational data, with the alphabetical section in its index form playing a minor role; or the systematic section and the alphabetical section may have equal status, the relational data being divided between them, or provided in full under both sections of the thesaurus.

The link between the two systems is usually the notation (i.e., an address code of numbers and letters – see F3), which is added to the systematic section and which functions as a reference in the alphabetical thesaurus.

A systematic display provides an 'overall structure or macroclassification' (ISO 2788) within which the relations between hierarchies (see F1.2) and groups of terms otherwise related (see F1.1 and F1.3) may be clarified and presented. The creation of systematic displays is discussed more fully at F2.3 and J7.2.1. There are several options to consider when developing this type of display, including:

- Broad subject groups, versus detailed systems
- Faceted classification, versus enumerative, non-facet systems
- Primary arrangement by discipline or subject field, versus fundamental facets
- The systematic display as the source of the alphabetical display versus a separate classification having a different structure against which the indexing terms are arranged

Figure 16. Broad subject groups
Thesaurus of ERIC descriptors

INITIAL TEACHING ALPHABET
INTERPRETIVE READING (1966 1980)
LITERACY
LITERACY EDUCATION
MISCUE ANALYSIS
ORAL READING
PHONICS
PREREADING EXPERIENCE
READABILITY
READABILITY FORMULAS
READER TEXT RELATIONSHIP
READING
READING ABILITY
READING ACHIEVEMENT
READING ALOUD TO OTHERS
READING ASSIGNMENTS
READING ATTITUDES
READING CENTERS
READING COMPREHENSION
READING DEVELOPMENT (1966 1980)
READING DIAGNOSIS
READING DIFFICULTIES
READING DIFFICULTY (1966 1980)
READING FAILURE
READING GAMES
READING HABITS
READING IMPROVEMENT
READING INSTRUCTION
READING INTERESTS
READING LEVEL (1966 1980)
READING MATERIAL SELECTION
READING PROCESSES
READING PROGRAMS
READING RATE
READING READINESS
READING SKILLS
READING STRATEGIES
READING WRITING RELATIONSHIP
RECREATIONAL READING
REMEDIAL READING
SIGHT METHOD
SIGHT VOCABULARY
SILENT READING
SPEED READING
STORY GRAMMAR
STORY READING
SUPPLEMENTARY READING MATERIALS
SUSTAINED SILENT READING
TEXT STRUCTURE
WORD RECOGNITION
WORD STUDY SKILLS

470 PHYSICAL EDUCATION AND RECREATION

AEROBICS
AQUATIC SPORTS
ARCHERY
ATHLETES
ATHLETIC COACHES
ATHLETIC FIELDS
ATHLETICS
BADMINTON
BASEBALL
BASKETBALL
BICYCLING
BOWLING
CALISTHENICS
CAMPING
CHILDRENS GAMES
COLLEGE ATHLETICS
COMMUNITY RECREATION PROGRAMS
DAY CAMP PROGRAMS
DIVING
EXERCISE
EXERCISE (PHYSIOLOGY) (1969 1980)
EXTRACURRICULAR ACTIVITIES
EXTRAMURAL ATHLETICS
FENCING (SPORT)
FIELD HOCKEY
FOOTBALL
GAMES
GOLF
GYMNASTICS
HANDBALL
HOBBIES

HORSEBACK RIDING
ICE HOCKEY
ICE SKATING
INTRAMURAL ATHLETICS
LOGGING
LACROSSE
LEISURE TIME
LIFETIME SPORTS
MOVEMENT EDUCATION
OLYMPIC GAMES
ORIENTEERING
OUTDOOR ACTIVITIES
PHYSICAL ACTIVITIES
PHYSICAL EDUCATION
PHYSICAL RECREATION PROGRAMS
PLAY
PLAYGROUND ACTIVITIES
PLYOMETRICS
RACQUET SPORTS
RACQUETBALL
RECESS BREAKS
RECREATION
RECREATIONAL ACTIVITIES
RECREATIONAL PROGRAMS
RECREATIONISTS
RESIDENT CAMP PROGRAMS
ROLLER SKATING
RUNNING
SAILING
SCHOOL RECREATIONAL PROGRAMS
SKIING
SOCCER
SOFTBALL
SPORTSMANSHIP
SQUASH (GAME)
SURFING
SWIMMING
TABLE TENNIS
TEAM HANDBALL
TEAM SPORTS
TENNIS
TOYS
TRACK AND FIELD
TUMBLING
UNDERWATER DIVING
VOLLEYBALL
WATER POLO
WATERSKIING
WEIGHTLIFTING
WINTER SPORTS
WOMENS ATHLETICS
WRESTLING

480 MATHEMATICS

ADDITION
ALGEBRA
ALGORITHMS
ANALYTIC GEOMETRY
AREA
ARITHMETIC
BAYESIAN STATISTICS
CALCULUS
COLLEGE MATHEMATICS
COMPUTATION
CONGRUENCE (MATHEMATICS)
DECIMAL FRACTIONS
DIFFERENTIAL EQUATIONS
DISTANCE
DIVISION
ELEMENTARY SCHOOL MATHEMATICS
EQUATIONS (MATHEMATICS)
ESTIMATION (MATHEMATICS)
EXPECTANCY TABLES
FRACTIONS
FUNCTIONS (MATHEMATICS)
GENERAL MATHEMATICS
GEOMETRIC CONCEPTS
GEOMETRIC CONSTRUCTIONS
GEOMETRY
INCIDENCE
INEQUALITY (MATHEMATICS)
INTEGERS
LINEAR PROGRAMMING
LOGARITHMS
MARKOV PROCESSES

MATHEMATICAL APPLICATIONS
MATHEMATICAL APTITUDE
MATHEMATICAL CONCEPTS
MATHEMATICAL ENRICHMENT
MATHEMATICAL EXPERIENCE (1966 1980)
MATHEMATICAL FORMULAS
MATHEMATICAL LOGIC
MATHEMATICAL VOCABULARY
MATHEMATICS
MATHEMATICS ACHIEVEMENT
MATHEMATICS ANXIETY
MATHEMATICS CURRICULUM
MATHEMATICS EDUCATION
MATHEMATICS INSTRUCTION
MATHEMATICS SKILLS
MATRICES
METRIC SYSTEM
MODERN MATHEMATICS
MODULAR ARITHMETIC
MULTIPLICATION
NONPARAMETRIC STATISTICS
NUMBER CONCEPTS
NUMBER SYSTEMS
NUMBERS
NUMERACY
ORTHOGRAPHIC PROJECTION
PERCENTAGE
PLACE VALUE
PLANE GEOMETRY
POLYGONS
POLYNOMIALS
PRIME NUMBERS
PROBABILITY
PROOF (MATHEMATICS)
PROPERTIES (MATHEMATICS)
RATIONAL NUMBERS
RATIOS (MATHEMATICS)
RECIPROCALS (MATHEMATICS)
REGRESSION (STATISTICS)
REMEDIAL MATHEMATICS
SECONDARY SCHOOL MATHEMATICS
SET THEORY
SOLID GEOMETRY
STATISTICAL DISTRIBUTIONS
STATISTICAL INFERENCE
STATISTICS
SUBTRACTION
SYMBOLS (MATHEMATICS)
SYMMETRY
TECHNICAL MATHEMATICS
TOPOGRAPHY
TOPOLOGY
TRANSFORMATIONS (MATHEMATICS)
TRIGONOMETRY
VECTORS (MATHEMATICS)
VOLUME (MATHEMATICS)
WHOLE NUMBERS
WORD PROBLEMS (MATHEMATICS)

490 SCIENCE AND TECHNOLOGY

ACCELERATION (PHYSICS)
ACOUSTICS
AEROSPACE EDUCATION
AEROSPACE TECHNOLOGY
AIR FLOW
AIR TRAFFIC CONTROL
ALTERNATIVE ENERGY SOURCES
ANATOMY
ANIMALS
ASTRONOMY
ATOMIC STRUCTURE
ATOMIC THEORY
AUTOMATION
AVIATION EDUCATION
AVIATION TECHNOLOGY
BACTERIA
BIOCHEMISTRY
BIOFEEDBACK
BIOLOGICAL SCIENCES
BIOLOGY
BIOMECHANICS
BIONICS
BIOPHYSICS
BIOTECHNOLOGY

In this manual, systematic thesauri and hierarchies are grouped into three main categories: (1) broad subject groups; (2) tree structures and enumerative classification; (3) detailed faceted classification.

H4.1. Broad subject groups

In this type of layout the indexing terms are arranged in alphabetical order under appropriate broad subject groups or facets. The notation for the subject group is shown against the indexing term in the alphabetical section. This type of display is found in many thesauri in which the main emphasis is on the alphabetical section. Figure 16 shows the descriptor group display of *Thesaurus of ERIC descriptors* (Thesaurus, 1995) and Figure 17 a page from the *UNESCO:IBE education thesaurus's* (International, 1984) faceted array of descriptors and identifiers.

H4.1.1. 'Themes'

This is a style of thesaurus developed by Jean Viet in France, which has been used in the layout of numerous thesauri for international organizations, mainly in the social sciences. The systematic section may be the main part of the thesaurus, as in the *ILO thesaurus* (International, 1992) (Figure 18), consisting of broad groups, sometimes known as 'themes'. The themes are further divided into subgroups. Within the subgroups, the preferred terms are listed alphabetically, accompanied by scope notes, synonyms, and broader, narrower and related terms.

Example:

13	**LABOUR AND EMPLOYMENT**
13.07	**WAGES AND WAGE PAYMENT SYSTEMS**

3034	EQUAL PAY RT DISCRIMINATION WAGE DETERMINATION
3035	FEE Remuneration of professional workers such as doctors and lawyers in return for their services. BT WAGE NT USERS FEES
3040	MINIMUM WAGE UF GUARANTEED WAGE

Access to the terms is by a KWOC index, consisting of preferred and non-preferred terms only.

Figure 17. Broad subjects groups
UNESCO: IBE education thesaurus

100 ABSTRACT IDEAS

CHILD WELFARE
EDUCATIONAL FUTUROLOGY
FREEDOM OF SPEECH
HUMAN DIGNITY
HUMAN RIGHTS
MORAL ISSUES
NEEDS
OPPORTUNITIES
POLITICAL ISSUES
PRODUCTIVE LIVING
PUBLIC SUPPORT
SOCIAL WELFARE
WELFARE
YOUTH OPPORTUNITIES
YOUTH WELFARE
   A FREEDOM OF ASSOCIATION

101 POLICIES

CITIZENSHIP
COLLECTIVISM
COLONIALISM
DEMOCRACY
DEVELOPED COUNTRIES
DEVELOPING COUNTRIES
INTERNATIONAL
   UNDERSTANDING
NATIONAL INTEGRATION
NATIONALISM
PATRIOTISM
POLICIES
POLITICAL THEORIES
RACISM
STATE CHURCH SEPARATION
WORLD PROBLEMS
   A FEMINISM

102 POLITICAL STRUCTURE

COMMUNITY
COMMUNITY CONTROL

COORDINATION
FEDERATIVE STRUCTURE
FOREIGN POLICY
GEOGRAPHIC REGIONS
GOVERNMENT
MUNICIPALITIES
POLICY MAKING
PROVINCIAL POWERS
VOTING
   A COMMUNITY ACTION

103 CENTRAL AGENCIES

AGENCIES
CENTRAL GOVERNMENT
GOVERNMENTAL STRUCTURE
INTERNATIONAL AGENCIES
REGIONAL AGENCIES
SOCIAL AGENCIES
WELFARE AGENCIES
YOUTH AGENCIES
   A ADULT EDUCATION
   AGENCIES
   A COORDINATING AGENCIES

**104 INTERMEDIATE, LOCAL
   AGENCIES**

CITY GOVERNMENT
COMMUNITY AGENCIES
   (PUBLIC)
LOCAL GOVERNMENT
PROVINCIAL AGENCIES
PROVINCIAL GOVERNMENT

**105 AGENCY ROLE,
   RELATIONSHIP**

AGENCY ROLE
CENTRAL PROVINCIAL
   RELATIONSHIP
CITIZEN PARTICIPATION

Figure 18. Themes
ILO thesaurus
Systematic Display

	English	French	Spanish
	BT WORKERS PARTICIPATION RT WORKERS BUYOUT	BT PARTICIPATION DES TRAVAILLEURS RT RACHAT D'UNE ENTREPRISE PAR SES SALARIES	BT PARTICIPACION DE LOS TRABAJADORES RT COMPRA DE UNA EMPRESA POR SUS TRABAJADORES
3063	YEAR END BONUS 1983 BT WAGE INCENTIVE	PRIME DE FIN D'ANNEE 1983 BT PRIME DE SALAIRE	AGUINALDO 1983 BT INCENTIVO EN METALICO

13.08 WELFARE FACILITIES / SERVICES SOCIAUX POUR LES TRAVAILLEURS / SERVICIOS SOCIALES PARA LOS TRABAJADORES

3064	CANTEEN 1982
	BT FOOD SERVICE
	   WELFARE FACILITIES
	RT PROVISION OF MEALS
		RESTAURANT DU PERSONNEL 1982
		BT SERVICE DE RESTAURATION
		   SERVICES SOCIAUX POUR LES TRAVAILLEURS
		RT FOURNITURE DE REPAS
			RESTAURANTE DE EMPRESA 1982
			BT SERVICIO DE RESTAURACION
			   SERVICIOS SOCIALES PARA LOS TRABAJADORES
			RT SUMINISTRO DE COMIDAS

3065	CHILD CARE FACILITIES 1989
	UF CHILDMINDING SERVICE
	   CRECHE
	   DAY CARE
	   WORKPLACE NURSERY
	RT CHILD
	   CHILD CARE
	   WELFARE FACILITIES
	   WOMAN WORKER
	   WOMEN
		SERVICES DE GARDE D'ENFANTS 1989
		UF GARDERIE D'ENFANTS
		   CRECHE
		   JARDIN D'ENFANTS
		RT ENFANT
		   SOINS AUX ENFANTS
		   SERVICES SOCIAUX POUR LES TRAVAILLEURS
		   TRAVAILLEUSE
		   FEMMES
			GUARDERIA INFANTIL 1989
			UF JARDIN DE INFANTES
			
			RT NINO
			   CUIDADO INFANTIL
			   SERVICIOS SOCIALES PARA LOS TRABAJADORES
			   TRABAJADORA
			   MUJERES

3066	PROVISION OF MEALS BT WELFARE FACILITIES RT CANTEEN	FOURNITURE DE REPAS RT SERVICES SOCIAUX POUR LES TRAVAILLEURS RT RESTAURANT DU PERSONNEL	SUMINISTRO DE COMIDAS BT SERVICIOS SOCIALES PARA LOS TRABAJADORES RT RESTAURANTE DE EMPRESA

3067	WELFARE FACILITIES 1984
	NT CANTEEN
	   OCCUPATIONAL HEALTH SERVICE
	   PROVISION OF MEALS
	   RECREATION SERVICE
	RT CHILD CARE FACILITIES
	   FITNESS PROGRAMME
	   WORKERS HOUSING
	   WORKERS TRANSPORT
		SERVICES SOCIAUX POUR LES TRAVAILLEURS 1984
		NT RESTAURANT DU PERSONNEL
		BT SERVICE DE MEDECINE DU TRAVAIL
		   FOURNITURE DE REPAS
		   SERVICE RECREATIF
		RT SERVICES DE GARDE D'ENFANTS
		   PROGRAMME DE MISE EN FORME PHYSIQUE
		   LOGEMENT DES TRAVAILLEURS
		   TRANSPORT DES TRAVAILLEURS
			SERVICIOS SOCIALES PARA LOS TRABAJADORES 1984
			NT RESTAURANTE DE EMPRESA
			   SERVICIO DE MEDICINA DEL TRABAJO
			   SUMINISTRO DE COMIDAS
			   SERVICIO RECREATIVO
			RT GUARDERIA INFANTIL
			   PROGRAMA DE ACONDICIONAMIENTO FISICO
			   VIVIENDA DE LOS TRABAJADORES
			   TRANSPORTE DE TRABAJADORES

3068	WORKERS HOUSING 1983 UF STAFF ACCOMMODATION BT HOUSING RT WELFARE FACILITIES	LOGEMENT DES TRAVAILLEURS 1983 BT LOGEMENT RT SERVICES SOCIAUX POUR LES TRAVAILLEURS	VIVIENDA DE LOS TRABAJADORES 1983 BT VIVIENDA RT SERVICIOS SOCIALES PARA LOS TRABAJADORES

3069	WORKERS TRANSPORT 1983
	BT TRANSPORT
	RT COMMUTING
	   WELFARE FACILITIES
		TRANSPORT DES TRAVAILLEURS 1983
		BT TRANSPORT
		RT MOUVEMENTS PENDULAIRES
		   SERVICES SOCIAUX POUR LES TRAVAILLEURS
			TRANSPORTE DE TRABAJADORES 1983
			BT TRANSPORTE
			RT MIGRACION PENDULAR
			   SERVICIOS SOCIALES PARA LOS TRABAJADORES

13.09 SPECIAL CATEGORIES OF WORKERS / CATEGORIES SPECIFIQUES DE TRAVAILLEURS / CATEGORIAS ESPECIFICAS DE TRABAJADORES

13.09.1 Workers by employment status / Travailleurs selon leur situation dans la profession / Trabajadores según su situación en la ocupación

3070	AUXILIARY WORKER BT WORKER	TRAVAILLEUR AUXILIAIRE BT TRAVAILLEUR	TRABAJADOR AUXILIAR BT TRABAJADOR

3071	CASUAL WORKER
	Worker without a contract
	BT WORKER
	RT ATYPICAL EMPLOYMENT
	   SEASONAL UNEMPLOYMENT
		TRAVAILLEUR OCCASIONNEL
		Travailleur sans contrat
		BT TRAVAILLEUR
		RT TRAVAIL ATYPIQUE
		   CHOMAGE SAISONNIER
			TRABAJADOR OCASIONAL
			Trabajador sin contrato
			BT TRABAJADOR
			RT TRABAJO ATIPICO
			   DESEMPLEO ESTACIONAL

3072	EMPLOYEE
	A person who works for a public or private employer and receives remuneration in wages, salary, commission, tips, piece-rates or pay in kind.
	RT EMPLOYEES ASSOCIATION
	   EMPLOYEES ATTITUDE
	   WORKERS RIGHTS
		SALARIE
		Personne qui travaille pour un employeur public ou privé et qui reçoit une rémunération sous forme de traitement, salaire, commission, pourboire, salaire aux pièces ou paiement en nature.
		RT ASSOCIATION DE SALARIES
		   ATTITUDE DES SALARIES
		   DROITS DES TRAVAILLEURS
			EMPLEADO
			La persona que trabaja para un empleador público o privado y percibe una remuneración en forma de salario, sueldo, comisiones, propinas, pagos a destajo o pagos en especie.
			RT ASOCIACION DE EMPLEADOS
			   ACTITUD DE LOS TRABAJADORES
			   DERECHOS DE LOS TRABAJADORES

Example:

EQUAL
   EQUAL PAY 3034 (13.07)

GUARANTEED
   GUARANTEED WAGE $\longrightarrow$ MINIMUM WAGE
   3040 (13.07)

FEE
   FEE   3035 (13.07)

MINIMUM
   MINIMUM WAGE   3040 (13.07)

In the *Macrothesaurus* (Macrothesaurus, 1991) the roles of the systematic section and alphabetical section are reversed, and the relational detail is given under the indexing terms in the alphabetical section, which becomes the main part of the thesaurus, (Figure 19b, 1985 edition). The systematic display, consisting of preferred terms only, listed under themes without additional data, is reduced to an auxiliary position (Figure 19a, 1985 edition). Readers are advised that the method for the displays in the 1985 and 1991 editions is the same.

Another variant of this style is the 1995 edition of the *UNESCO thesaurus* (UNESCO, 1995) in which the alphabetical display is the main part of the thesaurus, and includes multilevel hierarchies. The systematic display, in an auxiliary position, includes themes known as 'microthesauri' within which preferred terms are listed in alphabetical order, accompanied by equivalent terms and multilevel narrower terms. Related terms are excluded. Except in the case of country names, indexing terms are assigned to only one 'microthesaurus'.

Example:

1.70   Educational facilities
Educational buildings
   UF Educational architecture
   NT1 Academic buildings
         NT2 University laboratories
   NT1 School buildings
         NT2 Classrooms
         NT2 School laboratories

Educational equipment
   UF Academic equipment
   UF School equipment
   NT1 School furniture

etc.

Figure 19a. Themes
Macrothesaurus (1985 edition)
Descriptor group display

01.
INTERNATIONAL COOPERATION
INTERNATIONAL RELATIONS

01.01
INTERNATIONAL COOPERATION

01.01.01
DEVELOPMENT AID
DEVELOPMENT ASSISTANCE
  USE: DEVELOPMENT AID
FIRST DEVELOPMENT DECADE
FOREIGN AID
HORIZONTAL COOPERATION
INTERNATIONAL ASSISTANCE
  USE: INTERNATIONAL COOPERATION
INTERNATIONAL COOPERATION
REGIONAL COOPERATION
SECOND DEVELOPMENT DECADE
THIRD DEVELOPMENT DECADE

01.01.02
AID BY RELIGIOUS BODIES
  USE: PRIVATE AID
BILATERAL AID
MULTILATERAL AID
PRIVATE AID

01.01.03
AID IN KIND
CAPITAL AID
  USE: FINANCIAL AID
ECONOMIC AID
ECONOMIC ASSISTANCE
  USE: ECONOMIC AID
EXTERNAL FINANCING
FINANCIAL AID
FINANCIAL ASSISTANCE
  USE: FINANCIAL AID
FOOD AID
GRANTS IN KIND
  USE: AID IN KIND
HEALTH AID
TECHNICAL ASSISTANCE
  USE: TECHNICAL COOPERATION
TECHNICAL COOPERATION
TRAINING ASSISTANCE

01.01.04
AID COORDINATION
AID EVALUATION
AID FINANCING
AID PROGRAMMES
GRANTS
PROGRAMME EVALUATION
TERMS OF AID
TIED AID
  USE: TERMS OF AID

01.01.05
COUNTERPART
COUNTERPART FUNDS
COUNTERPART PERSONNEL

01.01.06
DEVELOPMENT PROJECTS
FEASIBILITY STUDIES
JOINT PROJECTS
MULTIPURPOSE PROJECTS

01.01.06 (cont.)
NEEDS ASSESSMENT
PILOT PROJECTS
PLANS OF OPERATION
  USE: PROJECT DOCUMENTS
PROJECT APPRAISAL
PROJECT DESIGN
PROJECT DOCUMENTS
PROJECT EVALUATION
PROJECT FINANCING
PROJECT IMPLEMENTATION
PROJECT MANAGEMENT
PROJECT MONITORING
  USE: PROJECT MANAGEMENT
PROJECT PLANNING
  USE: PROJECT DESIGN
PROJECT REQUEST
PROJECT REVISION
PROJECT SELECTION

01.01.07
AID AGENCIES
  USE: AID INSTITUTIONS
AID INSTITUTIONS
CONSULTANTS
DEVELOPMENT CENTRES
DEVELOPMENT PERSONNEL
EXPERTS

01.01.08
PEACE CORPS
VOLUNTARY SERVICES
VOLUNTEERS

01.02
INTERNATIONAL RELATIONS

01.02.01
ALLIANCES
BILATERAL RELATIONS
BORDER INTEGRATION
COMMON MARKETS
COMPLEMENTARITY AGREEMENTS
ECONOMIC COOPERATION
ECONOMIC INTEGRATION
ECONOMIC INTERDEPENDENCE
ECONOMIC RELATIONS
FOREIGN RELATIONS
IMPERIALISM
INDUSTRIAL COOPERATION
INDUSTRIAL INTEGRATION
INTERNATIONAL AFFAIRS
  USE: INTERNATIONAL RELATIONS
INTERNATIONAL ECONOMIC
  RELATIONS
INTERNATIONAL POLITICS
INTERNATIONAL RELATIONS
INTERNATIONALIZATION
ISOLATIONISM
MILITARISM
MULTILATERAL RELATIONS
NEUTRALISM
NEUTRALITY
NEW INTERNATIONAL ECONOMIC
  ORDER
NON-ALIGNMENT
NORTH-SOUTH DIALOGUE
  USE: NORTH-SOUTH RELATIONS
NORTH-SOUTH RELATIONS
PROLETARIAN INTERNATIONALISM
REGIONAL INTEGRATION

01.02.02
ACCESS TO THE SEA
BORDERS
  USE: BOUNDARIES
BOUNDARIES
COASTAL AREAS
  USE: LITTORAL ZONES
EXCLUSIVE ECONOMIC ZONES
FRONTIERS
  USE: BOUNDARIES
TERRITORIAL SEA

01.02.03
AUTONOMY
  USE: INDEPENDENCE
COLONIAL COUNTRIES
COLONIES
  USE: COLONIAL COUNTRIES
DECOLONIZATION
ECONOMIC DEPENDENCE
INDEPENDENCE
SELF-DETERMINATION
TRUST TERRITORIES

01.02.04
CONVENTIONS
INTERNATIONAL AGREEMENTS
INTERNATIONAL CONTROL
INTERNATIONAL LAW
INTERNATIONAL NEGOTIATIONS
INTERNATIONAL SEA-BED
  AUTHORITY
LAW OF THE SEA
STATE LIABILITY
TREATIES
  USE: INTERNATIONAL AGREEMENTS

01.02.05
DIPLOMACY
FOREIGN INTERVENTION
FOREIGN POLICY
FOREIGN SERVICE

01.02.06
ARMAMENT
ARMED FORCES
ARMS EMBARGO
ARMS LIMITATION
  USE: DISARMAMENT
ARMS RACE
  USE: ARMAMENT
ARMY
  USE: ARMED FORCES
ATOMIC WEAPONS
  USE: NUCLEAR WEAPONS
BACTERIOLOGICAL WEAPONS
CONVENTIONAL WEAPONS
DEFENCE
DEFENCE POLICY
DISARMAMENT
MILITARY AID
MILITARY ASSISTANCE
  USE: MILITARY AID
MILITARY BASES
MILITARY EXPENDITURES
MILITARY PERSONNEL
MILITARY SERVICE
NUCLEAR DISARMAMENT
NUCLEAR WEAPONS
SOLDIERS
  USE: MILITARY PERSONNEL
WEAPON PROCUREMENT
WEAPONS

Figure 19b. Themes
Macrothesaurus (1985 edition)
Alphabetical descriptor display

ABACA
ABACA / ABACA – 07.07.07
  UF: MANILA HEMP
  TT: FIBRES
        PRODUCTS
  BT: SOFT FIBRES
        TEXTILE FIBRES
  RT: HEMP

ABANDONED CHILDREN
ENFANTS ABANDONNES / NINOS
ABANDONADOS – 02.04.02
  TT: AGE GROUPS
  BT: CHILDREN
  RT: ORPHANAGES

ABBREVIATIONS
ABBREVIATIONS / ABREVIATURAS – 19.02.07
  RT: INDEXING

ABILITY GROUPING
GROUPEMENT PAR APTITUDES /
AGRUPAMIENTO POR APTITUD – 06.04.10
  UF: STREAMING
  RT: CLASSES

ABORIGINAL POPULATION
  USE: INDIGENOUS POPULATION – 14.03.01

ABORTION
AVORTEMENT / ABORTO – 14.06.02
  NT: LEGAL ABORTION
  RT: PREGNANCY

ABRASIVES
ABRASIFS / ABRASIVOS – 08.12.08

ABSENTEEISM
ABSENTEISME / AUSENTISMO – 13.05.00
  RT: LEAVE OF ABSENCE

ABSORPTIVE CAPACITY
CAPACITE D'ABSORPTION / CAPACIDAD DE
ABSORCION – 11.02.06
  RT: DEVELOPMENT AID
        INVESTMENTS

ABSTRACTING SERVICES
  USE: BIBLIOGRAPHIC SERVICES – 19.01.03

ABSTRACTS
RESUMES / RESUMENES ANALITICOS –
19.02.07
  TT: DOCUMENTS
  BT: SECONDARY DOCUMENTS

ABUNDANCE
ABONDANCE / ABUNDANCIA – 03.02.05
  RT: AFFLUENT SOCIETY
        WEALTH

ACADEMIC FREEDOM
LIBERTE DE L'ENSEIGNEMENT / LIBERTAD
DE ENSENANZA – 04.02.02
  TT: FREEDOM
  BT: CIVIL LIBERTIES
  RT: EDUCATIONAL SYSTEMS

ACAST
CCAST / CCACT – 01.03.02
*USE FOR ADVISORY COMMITTEE ON THE
APPLICATION OF SCIENCE AND TECHNOLOGY
TO DEVELOPMENT PRIOR TO JULY 1980 AND
THE ADVISORY COMMITTEE ON SCIENCE AND
TECHNOLOGY FOR DEVELOPMENT
THEREAFTER*
  TT: INTERNATIONAL ORGANIZATIONS
  BT: CSTD
  RT: SCIENCE
        TECHNOLOGY

ACCELERATED COURSES
COURS ACCELERES / CURSOS INTENSIVOS –
06.06.01
  UF: INTENSIVE COURSES
  TT: CURRICULUM
  BT: COURSES

ACCESS TO CULTURE
ACCES A LA CULTURE / ACCESO A LA
CULTURA – 05.02.03
  RT: CULTURE
        RIGHT TO EDUCATION

ACCESS TO EDUCATION
AMCCES A L'EDUCATION / ACCESO A LA
EDUCACION – 06.02.02
  RT: EDUCATIONAL OPPORTUNITIES
        EDUCATIONAL SELECTION
        RIGHT TO EDUCATION

ACCESS TO INFORMATION
ACCES A L'INFORMATION / ACCESO A LA
INFORMACION – 19.01.01
  RT: DATA PROTECTION
        INFORMATION
        INFORMATION DISSEMINATION
        INFORMATION EXCHANGE
        INFORMATION SOURCES
        INFORMATION USERS

ACCESS TO MARKETS
ACCES AUX MARCHES / ACCESO A LOS
MERCADOS – 09.03.01
  UF: MARKET ACCESS
  RT: BOYCOTT
        EMBARGO
        MARKET
        TRADE AGREEMENTS

→ **ACCESS TO THE SEA**
ACCES A LA MER / ACCESO AL MAR – 01.02.02
  RT: LANDLOCKED COUNTRIES
        RESOURCES EXPLOITATION

ACCESSIONS LISTS
LISTES D'ACQUISITIONS / CATALOGOS DE
ACQUISICIONES – 19.02.07
  TT: DOCUMENTS
  BT: SECONDARY DOCUMENTS
  RT: ACQUISITIONS

ACCIDENT INSURANCE
ASSURANCE CONTRE LES ACCIDENTS /
SECURO CONTRA ACCIDENTES – 11.02.03
  TT: SERVICE INDUSTRY
  BT: INSURANCE
  RT: ACCIDENTS

ACCIDENT PREVENTION
  USE: SAFETY – 16.04.01

ACCIDENTS
ACCIDENTS / ACCIDENTES – 02.04.02
  NT: NUCLEAR ACCIDENTS
        OCCUPATIONAL ACCIDENTS
        TRAFFIC ACCIDENTS
  RT: ACCIDENT INSURANCE
        CAUSES OF DEATH
        DAMAGE
        SAFETY

ACCLIMATIZATION
ACCLIMATATION / ACLIMATACION – 17.02.01
  RT: CLIMATE

ACCOUNTANTS
COMPTABLES / CONTADORES – 13.09.09
  TT: HUMAN RESOURCES
        OCCUPATIONS
  BT: OFFICE WORKERS
  RT: ACCOUNTING

ACCOUNTING
COMPTABILITE / CONTABILIDAD – 12.09.00
  UF: BOOKKEEPING
  NT: COST ACCOUNTING
        NATIONAL ACCOUNTING
        PUBLIC ACCOUNTING
  RT: ACCOUNTANTS
        AUDITING

ACCT
ACCT / ACCT – 01.03.03
*AGENCY FOR CULTURAL AND TECHNICAL CO-
OPERATION (AMONG FRENCH-SPEAKING
COUNTRIES)*
  TT: INTERNATIONAL ORGANIZATIONS
  BT: INTERGOVERNMENTAL
        ORGANIZATIONS

ACCULTURATION
ACCULTURATION / ACULTURACION – 05.02
.02
  RT: CULTURAL CHANGE
        CULTURAL IDENTITY
        CULTURAL RELATIONS
        CULTURE
        MIGRANT ASSIMILATION

ACCUMULATION RATE
TAUX D'ACCUMULATION / TASA DE
ACUMULACION – 03.01.02
  RT: CAPITAL FORMATION
        GROWTH RATE
        INVESTMENTS

ACDA
USE: APDAC – 01.03.03

ACIDS
ACIDES / ACIDOS – 06.12.04
  NT: AMINO ACIDS
        INORGANIC ACIDS

ACOUSTIC POLLUTION
POLLUTION ACOUSTIQUE /
CONTAMINACION ACUSTICA – 16.03.04
  TT: POLLUTION
  BT: POLLUTION
  RT: NOISE
        NOISE CONTROL

ACOUSTICS
ACOUSTIQUE / ACUSTICA – 06.10.01
  TT: NATURAL SCIENCES

H.4.2. Tree structures and enumerative classification

H4.2.1. Medical Subject Headings (MeSH) tree structures

MeSH tree structures are hierarchies of broader/narrower terms of up to several levels, arranged within broad classes and subclasses (see Figure 20a). Terms may appear in more than one hierarchy. Within the same hierarchical level the terms are ordered alphabetically. An expressive notation (see F3.2) links the terms in the tree structures with the alphabetical section of *Medical subject headings (MeSH)* (Medical). The tree structures do not include scope notes, synonyms or related terms.

The alphabetical display (see Figure 20b) includes a notation indicating the place(s) of the term in the tree structures, scope notes, annotations, and 'see' and 'see related' references indicating equivalent and related terms, but no hierarchical information. The *Annotated alphabetical list* (Figure 20b), designed for indexers and searchers, includes more detail than the *Supplement to Index Medicus* designed for end users.

The *EMTREE thesaurus* (EMTREE) of the medical database EMBASE has a similar polyhierarchical tree structure, arranged under broad groups. Terms in the tree structure are either 'explosion terms' printed in bold and corresponding directly with the hierarchically arranged notation, or 'non-explosion terms', which are more specific terms associated with the 'explosion' terms and having no further narrower terms. These are retrieved either in the 'explosion' searches, or when searched as individual terms.

Example:

G1.680.675	**.. Pharmacogenetics**	← *Explosion term*
	... Acetylator phenotype	← *Non-explosion term*
G1.680.680	**.. Pharmacokinetics**	← *Explosion term*
	... Area under the curve	← *Non-explosion term*
	... Bioequivalence	← *Non-explosion term*
	... Drug absorption	← *Non-explosion term*
	⋮	
G1.680.680.230	**... Drug metabolism**	← *Explosion term*
	.... Drug degradation	← *Non-explosion term*

The alphabetical section includes 'see' references from non-preferred to preferred terms, 'see under' references from 'non-explosion terms' to 'explosion terms', 'see also' references, and term histories.

H4.2.2. Enumerative classification

In this type of display the enumerative classification may be a separate classification, against which indexing terms are mapped or related in some way. The *INSPEC thesaurus* (INSPEC, 1995) is an example of a thesaurus related to a classification system in this way.

Figure 20a. Tree Structures
Medical Subject Headings – tree structures
(Codes in small type indicate locations of terms in other hierarchies)

Eye Diseases

C11 – DISEASES-OCULAR

Eye Diseases	C11		
Asthenopia	C11.93		
Conjunctival Diseases	C11.187		
Conjunctival Neoplasms	C11.187.169	C4.588.364	C11.319.217
Conjunctivitis	C11.187.183		
Conjunctivitis, Allergic	C11.187.183.200	C20.543.480	
Conjunctivitis, Bacterial	C11.187.183.220	C1.252.354	C1.539.375
		C11.294.354	
Conjunctivitis, Inclusion	C11.187.183.220.250	C1.252.354	C1.252.400
		C1.539.375	C11.294.354
Ophthalmia Neonatorum	C11.187.183.220.538	C1.252.354	C1.252.400
		C1.539.375	C11.294.354
		C16.614.677	
Trachoma	C11.187.183.220.889	C1.252.354	C1.252.400
		C1.539.375	C11.204.813
		C11.294.354	
Conjunctivitis, Viral	C11.187.183.240	C2.325.250	C11.294.800
Conjunctivitis, Acute Hemorrhagic	C11.187.183.240.216	C2.325.250	C2.782.687
		C2.782.687	C11.294.800
Keratoconjunctivitis	C11.187.183.394	C11.204.564	
Keratoconjunctivitis, Infectious	C11.187.183.394.520	C1.252.354	C1.539.375
		C11.204.564	C11.294.354
		C22.500	
Keratoconjunctivitis, Sicca	C11.187.183.394.550	C11.204.564	C11.406.260
→ Reiter's Disease	C11.187.183.749	C1.539.717	C5.550.114
		C12.777.767	C20.111.782
Pterygium	C11.187.781		
Xerophthalmia	C11.187.810	C11.496.260	
Corneal Diseases	C11.204		
Corneal Dystrophies, Hereditary	C11.204.236	C11.270.162	C16.131.410
Fuchs' Endothelial Dystrophy	C11.204.236.438	C11.270.162	C16.131.410
Corneal Edema	C11.204.267		
Corneal Neovascularization	C11.204.290	C23.739.589	
Corneal Opacity	C11.204.299		
Arcus Senilis	C11.204.299.70		
Keratitis	C11.204.564		
Acanthamoeba Keratitis	C11.204.564.112	C3.300.125	C3.752.700
		C11.294.725	
Corneal Ulcer	C11.204.564.225	C1.539.375	C11.294.177
Keratitis, Herpetic	C11.204.564.425	C2.256.466	C2.325.465
		C11.294.800	
Keratitis, Dendritic	C11.204.564.425.450	C2.256.466	C2.325.465
		C11.294.800	
Keratoconjunctivitis	C11.204.564.585	C11.187.183	
Keratoconjunctivitis, Infectious	C11.204.564.585.500	C1.252.354	C1.539.375
		C11.187.183	C11.294.354
		C22.500	
Keratoconjunctivitis Sicca	C11.204.564.585.630	C11.187.183	C11.496.260
Keratoconus	C11.204.627		
Trachoma	C11.204.813	C1.252.354	C1.252.400
		C1.539.375	C11.187.183
		C11.294.354	
		C16.131.384	
Eye Abnormalities	C11.250	C16.131.384	
Aniridia	C11.250.60	C11.270.60	C11.941.375
		C16.131.384	C16.131.410
WAGR Syndrome	C11.250.60.950	C4.557.435	C10.496.966
		C11.270.60	C11.941.375
		C12.740.700	C13.371.820
		C16.131.384	C16.131.410
		C16.131.939	F3.709.346
Anophthalmos	C11.250.80	C16.131.384	
Blepharophimosis	C11.250.90	C11.338.190	C16.131.384
Coloboma	C11.250.110	C16.131.384	
Ectopia Lentis	C11.250.300	C11.510.598	C16.131.384
Hydrophthalmos	C11.250.480	C11.525.381	C16.131.384
		C16.614.438	
Microphthalmos	C11.250.566	C16.131.384	
Retinal Dysplasia	C11.250.666	C11.270.660	C11.768.660
		C16.131.384	C16.131.410
Eye Diseases, Hereditary	C11.270	C16.131.410	

Figure 20b. Tree Structures
Medical Subject Headings – Annotated alphabetical list

Reimbursement Mechanisms
N3.219.521.710.305+
79

Reimbursement, Prospective see Prospective Payment System
N3.219.521.710.305.200+

Reimplantation see Replantation
E4.936.494+

Reimplantation, Tooth see Tooth Replantation
E4.833.876   E4.936.494.711
E6.397.898   E6.892.876

Reindeer
B2.649.77.380.373.644
IM; qualif permitted
68; CARIBOU was heading 1975–94 (see under REINDEER 1975–90)
use REINDEER to search CARIBOU 1975–94
X Caribou

Reinforcement (Psychology)
F2.463.425.770+
human & animal; no qualif; DF:
REINFORCEMENT
65; was REINFORCEMENT LEARNING 1963–64
X Negative Reinforcement
X Positive Reinforcement

Reinforcement Schedule
F2.463.425.770.644
human & animal; no qualif
69(66)

Reinforcement, Social
F2.463.425.770.706
no qualif
69
X Social Reinforcement

Reinforcement, Verbal
F2.463.425.770.769
no qualif
69(66)

Reinforcing Factors see Causality
G3.850.490.625+   N5.715.350.200+

→ **Reiter's Disease**
C1.539.717   C5.550.114.782
V11.187.183.749   C12.777.767.851.644
C20.111.782
nongonococcal urethritis with conjunctivitis & arthritis
XR Arthritis, Reactive
XR Erythema Multiforme

Rejection (Psychology)
F1.145.76.850
no qualif; DF: REJECTION
75

Rejuvenation
E2.40.730   E2.849

rel Genes see Oncogenes
G5.275.740+

Relapse see Recurrence
C23.280.734   N1.407.306.750

Relapsing Fever
C1.252.400.155.644   C1.252.400.825.750

C1.252.847.193.644
a disease entity caused by Borrelia: not for 'recurrent fever' (= FEVER
(IM) + RECURRENCE (NIM)); tick-borne dis

Relative Biological Effectiveness
G3.850.810.250.275
NIM; no qualif; DF: RBE
77

Relative Risk see Risk
E5.318.740.600.800+   G3.850.520.830.600.800+
H1.548.832.672.734+   N5.715.360.750.625.700+

Relative Value Scales
N3.219.521.710.305.500 N4.452.313.500
'coded listing of physician or other professional services using units that indicate the relative value of the various services they perform'; no qualif; DF: RELAT VALUE SCALES
90
X Relative-Value Schedules
X Resource-Based Relative Value Scale
XR Fees, Medical
XR Rate Setting and Review

Relative-Value Schedules see Relative Value Scales
N3.219.521.710.305.500 N4.452.313.500

Relaxation
I3.450.769+
note category: not for muscle relaxation (= MUSCLE RELAXATION):/physiol/psychol permitted

Relaxation Techniques
E2.40.750+   F4.754.137.750+
a behavior technique: do not confuse with RELAXATION (I3); not for physiological relaxation of muscles (= MUSCLE RELAXATION) CATALOG: do not use/laboratory manuals
91; was RELAXATION TECHNICS 1976–90
use RELAXATION TECHNIQUES to search RELAXATION TECHNICS 1976–90
X Relaxation Therapy

Relaxation Therapy see Relaxation Techniques
E2.40.750+   F4.754.137.750+

Relaxin
D6.472.866.362.769
/biodyn/physiol permitted

Reliability and Validity see Reproducibility of Results
E5.318.780.725   E5.337.851
G3.850.520.840.725   H1.770.644.601
N5.715.360.780.685

Relief Work
G3.230.100.300   I1.880.787.839
coord IM with agency supplying the relief (IM) if pertinent; specify geog if pertinent CATALOG: / geog/form
91(75); was see under DISASTERS 1968–90; was see under DISASTERS & INDIGENT CARE 1963–67
search DISASTERS 1968–74 & DISASTERS & INDIGENT CARE 1966–67
XR Disasters
XR Natural Disasters
XR Rescue Work
XR Social Work

H4.3. Detailed faceted thesauri

This type of thesaurus arrangement involves the development of a faceted classification (see F2.3) as the systematic section, complemented by an alphabetical index or a full alphabetical thesaurus. In this type of display the indexing terms are not mapped against a separate structure but themselves form the faceted classification.

A faceted classification is the most suitable type of classification to use in a thesaurus because of its analytical/synthetic nature, which make it compatible with thesaurus structure.

Existing classified thesauri and faceted classification systems, such as the *Bliss classification* (Mills and Broughton, 1977) may be used as a source of arrangement and terminology (see F2.1.1)

Since the first faceted classified thesaurus *Thesaurofacet* (Aitchison, 1969) there have been a number of versions differing from each other in the varying distribution of relational data between the systematic and alphabetical sections of the thesaurus.

H4.3.1. Thesaurofacet

In *Thesaurofacet* (Aitchison, 1969) the division of information between the systematic and the alphabetical sections was about equal, with the classification displaying the main hierarchies and related terms in a particular field, and the alphabetical section providing the information on scope notes, synonyms, and related terms in other fields. The alphabetical section also provided information on polyhierarchies, indicated by the codes BT(A) and NT(A) (see Figure 21).

Example:

Systematic section		**Alphabetic section**		
H	**Mechanical components**	Fibre ropes	HTN	
HT	Ropes	UF	Textile ropes	
		BT(A)	Textile products	
	(Components)	Ropes	HT	
HTC	Strands	SN	A length of strong line made of fibrous material, metal wire, etc.	
		NT(A)	Gymnastic ropes	
	(Types – by material)	RT	Rescue equipment	
HTN	Fibre ropes	Strands	HTC	
HTR	Wire ropes	Wire ropes	HTR	
		RT	Wires	

H4.3.2. Art and Architecture Thesaurus

The *Art and architecture thesaurus (AAT)* (Art, 1994) consists of two parts: the hierarchies, displayed within fundamental facets (see F2.3.2), and an alphabetical display. The hierarchical display (see Figure 22a) consists of generically-related or whole-part hierarchically-related terms, arranged into sub-hierarchies according to characteristics of division, preceded by guide terms (i.e., facet indicators or node labels), shown in angle brackets in the example below. 'Single built works' is the name

Figure 21. Detailed faceted classification
Thesaurofacet

Systematic display	Alphabetical display

Fuel technology   V

Fuel Rating (i.c. engines) *use*
Antiknock Rating

Systematic	Alphabetical
V **FUEL TECHNOLOGY**	**Fuel Rating (nuclear)** EGB
*Power industries ZKT	UF Heat development on nuclear
	reactors
→ V2 **Fuels**	RT Nuclear fuels
*Nuclear fuels SE	BT(A) Rating
Subdivide by source	
V2B Fossil fuels	→ **Fuels** VZ
*Coal V3B	RT Antiknock ratings
*Fuel oils V5E	Bunkers
*Gasoline V5C	Fuel consumption (i.c. engines)
*Kerosene V5B	Fuel distribution (i.c. engines)
*Natural gas V7A	Fuel systems
*Peat V3R	Heat processes (chemical
*Petroleum V4D	engineering)
Subdivide by phase	NT(A) Nuclear fuels
V2C Solid fuels	BT(A) Materials by purpose
*Coal V3B	
*Peat V3R	**Fuel Sprays** OIM
*Solid propellants V2T	UF Sprays (fuel)
*Wood VJ2	BT(A) Sprays
V2D Pulverised fuels	
V2E Liquid fuels	**Fuel Systems** OI
*Fuel oils V5E	RT Bunkers
*Gasoline V5C	Fuel filters
*Kerosene V5B	Fuels
*Liquid propellants V2M	BT(A) Rocket engine components
*Petroleum V4D	
*Natural gas liquids V5J	**Fuel Tanks** OIU
V2G Gaseous fuels	RT External stores
*Gaseous propellants V2L	BT(A) Tanks
*Manufactured gas V70	
*Natural gas V7A	**Fuel Technology** V
Subdivide by application	RT Power industries
V2H Illuminating fuels	
V2I Aviation fuels	**Fugacity** COS
V2J Jet fuels	RT Vapour pressure
V2K Propellants	
V2L Gaseous propellants	**Full** AMN
V2M Liquid propellants	
V2N Monopropellants	**Full Employment** ZJWHB
V2O Bipropellants	
V2P Tripropellants	**Full Lift Single Seat Relief Valves**
V2R Hybrid propellants	PNF/POC/PPL
V2T Solid propellants	*Synth*
V2U Homogenous solid	S BT(A) Full lift valves
propellants	S Relief valves
V2V Composite solid	Single seat valves
propellants	
For others, synthesise, for	**Full Lift Valves** POC
example:	NT(A) Full lift single seat relief valves
V2K/F7Q Gelled propellants	
V2J/UNN Slurried propellants	**Full Pitch Windings** KHQ
V2X Motor fuels	
V2Y Diesel fuels	**Fulltime Work** ZFEBB
V3 **COAL TECHNOLOGY**	**Full Wave Rectification** *use*
*Coal mining SUU	**Rectification**
*Coal mining industry ZKBA	
	Full Wave Rectifiers *use*
By products:	**Rectifiers**
	Fullway Valves *use*
V3B Coal	**Gate Valves**
V3C Anthracite	
	Fully Developed Flow CUD
	Fully Submerged Hydrofoil Craft RDJ
	Fumaric Acids HUFU(528)
	Functional Analysis BF8
	RT Functionals
	Function spaces
	BT(A) Spaces (mathematics)
	Functional Block Diagrams *use*
	Circuit Diagrams

Figure 22a. Detailed faceted classification
Art and architecture thesaurus
Hierarchical display

prints
  <prints by function>
    <proofs: prints>
      trial proofs

VC.442	color proofs
VC.443	printers' proofs
VC.444	progressive proofs
VC.445	surimono
VC.446	*<prints by process or technique>*
VC.447	black-and-white prints
VC.448	cellocuts
VC.449	collagraphs
VC.450	color prints
VC.451	embossed prints
VC.452	glass colored prints
VC.453	ishizuri-e
VC.454	maculatures
VC.455	mizu-e
VC.456	nature prints
VC.457	paste prints
VC.458	plaster prints
VC.459	*<prints by process: transfer method>*
VC.460	intaglio prints
VC.461	crayon manner prints
VC.462	engravings
VC.463	copper engravings
VC.464	drypoints
VC.465	line engravings
VC.466	mezzotints
VC.467	niello prints
VC.468	steel engravings
VC.469	stipple engravings
VC.470	etchings
VC.471	aquatints
VC.472	sandpaper aquatints
VC.473	soft-ground etchings
VC.474	planographic prints
VC.475	lithographs
VC.476	color lithographs
VC.477	chromolithographs
VC.478	oleographs
VC.479	lithotints
VC.480	offset lithographs
VC.481	monotypes
VC.482	relief prints
VC.483	cardboard relief prints
VC.484	linocuts
VC.485	metal cuts
VC.486	dotted prints
VC.487	relief etchings
VC.488	white line engravings
VC.489	wood engravings
VC.490	color wood engravings

May be used in combination with other descriptors, for example, **over life-size + statues; tempera + paintings; Late Baroque + portraits; landscape (representation) + sketches; still life + painters (artists).**

of the hierarchy and RK the hierarchy code. The notation is a simple, non-expressive line code. The terms in the hierarchies and sub-hierarchies below the guide terms are arranged in alphabetical order. There are no scope notes (SN), use for (UF) references, or related terms (RT) in the hierarchies.

Example:

SINGLE BUILT WORKS (RK)
<single built works by specific type>
<single built works by function>

RK.199	*<communications structures>*
RK.200	**communications buildings**
RK.201	**computer centres**
RK.202	*<telecommunications buildings>*
RK.203	**broadcasting stations**
RK.204	**radio stations**
RK.205	**television stations**

(Found on page 15 of 'Guide to indexing and cataloging with the Art and architecture thesaurus' (Petersen and Barnett, 1994))

The alphabetical display (Figure 22b) serves as an index to the terms in the hierarchies. It shows the notation, or line number (RK 203 for 'broadcasting stations' in the example below), scope notes (SN) and history notes (HN), details of the term's sources (B, H and L in the example below), equivalent terms (USE/UF) and alternative forms (ALT), British term equivalents (UK) and British term alternative (UKA).

Example:

broadcasting stations
      RK.203   (B,H,L)

HN	March 1993 related term added
	April 1990 scope note changed
ALT	broadcasting station
UK	broadcasting houses
UKA	broadcasting house
SN	Telecommunications buildings containing studios, production and technical offices, equipment spaces ....
UF	houses, broadcasting
	stations, broadcasting
RT	broadcasting studios

(Found on page 14 of the 'Guide to indexing and cataloging with the Art and architecture thesaurus' (Petersen and Barnett, 1994))

The BT/NT relationships shown in the hierarchies are not included in the alphabetical display. The alphabetical display does include related terms (RTs), although there are no related terms displayed in the hierarchies.

A thesaurus with a faceted hierarchical display similar to that found in the *Art and architecture thesaurus* is the *ASIS thesaurus of information science and librarianship*

Figure 22b. Detailed faceted classification
Art and architecture thesaurus
Alphabetical display

color diagrams
  USE   color charts

color, dry
  USE   dry color

color dye coupler processes
  USE   chromogenic processes

color, earth
  USE   natural inorganic pigment

<color effects>
  HN   February 1992 guide term
       deleted

color, encaustic
  USE   encaustic paint

Color-field
       FL.3857   (L.R)
  SN   Encompasses both Abstract
       Imagist painting and works of
       the 1960s derived from it.
  UF   Abstraction, Chromatic
       Abstraction, Post-painterly
       Chromatic Abstraction
       Post-painterly Abstraction

color film
       MT.2370   (L)
  HN   April 1992 descriptor moved
  UK   colour film
  UF   film, color
       film, colour

color, film
  USE   film color

color filters
  USE   light filters

color, full
  USE   full-color printing

color lightfastness
  USE   lightfastness

color lithographs
       VC.476
  ALT color lithograph
  UK   colour lithographs
  USA colour lithograph
  SN   Lithographs printed in several
       colors
  UF   lithographs, color
       lithographs, colour
       lithographs, multicolor
       lithographs, multicolour
       multicolor lithographs
       multicolour lithographs
  RT   color prints

color lithography
       KT.687   (R)
  HN   March 1991 descriptor added
  UK   colour lithography
  SN   Printing by lithography using
       a separate stone or plate for
       each color. (LG)
  UF   lithography, color
       lithography, colour

color, local
  USE   local color

color, lost
  USE   lost color

color, luminous
  USE   luminous color

color makers
  USE   artists' colormen

color, mass
  USE   mass color

color measurement
  USE   colorimetry

<color measuring devices>
       TN.323

color media
  USE   filters

color mediums
  USE   filters

color, metallic
  USE   metallic pigment

color mixture
       DL.21
  HN   February 1992 descriptor
       moved
  UK   colour mixture
  UF   colorant mixture
       mixture, color
       mixture, colour
       mixture, optical
       optical mixture

color mixture, additive
  USE   additive mixture

color mixture, subtractive
  USE   subtractive mixture

color negatives
       VC.291
  HN   April 1992 descriptor moved
  ALT color negative
  UK   colour negatives
  UKA colour negative
  SN   Use for photographic negatives
       that record on a single base the
       hue and lightness of a scene in
       complementary relation to the
       scene's perceived values: e.g.,
       light blue is recorded as dark
       yellow. Use color separation
       negatives for images in which
       each color is recorded on a
       physically separate negative
  UF   negatives, color
       negatives, colour

color, oil
  USE   oil paint

Color, Party of
  USE   Rubenism

color photographs
       VC.348
  HN   April 1992 descriptor moved
  ALT color photograph
  UK   colour photographs
  UKA colour photograph
  SN   Use for the broad class of
       photographs whose images are
       composed of more than one

hue, plus the neutral tones. For
photographs having a range of
tones within one hue, use
black-and-white photographs
  UF   photographs, color
       photographs, colour

color photography
       KT.569   (L,R)
  UK   colour photography
  UF   chromophotography
       heliochromy (color
       photography)
       photography, color
       photography, colour

color photoprints
  USE   color prints (photographs)

color, polymer
  USE   polymer paint

color, poster
  USE   poster color

color printing
       KT.647   (L,R)
  HN   January 1993 related terms
       added
       October 1991 descriptor moved
       May 1991 related term added
  UK   colour printing
  UF   chromotypography
       printing, color
       printing, colour
  RT   color blocks
       color prints
       key blocks
       key plates

color printing, process
  USE   full-color printing

color prints
       VC.450   (L)
  ALT color print
  UK   colour prints
  UKA colour print
  SN   Images printed in two or more
       colors: if color is applied after
       printing, use colored (ALT of
       coloring) + prints. For color
       photographs, use color prints
       (photographs)
  UF   prints, color
       prints, colour
  RT   color lithographs
       color printing
       color prints (photographs)
       color proofs
       color wood engravings
       color woodcuts

color prints (photographs)
       VC.317
  HN   April 1993 scope note changed
       April 1992 descriptor moved
       May 1991 related term added
  ALT color print (photograph)
  UK   colour prints (photographs)
  UKA colour print (photograph)
  SN   Use for photographic prints
       whose images are composed of
       more than one hue, plus the
       neutral tones. For photographic

(Milstead, 1994). In this thesaurus the hierarchical display, with terms arranged under facet and sub-facet indicators, plays a subordinate role to the alphabetical display, which includes scope notes, and all relationships, including broader and narrower terms at one hierarchical level.

H4.3.3. BSI ROOT Thesaurus style

In other faceted thesauri a style has developed in which all the elements and relationships are given in the systematic display, so that a full alphabetical thesaurus may be derived from it automatically, if required. This style is epitomised in the BSI *ROOT thesaurus* (British, 1985b) format.

The BSI *ROOT thesaurus* (Figure 23) and thesauri using the *ROOT* format such as the *International thesaurus of refugee terminology* (Aitchison, 1996) and the *Royal Institute of International Affairs Library thesaurus* (*RIIA Library thesaurus*) (Aitchison, 1992a) (Figures 24a and 24b), place all definitional and relational data in the systematic section, i.e., scope notes (SN), equivalence relationships (UF) and main broader, narrower and related terms shown by indenting (see F1.3.4a). Additional related terms are indicated by *RT and polyhierarchies are indicated by *BT/*NT (see also F1.3.4b). References to polyhierarchical and related terms in other parts of the display are accompanied by the notation showing where the term is located.

Example:

BSI ROOT thesaurus style systematic display

H   Mechanical components
HT   Ropes
                    SN A length of strong line made of fibrous material, metal wire, etc.
          *NT Gymnastic ropes XVG.N
          *RT Rescue equipment SNK

                    (Components)
NTC *(RT)*   Strands

                    (Types – by material)
HTN   Fibre ropes
               UF Textile ropes
             *BT Textile products UMN
HTR   Wire ropes
             *RT Wires PVL

The amount of information in the alphabetical section may vary. As the systematic section gives all relational information, an alphabetical index may suffice, with only preferred and non-preferred terms included, as in *Thesaurus on youth* (Aitchison, 1981c). *The Martindale online drug information thesaurus* (Royal, 1990) which has many features of the *ROOT thesaurus* style in its systematic display, also has a simple index of preferred and non-preferred terms in its alphabetical display. Another option is to produce a partial alphabetical thesaurus that includes scope notes, equivalent terms, 'additional' BT/NTs and RTs only. This type of display is found in *DIAL UK classification* (DIAL UK, 1996).

Figure 23. Detailed faceted classification
ROOT thesaurus

Systematic display

K	**Electrotechnology**

KB/KO   **Electrical engineering** (continued)
KE/KJ   **Electrical equipment** (continued)
KIP   **Electrical protection equipment** (continued)
KIP.V   Electric contact protection
                * – Electric contacts   KNR

                (By construction)

KIP.W   Double electrical insulation
                * – Electrical insulation   CYB.K
                * – Electrical insulation devices   KNX

                (By connection to earth)

KIP.X   Earthing
                = Earth (electric)
                = Earthing systems
                = Electric grounding
                = Grounding (electric)
                * – Earthing reactors   KHC.E
KIP.XE   Earth electrodes
                * – Electrodes   KNW
KIP.XH   Earth conductors
                = Protective conductors
                * <Electric conductors   KNN
KIP.XN   Earthing switches
                = Automatic earthing switches
                * <Switches   KJH
KIP.XR   Neutral conductors
                * <Electric conductors   KNN

KJ   **Switchgear**
                * >Fuses   KIP.M
                * – Bus-bars   KNN.B
                * – Electric control equipment   KIB
                * – Switching substations   KDS.SH
KJC   ⟶   Circuit-breakers
                = Air-break circuit-breakers
                = Air circuit-breakers
                * >Earth-leakage circuit-breakers
                                        KIP.Q
                * >Relay circuit-breakers   KIP.PC
                * – Operating time   MBC.DP
                * – Switch-fuses   KJH.C
                * – Switches   KJH

                (By size)

KJC.C   Miniature circuit-breakers
                * – Fuses   KIP.M

                (By operating medium)

KJC.E   Oil circuit-breakers
KJC.G   Gas-blast circuit-breakers
KJC.GC   Air-blast circuit-breakers
KJC.H   Vacuum circuit-breakers
                * <Vacuum devices   NPT

                (By design)

KJC.M   Tri-pole circuit-breakers
                = Triple-pole circuit-breakers

Alphabetical display

Cinematography   LPM
    <   Photography
    –   Sprockets (cinematography)
    * – Film-making   ZWW.CW
    * – Film studios   RDH.X
    * – Location lighting   RLH.T
    * – Motion-picture cameras   LQB.C
    * – Motion-picture projectors   LQD.C
    * – Recording engineering   LN
    * – Special effects (photography)   LPO

Cineole   DVG.P
    –   Terpene hydrocarbons

Cinnamon   IIG.I
    <   Spices

Cinnamon   IIG.I
    +   Essential oils   VMF/VMH
    =** Oil of cinnamon   VMG.D

Circles (geometry)   CCG.J
    –   Arcs of a circle
    –   Geometry

Circling guidance lights
    →   Aeronautical ground lights   RLH.S

Circlips   NWU.FF
    <   Spring retaining rings

Circuit analysis
    →   Network analysis (circuits)   KPE

Circuit-breaker components   KJC.R
    >   Arc control devices
    >   Interrupters (circuit-breakers)
    >   Tripping mechanisms (circuit-breakers)
    –   Circuit-breakers

⟶ **Circuit-breakers**   KJC
    =   Air-break circuit-breakers
    =   Air circuit-breakers
    <   Switchgear
    >   Gas-blast circuit-breakers
    >   Miniature circuit-breakers
    >   Oil circuit-breakers
    >   Overcurrent circuit-breakers
    >   Tri-pole circuit-breakers
    >   Vacuum circuit-breakers
    –   Breaking capacity
    –   Circuit-breaker components
    –   Making capacity
    –   Recovery voltage
    * > Earth-leakage circuit-breakers   KIP.Q
    * > Relay circuit-breakers   KIP.PC
    * – Operating time   MBC.DP
    * – Switch-fuses   KJH.C
    * – Switches   KJH

Circuit design
    →   Network synthesis   KPG

On the other hand, a full alphabetical thesaurus is a useful format for screen display and acceptable to the end user. Such a thesaurus is included in the BSI *ROOT thesaurus* (Figure 23), the *RIIA Library thesaurus* (Figure 24b), and other similar thesauri. The alphabetical display repeats all the relationships shown in the systematic display, except that the broader and narrower terms are limited to one hierarchical level only. The indented terms in the systematic display, which are associatively related and not narrower terms to their superordinate terms, for example, 'Strands' in the above display (see above), should be coded (RT) to 'Ropes' (i.e., not NT) before the alphabetical display is generated (see also F1.3.4a).

Example:

BSI ROOT thesaurus style alphabetical thesaurus

Fibre ropes   HTN
    UF   Textile ropes
    BT   Ropes
  *BT   Textile products   UMN

Ropes   HT
    SN   A length of strong line made of fibrous material, metal wire, etc.
    BT   Mechanical components
    NT   Fibre ropes
    NT   Wire ropes
    RT   Strands
  *NT   Gymnastic ropes   XVG.N
  *RT   Rescue equipment   SNK
Strands   HTC
    RT   Ropes
Wire ropes   HTR
    BT   Ropes
  *RT   Wires   PVL

The example above shows that there are two sequences of broader, narrower and related terms. The first sequence without asterisks is generated from the terms immediately above and below the preferred term in the systematic display. The second, asterisked sequence is derived from the cross-references in the display and includes terms located elsewhere in the schedules. In an alternative layout, the asterisked *BT/*NT/*RT sequence may be interfiled with the BT/NT/RT sequence. In this case the classmarks against each term in the entry indicate the location of the terms in the display.

Example:

Ropes HT
    SN   A length of strong line ...
    BT   Mechanical components   H
    NT   Fibre ropes   HTN
    NT   Gymnastic ropes   XVG.N
    NT   Wire ropes   HTR
    RT   Rescue equipment   SNK
    RT   Strands   HTC

Figure 24a. Detailed faceted classification
RIIA Library thesaurus
Classification schedules

M/P   01 **POLITICAL SCIENCE**

N/P   02 **INTERNATIONAL RELATIONS** (Cont)
NC/NG   04 **FOREIGN RELATIONS** (Cont)
NF   06 Foreign services (Cont)

                      07 *(Departments of state)*
NFC   –   08 Foreign offices
                           UF Departments of state for foreign affairs
                           *BT Government departments *MQL.CM**

NFC.F –   09 Foreign secretaries
                         UF Foreign ministers
                         UF Secretaries of state for foreign affairs
                         *RT Cabinets *MPS**
                         *RT Foreign secretaries meetings *NBF**

→NFP   07 Diplomatic services
                     UF Consular services

                   08 *(Law)*
NFP.5X –   09 Diplomatic law
                       *BT International law *IN/IZ**

                   10 *(Agreements)*
NFP.5XD –   11 Diplomatic law agreements
                         UF Vienna Convention on Diplomatic Relations
                       *BT International agreements *NH**

                   10 *(Immunity and privilege)*
NFP.5XI   11 Diplomatic immunity
                       UF Diplomatic privilege
                       UF Immunity (diplomatic)
                       UF Privilege (diplomatic)
                       *BT State immunity *IUF.I*
                       *RT Extraterritoriality *IUL.T*
                       *RT UN delegates *NKB.D*

                   08 *(Personnel)*
NFP.K –   09 Diplomatic corps
                     UF Ambassadors
                     UF Attaches
                     UF Charges d'affaires
                     UF Consuls
                     UF Diplomats
                     UF Envoys
                     UF Plenipotentiaries
                     *RT Diplomat expulsion *NGK*

                   08 *(Establishments)*
NFP.M –   09 Embassies
                     UF Consulates
                     UF Legations

                   08 *(Activities)*
NFP.S –   09 Intelligence gathering (diplomacy)
                     UF Foreign intelligence gathering (diplomacy)
                     UF Information gathering (diplomacy
                     *RT Secret services *NWS*

Figure 24b. Detailed faceted classification
RIIA Library thesaurus
Alphabetical thesaurus

Diplomatic services

→**Diplomatic services** *NFP*
        UF   Consular services
        BT   **Foreign services** *NF*
        RT   **Diplomatic corps** *NFP.K*
        RT   **Diplomatic intrigue** *NFP.U*
        RT   **Diplomatic law** *NFP.5X*
        RT   **Embassies** *NFP.M*
        RT   **Foreign diplomats** *NFP.X*
        RT   **Intelligence gathering (diplomacy)** *NFP.S*

Diplomats
        USE **Diplomatic corps** *NFP.K*

Diplomats (foreign)
        USE **Foreign diplomats** *NFP.X*

Direct taxation
        USE **Taxation** *KVT*

Directorates
        USE **Secretariats** *4BQ*

Directories *2NA*
        BT   **Form divisions** *2*

Dirty floating (exchange rates)
        USE **Managed flexibility (exchange rates)** *LGE.VM*

Disadvantaged people *HHD*
        BT   **Social problems** *HH/HZ*
      *BT   **Persons** *3A*
      *BT   **Social units** *FH/FZ*
      *NT   **Deprived people** *HI3.A*
      *NT   **Disaster victims** *AMD.3A*
      *NT   **Prisoners** *HSP.3A*
      *NT   **Refugees** *FP*
      *NT   **Stateless persons** *FNH*
      *NT   **Victims of repression** *MIR.B*
      *RT   **Minority groups** *FNV*

Disappeared persons *MIR.BD*
        BT   **Victims of repression** *MIR.B*
      *RT   **Crimes against humanity** *MGB*
      *RT   **Detention** *HSD*
      *RT   **Human rights violations** *MJF.V*
      *RT   **Kidnapping** *HVM.K*

Disarmament
        USE **Arms control** *PD/PI*

Disarmament agreements
        USE **Arms control agreements** *PDE*

Disarmament conferences
        USE **Arms control conferences** *PD4.D4*

Disarmament negotiations
        USE **Arms control negotiations** *PDC*

Disarmament organizations
        USE **Arms control organizations** *PD4*

The *ROOT* style of thesaurus is helpful to the compiler as all intellectual effort takes place at the stage of creating the systematic section. The alphabetical section may be derived by clerical effort or computer program from the systematic display (Dextre and Clarke, 1981).

H4.3.4. Polyhierarchies in faceted systematic displays

In most faceted thesauri polyhierarchies (see F1.2.4) are included in the systematic display. Polyhierarchies, however, are not included in the hierarchies of the *Art and architecture thesaurus* (Art, 1994), although they are shown in similar hierarchies in the *ASIS thesaurus* (Milstead, 1998) (see H4.3.2).

A method of displaying polyhierarchies in a systematic display is suggested in ISO 2788 and BS 5723, in which indexing terms with more than one broader term are placed in each appropriate hierarchy. The *Construction industry thesaurus* (Construction, 1976) deals with polyhierarchies in this way.

Example:

    Systematic display

H	**Mechanical components**
	...
HT	Ropes
	SN A length of strong line ...
	(Components)
HTC *(RT)*	Strands
	(Types – by material)
→ HTN	Fibre ropes
	UF Textile ropes
HTR	Wire ropes
	*RT Wires PVL
	(Types – by application)
→ HTW	Gymnastic ropes
	UF Climbing ropes
	...
UM	**Textile technology**
	...
UMN *(RT)*	Textile products
UMN.C	Yarn
UMN.K	Cloth
→ UMN.T	Fibre ropes
	UF Textile ropes
	...

XV	**Leisure equipment**
XVG	Gymnastic equipment
XVG.C	Springboards
XVG.E	Wall bars
XVG.G	Vaulting bars
→ XVG.N	Gymnastic ropes
	UF Climbing ropes

Alphabetical display

Fibre ropes   HTN; UMN.T
  UF   Textile ropes
  BT   Ropes
  BT   Textile products
Gymnastic ropes   HTW; XVG.N
  UF   Climbing ropes
  BT   Gymnastic equipment
  BT   Ropes
Ropes   HT
  SN   A length of strong line ...
  BT   Mechanical components
  NT   Fibre ropes
  NT   Gymnastic ropes
  NT   Wire ropes
  RT   Strands
Strands   HTC
  RT   Ropes
Wire ropes   HTR
  BT   Ropes
  RT   Wires   PVL

This method differs from the *ROOT thesaurus* approach which places an indexing term in one preferred hierarchy and makes reference from it to broader terms in other hierarchies using the code *BT followed by the appropriate classmark. Under these broader terms reciprocal *NT references are made to the indexing term. In screen displays, the terms in the polyhierarchies, indicated by the asterisked cross-references, may be viewed in full, by easy switching to the appropriate location (see H4.3.3, J7.2.1.b and Figure 23).

The multiple placing of indexing terms gives the most detailed analysis of each subject field, as in each location the indexing term has to be placed in the correct facets and arrays. There is then no bias in favour of analyzing one subject field more fully than another. Another advantage is that a term may be retrieved in a truncated, or 'explosion', search on notation for all its broader terms. For example, searching on HT* 'Ropes' or UMN* 'Textile products' will retrieve 'Fibre ropes' whereas, in the 'preferred-term layout' a search on UMN* would not retrieve the term as it lacks a classmark in the textile field. On the other hand, this layout demands more effort by the compiler, and frequent repetition of lengthy hierarchies may overload the display.

H5. Graphic displays

Indexing terms and their inter-relationships may be displayed in the form of a two-dimensional figure from which the user may select those terms that are appropriate. Graphic displays help to improve access and may also be a useful tool during thesaurus construction in bringing related terms together in semantic clusters (see J7.2.2). Early reviews of types of graphic displays were made by Gilchrist and Foskett (Gilchrist 1971, p. 35–38, 89–92, and Foskett, D.J., 1981).

Recently, computerized graphic displays of information have become increasingly common. Craven gives a review, citing the literature up to 1991, of ideas on computerized displays of concept networks, applicable to graphic displays of thesauri and related purposes (Craven, 1992a), and compares general purpose and specially designed software for thesaurus display, concluding the latter gives better results (Craven, 1992b).

However, this form of display has yet to achieve wide use with practical thesauri, despite numerous examples in the literature. The inherent difficulty of effectively displaying detailed hierarchies and numerous related terms without overcrowding, and the lack of suitable software to address this problem and to rapidly generate the display, is undoubtedly a major factor.

There are three main types of graphic display: family tree structures, arrowgraphs, and terminographs or box charts.

H5.1. Family tree structures

In this layout the broadest term occurs at the head of the display and narrower terms are printed in subordinate positions, the relationship being indicated by vertical connecting lines. Scope notes, equivalence relationships, polyhierarchies and related terms are usually shown only in the accompanying alphabetical section. Each family tree diagram is given a notation, which is quoted as the address of all the terms in the diagram.

Example:

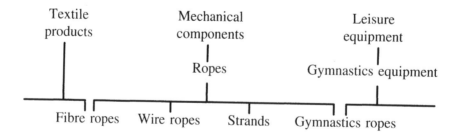

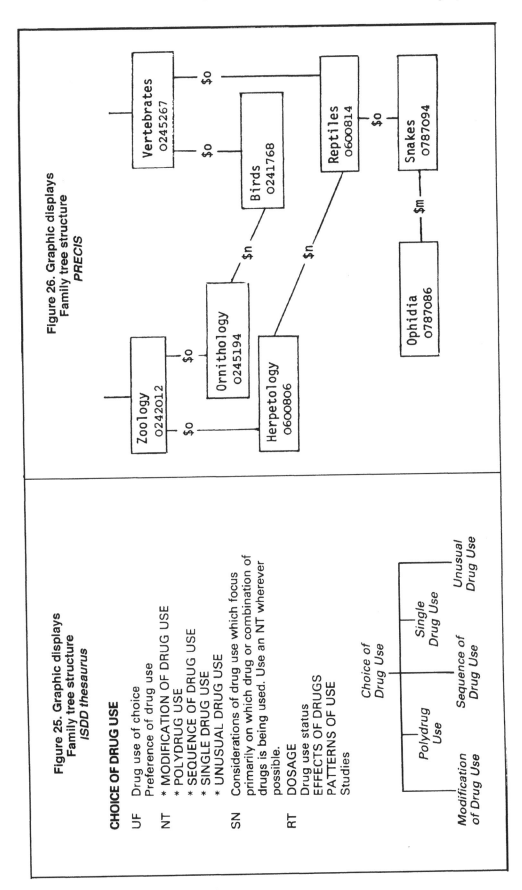

Figure 26. Graphic displays
Family tree structure
PRECIS

Figure 25. Graphic displays
Family tree structure
ISDD thesaurus

CHOICE OF DRUG USE

UF   Drug use of choice
     Preference of drug use

NT   * MODIFICATION OF DRUG USE
     * POLYDRUG USE
     * SEQUENCE OF DRUG USE
     * SINGLE DRUG USE
     * UNUSUAL DRUG USE

SN   Considerations of drug use which focus
     primarily on which drug or combination of
     drugs is being used. Use an NT wherever
     possible.

RT   DOSAGE
     Drug use status
     EFFECTS OF DRUGS
     PATTERNS OF USE
     Studies

See also Figure 25, an extract from the Institute for the Study of Drug Dependence's *ISDD thesaurus* (Defriez, 1993). The family tree structures in this thesaurus are the graphic equivalent of separate machine-derived hierarchies, as found in the *INSPEC thesaurus* and others (see H3.1). The tree structures are located via the TT (top term) code in the alphabetical display. Unlike the *INSPEC thesaurus* hierarchies, these tree structures were the source of, and not derived from, the hierarchical relationships in the alphabetical display. Another thesaurus containing tree structures is the *Thesaurus of terms in copper technology* (Black, 1981).

Family tree structures may lack equivalence relationships and do not usually differentiate between broader and narrower and related terms in the diagram itself. However, these relationships are shown in the *PRECIS* thesaurus networks (Figure 26). Vertical lines and the code $o show general BT/NT relationships, horizontal lines and code $m equivalence relationships, and inclined lines and code $n associative relationships.

H5.2. Arrowgraphs

Arrowgraphs are displays in the form of charts representing a number of specific subject fields and subfields. The chart may be marked with grids. Each chart has its own distinguishing notation, and the terms displayed in the chart may be located by the reference to the chart notation and to the specific grid reference number if a grid is used.

The broadest term is placed towards the centre of the chart in bold type (see Figure 27a). Narrower (and related) terms are printed in other positions within the grid, and hierarchical levels are shown by connecting arrows or lines pointing from the higher to the lower generic level; associatively related terms may be shown by connected two-way arrow systems or by broken lines. Reference is made to related indexing terms outside the groups represented in the chart, giving the relevant notation in the appropriate chart. Equivalence relations and scope notes are not usually shown on arrowgraphs. The alphabetical section may consist of no more than an index to the chart numbers of the indexing terms, but the data in the alphabetical section could include scope notes, equivalence relations, broader, narrower and related terms, as in Figure 27b. This form of layout is described fully in a paper by Rolling (Rolling, 1971).

The earliest diagram with arrows showing term relationships was the *TDCK circular thesaurus system* (Tuck, 1963) published by the Netherlands Armed Forces Technical Documentation and Information Centre. In 1966–67 Rolling compiled the *EURATOM thesaurus* (EURATOM, 1966) for the Commission of the European Communities, which featured arrowgraphs, and later he developed the trilingual SDIM thesaurus (Metallurgical, 1975) in the field of metallurgy. Arrowgraphs are also found in the multilingual *International road research documentation (IRRD) thesaurus* (International, 1985b) which includes about 50 arrowgraphs complemented by an alphabetical section (see Figure 28).

Figure 27a. Graphic display — arrowgraph

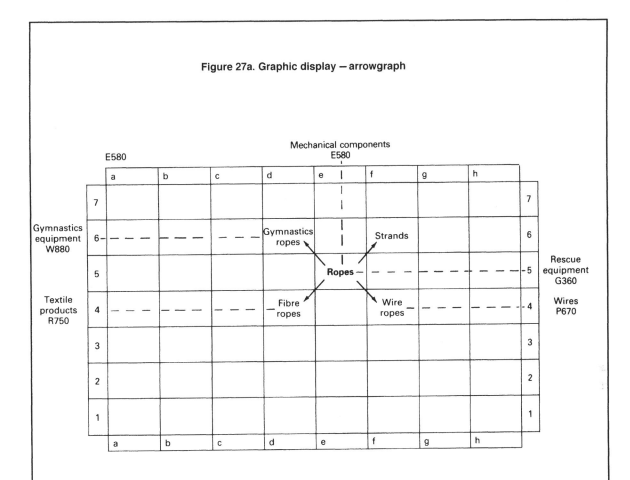

Figure 27b. Alphabetical index to arrowgraph

Fibre ropes	E580.d4	Ropes (cont.)	
BT Ropes		NT Fibre ropes	
Textile products		Gymnastics ropes	

Fibre ropes   E580.d4
  BT   Ropes
         Textile products

Gymnastics equipment   W880.d4
  NT   Gymnastics ropes

Gymnastics ropes   E580.d6
  BT   Gymnastics equipment
         Ropes

Mechanical components   E500.e5
  NT   Ropes

Rescue equipment   G360.c3
  RT   Ropes

Ropes   E580.e5
  BT   Mechanical components

Ropes (cont.)
  NT   Fibre ropes
         Gymnastics ropes
         Wire ropes
  RT   Rescue equipment
         Strands

Strands   E580.f6
  RT   Ropes

Textile products   R750.f3
  NT   Fibre ropes

Wire ropes   E580.f4
  BT   Ropes
  RT   Wires

Wires   P670.d5
  RT   Wire ropes

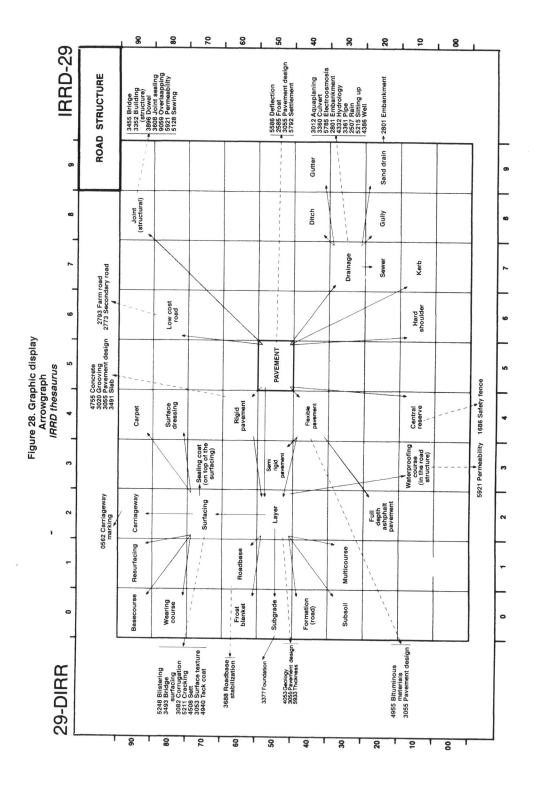

Figure 28. Graphic display
Arrowgraph
IRRD thesaurus

H5.3. Terminographs/box charts

Another type of graphic display is the terminograph or box chart found in Volume 3 of *SPINES thesaurus* (Spines, 1976) and in the *European education thesaurus*, formerly the EUDISED thesaurus, 1991. In the *European education thesaurus* (see Figure 29), there are 42 subfields or microthesauri, each represented by a terminograph, set out on a single page, which is identified in the bottom right-hand corner by a two-digit serial number followed by the title of the microthesaurus. Each terminograph contains an inner frame enclosing all the preferred terms in the microthesaurus. These preferred terms are listed hierarchically under the top terms (underlined) inside boxes. The steps of the hierarchy within the boxes are shown by the indenting of subordinate terms. Associative relationships between the preferred terms in the same microthesaurus are shown by lines linking the related terms. Outside the frame appear preferred terms referring to other microthesauri but linked to the preferred terms within the microthesaurus by some associative relationship or by a polyhierarchical relation. On the left of each external preferred term appears the number(s) of the microthesaurus to which it belongs. Non-preferred terms are not shown in the terminograph. The link between the terms in the alphabetical listing and in the terminograph is the terminograph number. All terms in the one microthesaurus have the same number but are not precisely located on the page by a specific grid reference number, as in the arrowgraph.

H6. Display in multilingual thesauri

In planning the layout of multilingual thesauri, one option is to include all languages in one volume. This is the layout preferred in the *ILO thesaurus* (ILO, 1992), where the systematic display contains the three language versions side-by-side (see Figure 18), with an alphabetical index to the display in each language. The *UNESCO thesaurus* (UNESCO, 1995) is also published in one volume, but has its main alphabetical section and its systematic section in English, with access for other languages via French and Spanish indexes.

Alternatively, a separate edition may be published for each language, in which alphabetical, systematic, permuted and all forms of display appear in the language of the edition. The edition may also include indexes in the other languages of the thesaurus. Examples of multilingual thesauri in separate volumes include *European education thesaurus* (European, 1991) and the *International thesaurus of refugee terminology* (Aitchison, 1966).

Alphabetical displays

In the main alphabetical display in multilingual thesauri, it is common practice to show the equivalent terms in other languages immediately below the preferred term, preceding any scope notes or non-preferred terms (see Figure 30 from *UNESCO thesaurus*).

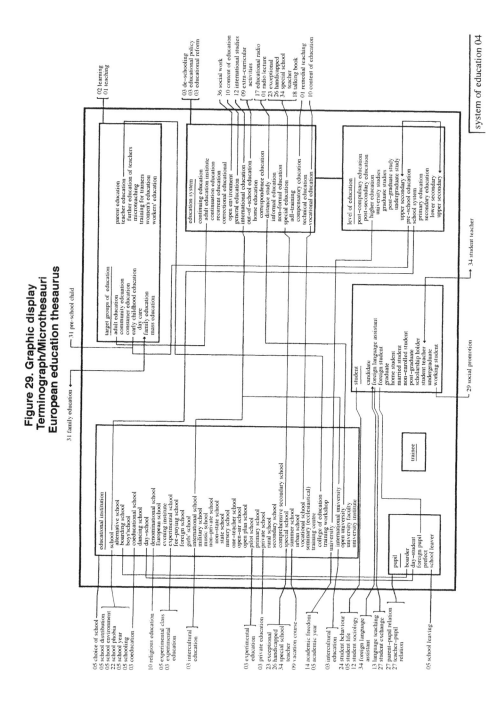

Figure 29. Graphic display
Terminograph/Microthesauri
European education thesaurus

Figure 30. Multilingual thesauri
Alphabetical display
UNESCO thesaurus

Engineers
MT   2.10 Science and research management
     FR   *Ingénieur*
     SP   *Ingeniero*
BT1   **Scientists**
     BT2 **Scientific personnel**
RT   **Engineering**
RT   **Occupations**

England
USE   UK (7.20)

English
MT   3.35 Languages
     FR   *Anglais*
     SP   *Inglés*
BT1   **Germanic language**
     BT2   **Indo-european languages**

English speaking Africa
MT   7.45 Linguistic groupings
     FR   *Afrique anglophone*
     SP   *Africa de habla inglesa*
NT1   **Bostwana**
NT1   **Gambia**
NT1   **Ghana**
NT1   **Kenya**
NT1   **Lesotho**
NT1   **Liberia**
NT1   **Malawi**
NT1   **Mauritius**
NT1   **Namibia**
NT1   **Nigeria**
NT1   **Seychelles**
NT1   **Sierra Lione**
NT1   **South Africa**
NT1   **Swaziland**
NT1   **Tanzania UR**
NT1   **Uganda**
NT1   **Zambia**
NT1   **Zimbabwe**

Engraving
MT   3.50 Visual arts
     FR   *Gravure*
     SP   *Grabado*
BT1   **Handcrafts**
RT   **Illustration printing**
RT   **Plastic arts**

Enrolment
MT   1.15 Educational planning
     FR   *effectifs*
     SP   *Matrícula*
SN   The total number of individuals registered as
     participants in a programme or activity
UF   *Educational registration*
BT1   **Educational statistics**
NT1   **Educational wastage**
     NT2   **Dropout rate**
     NT2   **Repetition rate**
RT   **Admission requirements**
RT   **Educational attendance**
RT   **School age population**

Enrolement:
     Girls enrolment
       USE Girls education (1.30)

Enrolment projections
MT   1.15 Educational planning
     FR   *Projection des effectifs*

Enrolment projections
     SP   *Proyecciones de la matricula*
BT1   **Educational forecasting**
     BT2   **Educational statistics**
RT   **Enrolment trends**

Enrolment ratio
MT   1.15 Educational planning
     FR   *Taux d'insription*
     SP   *Tasa de matrícula*
SN   Enrolment as percentage of relevant age
     group
BT1   **Educational statistics**
RT   **Enrolment trends**

Enrolment trends
MT   1.10 Educational policy
     FR   *Évolution des effectifs*
     SP   *Evolución de la matrícula*
BT1   **Educational trends**
     BT2   **Educational development**
RT   **Enrolment projections**
RT   **Enrolment ratio**

Enterprise:
     Culture of enterprise
       USE Culture of work (3.05)
     Size of enterprise (6.75)

Enterprises
MT   6.75 Organization and management
     FR   *Entreprise*
     SP   *Empresa*
UF   *Business*
NT1   **Agriculutral enterprises**
NT1   **Cooperatives**
     NT2   **Agricultural cooperatives**
NT1   **Industrial enterprises**
NT1   **Joint ventures**
NT1   **Private enterprises**
NT1   **Public enterprises**
     NT2   **Public utilities**
NT1   **Size of enterprise**
     NT2   **Small enterprises**
NT1   **Transnational corporations**
RT   **Administration**
RT   **Business economics**
RT   **Management**
RT   **Organizational change**
RT   **Organizations**

Enterprises:
     Agriculutral enterprises (6.75)
     Industrial enterprises (6.75)
     International business enterprises
       USE Transnational corporations (6.75)
     Multinational enterprises
       USE Transnational corporations (6.75)
     Nationalized enterprises
       USE Public enterprises (6.75)
     Private enterprises (6.75)
     Public enterprises (6.75)
     Small enterprises (6.75)

Entertainment
MT   3.65 Leisure
     FR   *Divertissement*
     SP   *Entretenimiento*
BT1   **Leisure time activities**
RT   **Clubs**
RT   **Cultural events**
RT   **Cultural industry**
RT   **Festivals**

Language indexes

The function of language indexes in multilingual thesauri is specifically to show equivalent terms in the other languages of the thesauri. For example, in the English language editions of the *International thesaurus of refugee terminology* (Aitchison, 1996), there is a French/English/Spanish index and a Spanish/English/French index.

Example:

French/English/Spanish Index

French	*English*	*Spanish*
Pompes	Pumps	Bombas
Ponts	Bridges	Puentes
Pouvoir judiciaire	Judicial power	Poder judicial

Spanish/English/French Index

Spanish	*English*	*French*
Bombas	Pumps	Pompes
Puentes	Bridges	Ponts
Poder judicial	Judicial power	Pouvoir judiciaire

Section I: Multilingual thesauri

General

The problems of multilingual thesaurus construction are no worse, in kind, than those of monolingual thesaurus construction; providing, of course, that there are competent linguists available. Perhaps the most difficult aspect is that of human organization, often involving the work of international committees.

The relevant standard here is ISO 5964: 1985: *Guidelines for the establishment and development of multilingual thesauri* (International, 1985a), the equivalent to British Standard 6723: 1985 (British, 1985a), which states clearly right at the start: 'The guidelines given in this International Standard should be used in conjunction with ISO 2788, and regarded as an extension of the scope of the monolingual guidelines. It is considered that the majority of procedure and recommendations contained in ISO 2788 are equally valid for a multilingual thesaurus'. This can be seen to be sound advice when it is considered that the majority of descriptors are nouns (see D3.1.1) and, more importantly, that thesaurus compilation is concerned with the identification of the concepts behind the words.

Thus, the handling of descriptors in multilingual thesauri is much the same as in monolingual work, with the added variety of morphologies arising from the different language forms. It may be useful, then, to know that languages are classified broadly into four forms.

- Inflectional languages, such as Latin, which use case-endings. These root-suffixes qualify the nouns and verbs.
- Agglutinative languages, such as Turkish, Finnish and Hungarian where the root-suffixes can, and regularly do, stand as separate words.
- Isolating languages, such as Chinese, which make no use of inflection, agglutination or prepositions.
- Analytical languages, such as English, which use word order, auxiliary words and some vestiges of inflection to provide the grammatical structure.

Clearly some of the rules discussed above such as plurals being preferred to singulars need to be reconsidered in the light of linguistic variations.

However, though the above knowledge may be useful, it is not so important as a good working knowledge of the languages being handled, including the socio-cultural nuances, particularly present in non-scientific subjects.

Aspects of display are discussed in Section H6, and aspects of software in Section K3.

I1. Source and target thesauri

The first decision to be made in the multilingual situation is which is to be the 'source language'; and this should obtain whether the work is to be started *ab initio* or existing schemes are to be reconciled and merged.

The source language is defined as 'that language which serves as a starting point when a preferred term is translated into its nearest equivalent term or terms in a second language'. This second language and any subsequent languages are known as 'target languages'. No implication of status should be made in the use of the terms 'source' and 'targets', and the choice of the source language should be made on pragmatic grounds, no one language having dominance over any other. Thus, in the compilation work, it will be important to feed back concepts and translations continuously from each target language, taken in turn, to the source language.

In practice, and more happily in some systems than in others, the target thesauri are not directly related to each other, leaving the source thesaurus in the hub position of a radial network.

I2. Equivalences

BS 6723 contains a table, reproduced in Figure 31, showing five degrees of equivalence, and these are discussed, in turn, below.

I2.1. Exact equivalence

This is the analogue of the true synonym and is dealt with straightforwardly, as in the following example.

English	French	German
PHYSICS	= PHYSIQUE	= PHYSIK

I2.2. Inexact equivalence

This is the analogue of the near synonym and, again, is dealt with as in monolingual thesauri, i.e., the near synonyms are regarded, for indexing purposes, as being equivalent, as in the following example.

German	French	English
GEDECK	= MENU	= MENUS

where the English equivalent is a 'loan term' from the French, and normally expressed in the plural, whereas the German and French standards prefer the singular form for descriptors.

I2.3. Partial equivalence

This is similar to the case of the near synonym but in which one of the terms strictly viewed denotes a slightly broader or narrower concept. Thus, the two terms can either be treated as synonyms, or one can be recognized as being broader, and dealt with accordingly. The example given in ISO 5964 is the well-known case of the German word '*Wissenschaft*' which has a broader connotation than the English word 'science'.

Figure 31. Degrees of equivalence

Case	Source language	Target language
1 - Exact equivalence		
2 - Inexact equivalence		
3 - Partial equivalence		
4 - Single-to-multiple equivalence		
5 - Non-equivalence		

acceptable term exists

acceptable term does not exist

I2.4. Single-to-multiple equivalence

This is the most complex situation and the one which requires the most thoughtful analysis. Essentially, there are three separate, though similar, situations, each having at least three solutions.

Situation 1: where a term does not exist in another language but two or more narrower terms do, which in combination cover the broader concept.

Situation 2: similar to situation 1, but where factoring (see E2.4.2) can be employed.

Situation 3: where two generic terms exist in one language and only one in another, it not being clear which of the two generic terms is the most appropriate.

The solutions differ in the degree of detail which can be incorporated and in the accuracy with which the concepts in the two languages are equated. One trick which is to be found throughout these examples is the use of the 'loan term'. For example, in the case of the German word 'Wissenschaft', this could be included in the English thesaurus clearly marked as a loan term from the German and shown as being a BT to science. Whereas this seems not only permissible but useful where a particular word has a local and socio-cultural content, it is to be avoided in those cases where the underlying concepts can be equated, as can be seen in the examples which follow.

Example of situation 1

The English word 'skidding' has no equivalent in German but there exist the two words, *Rutschen*, which means 'forward skidding', and *Schleudern*, which means 'sideways skidding'. Apart from the deprecated denoting of the English word 'Skidding' as a loan term to the German (or presumably both *Rutschen* and *Schleudern* to the English) there are two courses of action:

(a) to recognize 'skidding' as the addition of *Rutschen* and *Schleudern*

(b) to regard *Rutschen* and *Schleudern* as variations of an English homograph 'skidding'.

In practice the combination of (a) and (b) is the preferred solution, achieving all the equivalents, as shown below:

```
SKIDDING                = RUTSCHEN + SCHLEUDERN
                            D   Zu benutzen, wenn ein Dokument sowohl
                                Rutschen also auch Schleudern behandelt
NT SKIDDING (forwards)  =   UB RUTSCHEN
NT SKIDDING (sideways)  =   UB SCHLEUDERN

SKIDDING (forwards)     = RUTSCHEN
   BT SKIDDING            OB RUTSCHEN + SCHLEUDERN

SKIDDING (sideways)     = SCHLEUDERN
   BT SKIDDING            OB RUTSCHEN + SCHLEUDERN
```

Example of situation 2

The English phrase 'solar heating' can be expressed in French by the terms *chauffage* and *energie solaire*. Here it is possible, though again deprecated as being even more dangerous than the use of the loan term, to coin a new term, in this case *chauffage solaire*. However, factoring (see E2.4.2) will give a better result and, in this particular situation, can be solved in two ways, depending on the degree of usage of the term 'solar heating'.

Solution (a):
```
HEATING          = CHAUFFAGE
SOLAR ENERGY     = ENERGIE SOLAIRE
```

Solar heating
   USE HEATING + SOLAR ENERGY

Solution (b)
```
SOLAR HEATING    = CHAUFFAGE + ENERGIE SOLAIRE
HEATING          = CHAUFFAGE
SOLAR ENERGY     = ENERGIE SOLAIRE
```

Example of situation 3:

The French word *bétail* can be translated into English as 'livestock' which includes cattle and horses; but the French expression *gros bétail* which also includes cattle and horse has no clear equivalent in English. Here there are three solutions (again disregarding the use of loan terms), the third solution being the combination of the first two.

Solution (a) ignores one pair of generic terms:

GROS BETAIL   = CATTLE + HORSES
                            SN   Use this combination as an equivalent to the French
                                    term GROS BETAIL
                            NT   CATTLE
                            NT   HORSES

Solution (b) makes the two generic terms synonymous, and selects one as being equivalent to the generic term in the other language:

BETAIL   = LIVESTOCK
    EP Gros bétail   NT   CATTLE
    TS BOEUF   NT   HORSES
    TS CHEVAL

   Gros bétail
     EM BETAIL

This last situation is clearly one which calls for expert linguistic assistance, and will not be easily appreciated by the monoglot. In fact, one reputable dictionary gives *bétail* as being translatable to either 'cattle' or 'livestock', *gros bétail* as being only 'bovine cattle', and a third term, *menu bétail* as including 'sheep' and goats'. Thus *bétail* can be seen to either include or exclude 'horses', and *gros bétail* to definitely exclude 'horses'.

12.5. Non-equivalence

What this actually means is that there is no simply expressed equivalent, and the only two possible solutions are the loan term or the coined term. In both cases the introduced terms should be accompanied by scope notes.

In solution (a), the German term is lent to the English thesaurus:

BERUFSVERBOT   = BERUFSVERBOT
                          SN   Alleged prohibition of certain classes of persons
                                    from official employment. Loan term adopted from
                                    German; used only in some political contexts.

In solution (b), a French term is coined as being equivalent to the English:

STEAM CRACKING   = VAPOCRAQUAGE
                          NE   Craquage à la vapeur d'eau. Terme équivalent au
                                    terme anglais STEAM CRACKING.

13. Other considerations

In most other aspects the guideline for multilingual thesaurus compilation follow those for monolingual construction, but there are a few additional points to be made arising from the language problem and from variations in local usage. In all cases, two basic rules obtain: first, try to use the most familiar form of a term and second, cross refer from the others. Thus:

NETHERLANDS	= PAYS-BAS
UF Holland	EP Hollande
Holland	Hollande
USE NETHERLANDS	EM PAYS-BAS

While national institutions should appear the same in all versions (e.g., Royal Society), international institutions should be translated and cross-references made from their abbreviations, e.g.:

EUROPEAN COMMUNITIES	= COMMUNAUTES EUROPEENNES
UF EC	EP CE
EC	EM COMMUNAUTES EUROPEENNES
USE EUROPEAN COMMUNITIES	

The conventions governing the use of singulars and plurals may vary between languages. For example, French and German both prefer the singular:

| ANIMALS | ANIMAL | TIER |
| CHILDREN | ENFANT | KIND |

The homograph problem can now occur within one language or between several. The first instance is no different to the problem in monolingual work and is so treated:

TOUR (bâtiment)	= TOWERS
TOUR (outil)	= LATHES
TOUR (voyage)	= TOURS
TOUR (rotation)	= ROTATION

The homograph between languages will present a potential problem only if one alphabetical sequence is employed for some reason, and here a simple discriminating code can be used. Where the English/French equivalents are

| BEAMS (radiation) | = RAYON |
| RAYON | = SOIE ARTIFICIELLE |

confusion can be avoided by using RAYON(E) and RAYON(F).

The options and solutions offered by the Standards, and discussed above, are considered in a paper by Hudon concerned with how to achieve a fully developed thesaural structure in each language. In each case, the preferred option from the Standards, the one most truly capable of ensuring respect for a language and its speakers, is carefully selected (Hudon, 1997).

Finally, the abbreviations for thesaural relationships are given in English, French and German, together with a set of mathematical symbols which, being language-independent, might be preferred.

BT	Broader term	TG	Terme générique	OB	Oberbegriff	<
NT	Narrower term	TS	Terme spécifique	UB	Unterbegriff	>
RT	Related term	VA	Voir aussi	VB	Verwandter Begriff	—
USE	Use	EM	Employer	BS	Benutze	→
UF	Used for	EP	Employé pour	BF	Benutzt für	=
SN	Scope note	NE	Note explicative	D	Definition	

Section J: Construction techniques

In this section a step-by-step approach to thesaurus construction (subsequent to checking that a thesaurus is required – see B1) is given with illustrations from a hypothetical thesaurus. The section considers only the intellectual aspects of thesaurus construction. Automatic thesaurus construction is considered in F4.

The reader is referred for further information to seven publications which also include practical steps in thesaurus construction, namely Batty, 1980, 1989; Craven, 1997; Milstead, 1996; Orna, 1983; Soergel, 1974; Townley and Gee, 1980; and Will, 1996.

J1. Definition of subject field

As a first step, the subject field is defined, the boundaries of the subject are established, and a distinction is made between those parts which must be treated in depth and those of marginal importance (See also J7.1: preliminary organization of the subject field).

J2. Selection of thesaurus characteristics and layout

By this stage the compiler should have clarified his or her ideas as to what type of thesaurus is to be constructed, having already studied the overall system requirements (B2–B3), and should now know whether controlled language only, natural language alone, or a hybrid system of natural and controlled language is to be used. The compiler should know if the thesaurus is to serve as a macrothesaurus, a switching language, or a search thesaurus for a natural language system. A decision should have been made on features of the thesaurus, such as specificity, compound terms and the use of auxiliary precision devices. The compiler should also know how the thesaurus is to be presented, i.e., whether there is to be a graphical or a systematic display as well as an alphabetical display. In the case of the hypothetical thesaurus (on Catering) used here to illustrate construction techniques, it is assumed that a decision has been made that the thesaurus is to serve the needs of a database with controlled and natural language. It is to have a medium level of specificity and term pre-coordination. The preferred layout could be a systematic display supported by a full alphabetical thesaurus as in the BSI *ROOT thesaurus* (H4.3.3), though other options discussed in Section H, Thesaurus display, would be possible following the same construction steps. These options include an alphabetical display with single or multiple hierarchies (H2.2) accompanied by broad subject groups (H4.1) 'themes' (H4.1.1), other forms of detailed faceted classification (H4.3) or graphic displays (H5).

J3. Notification of intent

When the decision is made to produce a new thesaurus for eventual publication, notification of intent should be announced in an appropriate professional journal.

J4. Deductive versus inductive method

If a thesaurus is compiled using the deductive method, the examination of selected terms to find structure and to introduce vocabulary control is delayed until a sufficient number of terms have been collected. In contrast, if the inductive method is used, terms are admitted to the thesaurus and are used in indexing as soon as they are encountered in the literature. Vocabulary control is applied from the outset and the terms are allocated to one or more broader categories. Indexing is started earlier in the project, but there may have to be revision of the indexing at a later stage when the significance of the terms used is better appreciated.

In the steps outlined below, the deductive method is favoured, although some vocabulary control is applied early, as the controlled form of terms is recorded on the initial record forms during term collection, whenever this is possible, and terms are allocated to one or more of several broad subject fields, or facets, for later analysis. The terms would not be used for 'live' indexing until all relationships had been established, form and choice of term finalized, and the resulting thesaurus tested.

J5. Selection of terms

The task of assembling terms starts as soon as the subject field is defined. There are three main written sources of terminology: terms in standardized form, non-standardized terminology found in the literature, and terminology in users' recorded questions and profiles. The two unwritten sources are the knowledge and experience of users and experts, and the similar resources of the compiler.

J5.1. Terminological sources in standardized form

• Thesauri and lists of terms
These will include specialized thesauri, subject heading and term lists and the appropriate sections of general thesauri and subject headings. Thesauri are a source of synonyms, broader, narrower and related terms and, to a lesser extent, definitions. (For details of thesaurus bibliographies see B3.1.)

If there is a large number of small vocabularies and thesauri in the subject field, it might be useful to merge these, so that the terms they contain may be viewed more easily by scanning a single list.

• Classification schemes
These include specialized schemes and the appropriate sections of general schemes such as the *Universal decimal classification*, the *Library of Congress classification*, and *BC2*. Classification schemes may lack the word form control and precise display of

relationships necessary for a thesaurus, but may be rich in terminology. The *Bliss classification* (see also F2.1.1.) includes many synonyms and some definitions as well as hierarchies of terms. (One of the bibliographies of thesauri mentioned in B3.1 also includes details of classification systems.)

- Encyclopaedias, lexicons, dictionaries, glossaries

These may be universal or discipline-oriented, monolingual, bilingual or multilingual. They may be alphabetically organized or concept-oriented (i.e., arranged systematically under concepts).

Always check that it is the latest edition that is being searched.

- Terminological databanks

Terminological databanks are another source of thesaurus terms. Databanks provide definitions, synonyms, and sometimes broader, narrower and related terms.

- Treatises on the terminology of a subject field
- Indexes of journals and abstract journals
- Indexes of other publications in the field

J5.2. Literature scanning

In all subject fields, and in particular in those which are developing rapidly, it is not sufficient to rely solely on 'pre-arranged' sources for term selection. The literature must be scanned for non-standardized, free-text terms. The literature scanned should not be limited to monographs and journal articles but should extend to reports, pamphlets, product catalogues, conference papers, patent specifications and standards.

J.5.2.1. Manual selection

In manual selection, cards should be used to record terms and phrases considered significant. If a note is also kept on the card of the number of times that the term occurs in the literature, this will give an indication of the relative importance of the term. If clerical help is available, the compiler may underline the selected terms ready for typing on to cards or (preferably) on to a microcomputer to produce a machine-readable master file, from which may be produced lists in alphabetical order and also in descending order of frequency of occurrence. The frequency list will assist not only in suggesting the leading candidate terms, but also in the choice of preferred terms among synonyms.

J5.2.2. Automatic term selection

In automatic selection, lists of words are derived by computer from the title, abstracts and full text of documents, where available (see Gilchrist, 1971, p. 38, and Lancaster, 1986, Chapter 4). Ranked lists of most frequently used terms and phrases are output. Information on the frequency of co-occurrence of terms or phrases with other terms or phrases may also be derived, using statistical techniques. This provides guidance on term groupings and relationships.

J5.3. Question scanning

Terms found in questions put to the system have equal importance as candidates for the thesaurus as those taken from the literature. The questions should be collected from users (see J5.4) or from records of questions, searches and profiles already encountered. Analysis of user queries on a full-scale research project basis might be considered. This was done as a preliminary step before the 'Community information classification' (Bonner) was compiled. Several thousands of user profiles, held in a large number of community information and advice organizations in the United Kingdom, were computer-analyzed to show frequency of term use and co-occurrence of subjects.

J5.4. Users'/experts' experience and knowledge

The compiler should seek the advice and cooperation of users and user groups in term selection at all stages of compilation. At the stage of term gathering, users' opinions are invaluable. Compilation through a committee of experts may not be very satisfactory, but advice may be obtained in a more informal manner. Some suggestions as to how to go about this are listed below.

- Experts may be asked to assist in the scanning of the literature, indexing items with those terms they consider most appropriate.
- Experts may be asked to list terms of importance in their subject fields.
- Experts may be asked to list typical questions which they might put to the system.
- Experts may be shown lists of terms or draft classification schemes, in their own subject fields, and asked to comment, make amendments and add terms.
- Groups of experts may be asked to discuss the terminology and classification in subject areas which appear difficult to delineate and which require careful clarification.

J5.5. The compiler's experience and knowledge

The compiler's knowledge of the subject and familiarity with the terminology is an asset in term selection and rejection, but it is unwise for the compiler to rely on his or her own knowledge and memory to the exclusion of all other sources.

J6. Recording of the terms

It has already been suggested (J5.2.1) that a record (see Figure 32) should be kept of the terms selected on cards or, preferably, in machine-readable form. Information about the term might include definitions, synonyms, hierarchical and associative relations. In addition, the source of the term might be included: also its frequency of occurrence, and a field for entering a notation or broad subject heading to be used in the initial sorting of terms into subject groups for the process of finding structure. When selecting thesaural relationships from existing thesauri care should be taken not to record relationships which would be inappropriate for the particular bias of the thesaurus under construction. In any case some of these recorded relationships may be modified or discarded when the terms are analyzed, in relation to the other selected terms, during later construction processes.

Figure 32. Term record form

Term		Notation
CATERING EQUIPMENT		R/Z
UF Kitchen equipment	SN	
BT Domestic appliances	Includes food mixers, cooking-ware, tableware etc.	
NT Cookers Microwave ovens	Frequency 8	
RT	Source Journal articles BSI ROOT Thesaurus Library catalogue	

J7. Finding structure

J7.1. Preliminary organization of the subjects covered by the thesaurus

Before or during the period of term collection, the subjects covered by the thesaurus should be organized into main categories so that terms, on selection, may be sorted and filed under appropriate headings to await further analysis. This operation is necessary whether a systematic, graphic or solely alphabetical display is the goal, because it will reveal the coverage of the thesaurus, existence of gaps and overloaded areas, and, at the same time, by bringing like terms together, will facilitate the determination of their structural relationships.

The subject coverage of thesauri varies from the broad in scope to the limited and highly specific. Some thesauri are concerned with the whole of knowledge, although usually from a particular viewpoint, or with large sub-sections, such as the 'social sciences' or 'technology'. Other thesauri treat major disciplines, for example 'physics', 'medicine', 'education' or 'economics', while many are involved with narrower subject areas such as 'microbiology', 'welding', 'industrial relations' or 'drug dependence'. In most thesauri, apart from the very general, it is possible to discern at least one and usually several main subject areas which form the core of the thesaurus. Surrounding the core area will be marginal subjects, including common terms such as 'Geographic areas' and 'Form of document', and peripheral subjects which may be required to further define and supplement the terms in the main part of the thesaurus.

Having determined the main and subordinate areas of the thesaurus, it must next be decided whether the primary division of the subject area is to be by discipline or fundamental facets. It is more usual to divide first by discipline or subject field and then by facets within the subject fields and disciplines, as described in F2.3.1 above. There are, however, a few exceptions, when fundamental facets are preferred for the main divisions of the thesaurus (see F2.3.2). An advantage of a subject area partitioned initially by basic facets is that the arrangement may date more slowly than one organized by disciplines and subject fields. On the debit side, concepts expected to be found together in traditional groupings are separated.

There are differences between thesauri organized by disciplines and those arranged by subject field, but these are difficult to analyse. Discipline-based thesauri tend to group subjects according to academic consensus and to emphasize the study aspect, whereas the subject-field-based thesauri concentrate on the phenomena studied and may separate categories which might be closely associated in academic curricula. In practice the two systems overlap, with the subject-field-oriented thesaurus including some disciplines, and vice versa. The consistent use of commonly accepted disciplines is more usual in thesauri covering several fields of knowledge or for the classification of peripheral subject areas. Disciplines may also be preferred in thesauri covering well-defined, traditional subjects, where users would expect to find concepts grouped along familiar lines. If a discipline-oriented thesaurus is to be designed, the *Broad system of ordering* (BSO, 1978) is a useful source of structure, as is *BC2* (Mills and Broughton, 1977).

For the purpose of illustrating construction techniques it is supposed that a thesaurus is required for a database concerned with catering and related subjects. The scope of this field is wide ranging, but the areas of major and minor importance might be determined as follows:

Core area:	Catering

Closely related areas:	Household technologies
	   Hotel management
	   Home economics
	   Cleaning technologies
	Food technology

Peripheral areas:	All other areas of knowledge in outline, but in more detail Psychology, Education, Law, Medicine, and other related Technologies.
General concepts:	Geographical areas, etc.

In this Catering thesaurus, the primary organization might be as shown in Figure 33, where the core field of 'Catering' occurs at the end of a sequence of classes that begins with 'General concepts', including 'Geographical areas', 'Research', 'Design', and 'Testing'. Next come the peripheral subjects, organized into disciplines, and subject fields most closely related to 'Catering', for example, 'Food technology', 'Household technologies', 'Cleaning', 'Hotel management', and 'Home economics'. The final section is concerned with the subject of 'Catering' itself. All the terms occurring in the fields preceding 'Catering' may be used to further qualify the 'Catering' terms. For example, 'Training' from the 'Education' category may be used in combination with the term 'Waiters' to represent the concept of 'Training of waiters', or 'Engineering maintenance' from the 'Engineering' category may be used with 'Cookers' to represent the concept of 'Maintenance of cookers'.

Figure 33. Broad subject categories
Catering and related fields

General concepts

Geographical areas
Research, design and testing
Standardization
Management
Organizations

Peripheral subjects

Communication and information
  Computers
Philosophy
Mathematical sciences
Sciences
  Physical sciences
  Earth sciences
  Biology
Agriculture, Food production
Technology and Engineering
  including Construction
Biomedical sciences, Medicine
  Nutrition, Dietetics
  Environmental health
    Food hygiene
  Health services
    Hospitals
Psychology
Education
Social sciences
  Sociology
  Social problems and Welfare
  Politics and Government
    Armed forces
  Law
  Humanities, History, Religion
Arts, literature, leisure

Closely related subjects

Food technology
Household technologies
  Cleaning technology
  Corporate housekeeping
    Hotel management
  Home economics

Catering

J7.2. Analysis and grouping of terms within broad categories

Terms should be allocated to the appropriate broad category, and arranged within these, initially in alphabetical order (see Figure 34).

J7.2.1. Analysis using a systematic display

Each broad category should be taken in turn and its terms analyzed in relation to the other terms in the category to find a structural pattern. For example, supposing the Catering section of the Catering thesaurus is to be analysed, the first step would be as Step A in Figure 35.

J7.2.1a.

Step A (Figure 35)

In Step A, the basic facets are recognized and stated. In Figure 35 these are shown be to 'Personnel', 'Equipment', 'Operations' ('Catering management', 'Food preparation',

---

Figure 34. Allocation of terms to broad subject categories
Catering and related fields

General concepts
...
Management
    Catering management
    Catering managers
    Financial management
    Office management
    Personnel management
    Planning
    Purchasing
    Recruitment
    Work measurement

Peripheral subjects
...
Psychology
    Attitude
    Conflict
    Interpersonal relations
    Social interaction
    Stress

Education

    Colleges of further education
    Colleges of higher education
    Curricula
    Educational courses
    In-service training
    Polytechnics
    Practical training
    Schools
    Teachers
    Teaching
    Training
    Universities

etc.

etc.), 'Areas' ('Canteens', 'Kitchens', etc.), 'Food and meals' and 'Applications' ('Hospital catering', etc.). The terms are listed within the facets in alphabetical order.

J7.2.1b.

Step B (Figure 35)
In Step B, the terms within the basic facets are organized into arrays and hierarchies, showing subordinate terms indented under their superordinate terms. Both hierarchical and associative relationships may be indicated by indenting. Although most of the terms within the facets in Step B are generically related, a few are associatively related. For example, 'Catering personnel', 'Catering equipment', 'Catering areas', 'Food' and 'Meals' are all associatively related to 'Catering', the term for the subject field, and are not narrower terms. The hierarchical and associative relations are distinguished by an NT or RT, written in the margin against the term, marking its relation to the term one level above.

The display is written out, showing indenting and indicating the start of a new characteristics of division, or facet, by a facet indicator (or node label) in parentheses, preceding the array of terms.

Example:

	Catering	
	. *(Equipment)*	← *Facet indicator*
(RT)	. Catering equipment	← *Indented terms*
(NT)	.. Cooking appliances	*coded (NT) and (RT)*
(NT)	... Cookers	
(NT)	... Microwave ovens	
	. *(Operations)*	← *Facet indicator*
(NT)	. Catering operations	← *Indented terms*
(NT)	.. Catering management	*coded (NT)*
(NT)	... Food purchasing	
(NT)	... Restaurant management	
(NT)	.. Food preparation	
(NT)	... Cookery	
(NT)	.. Food service	
(NT)	... Waiting	

The use of classificatory techniques gives several benefits. By the grouping of terms, synonyms and near synonyms are brought together and the relationship is more easily recognized. For example, in the 'Food' group, the terms 'Convenience food' and 'Fast food' appear. Although these terms are not exact synonyms, in a small thesaurus it may be acceptable to treat them as such and to lead 'Fast food' into 'Convenience food'. The same treatment might be acceptable for the closely related terms 'Cooks' and 'Chefs', which appear together under 'Catering personnel'. Preference is given to 'Chefs' with 'Cooks' leading into it.

Classification also shows missing hierarchical levels. For example, 'Cookers' and 'Microwave ovens' brought together in the 'Catering equipment' facet suggests a

Figure 35. Subject field analysis and thesaurus derivation
Catering and related fields

Step A

Find facets/groups
(Arrangement of terms previously listed alphabetically under Catering)

CATERING

(Personnel)
Catering personnel
Catering managers
Chefs
Cooks
Waiters

(Equipment)
Catering equipment
Cooking appliances
Cookers
Microwave ovens

(Operations)
Catering management
Cookery
Food purchasing
Food preparation
Food service
Restaurant management
Waiting

(Areas)
Bars (licensed)
Canteens
Kitchens
Restaurants

Step B

Make hierarchies/arrays
Code terms NT/RT to term one step above

CATERING

(Personnel)
(RT) Catering personnel
(NT) Catering managers
(NT) Chefs
(NT) Waiters

(Equipment)
(RT) Catering equipment
(NT) Cooking appliances
(NT) Cookers
(NT) Microwave ovens

(Operations)
(NT) Catering operations
(NT) Catering management
(NT) Food purchasing
(NT) Restaurant management
(NT) Food preparation
(NT) Cookery
(NT) Food service
(NT) Waiting

(Areas)
(RT) Catering areas
(NT) Bars (licensed)
(NT) Canteens
(NT) Restaurants
(NT) Kitchens

Step C

Add SNs, UFs and BT/NT/RTs from terms in other subject fields, and within the catering field

CATERING

(Personnel)
(RT) Catering personnel
(NT) Catering managers
    BT Managers
    RT Catering management
(NT) Chefs
    UF Cooks
    RT Food preparation
(NT) Waiters
    RT Waiting

(Equipment)
(RT) Catering equipment
    SN Includes food mixers, cooking ware, tableware, etc.
    UF Kitchen equipment
    RT Dishwashers
(NT) Cooking appliances
    BT Domestic appliances
(NT) Cookers
(NT) Microwave ovens

(Operations)
(NT) Catering operations
(NT) Catering management
    BT Management
    RT Catering managers
(NT) Food purchasing
    BT Purchasing

Step D

Make conventional alphabetical display. (A few selected entries. See Figure 38 for complete thesaurus)

CATERING PERSONNEL
NT Catering managers
NT Chefs
NT Waiters
RT Catering

COOKING APPLIANCES
BT Catering equipment
BT Domestic appliances
NT Cookers
NT Microwave ovens

CATERING MANAGEMENT
BT Catering operations
BT Management
NT Food purchasing

(Food and meals)
Bakery products
Beverages
Convenience food
Dairy products
Fast food
Fish
Food
Food dishes
Fruit
Meals
Meat
Menus
Vegetables

(Applications)
(Not further analysed)
Educational catering
Hospital catering
Hotel catering
Institutional catering
School catering

(RT)   *(Food and meals)* Food
(NT)   *(Dishes)* Food dishes
(NT)   *(By special properties)* Convenience food
(NT)   *(Individual foods)* Beverages
(NT)   Meat
(NT)   Fish
(NT)   Dairy products
(NT)   Fruit
(NT)   Vegetables
(NT)   Bakery products
(RT)   Meals
(RT)   Menus

Restaurant management
(NT)   **RT   Restaurants**
(NT)   Food preparation **RT   Chefs**
(NT)   Cookery
(NT)   Food service
(NT)   Waiting **RT   Waiters**

(Areas)
(RT)   Catering areas
(NT)   Bars (licensed) **RT   Licensing laws**
(NT)   Canteens
(NT)   Restaurants **RT   Restaurant management**

(NT)   Kitchens

(Foods and meals)
(RT)   Food
(Dishes)
(NT)   Food dishes **RT   Meals**
(By special properties)
(NT)   Convenience food **UF   Fast food**
(Individual foods)
(NT)   Beverages **UF   Drinks**
(NT)   Meat
(NT)   Fish
(NT)   Dairy products
(NT)   Fruit
(NT)   Vegetables
(NT)   Bakery products
(RT)   Meals **RT   Food dishes**
(RT)   Menus **RT   Diet**

NT   Restaurant management
RT   Catering managers

FOOD SERVICE
BT   Catering operations
NT   Waiting

BARS (licensed)
BT   Catering areas
RT   Licensing laws

FOOD DISHES
BT   Food
RT   Meals

BEVERAGES
UF   Drinks
BT   Food

MEALS
RT   Catering
RT   Food dishes
RT   Menus

common broader term 'Cooking appliances', and the assembling of terms such as 'Catering management', 'Food preparation' and 'Food service' in another group, suggests the generic term 'Catering operations'. Classification may also show gaps in arrays. For example the 'Catering areas' facet includes 'Restaurants', 'Bars' and 'Kitchens', and it is easy to check what similar areas are missing. 'Snack bars', 'Canteens' and 'Dining rooms' are not represented, and might be added.

J7.2.1c.

Step C (Figure 35)

In Step C, details are added of scope notes (D5.2), equivalence relationships (F1.1), polyhierarchies (F1.2.4), and associatively-related terms (F1.3), which may already have been noted on the term record card or revealed during the classification process.

Scope note: Equivalence relationship

Examples:

Catering equipment
    SN Includes food mixers, cooking ware, tableware, etc.

Catering equipment
    UF Kitchen equipment

In the display in Figure 35 the entry appears as follows:

(Equipment)
Catering equipment
Add **SN Includes food mixers, cookingware, tableware, etc.**
Add **UF Kitchen equipment**

Polyhierarchies

Also to be added are polyhierarchies occurring in different subject fields or in the same field.

Example:

Cooking appliances
    BT Domestic appliances

In the display in Figure 35 the entry appears as follows:

(Equipment)
Cooking appliances
Add **BT Domestic appliances**

'Cooking appliances' in the display is shown in the 'Catering' field, although it is also a narrower term to the broader concept 'Domestic appliances', located in the display for the 'Household technologies' section. When the 'Household technologies' field is analyzed a reciprocal entry will be made:

Domestic appliances
Add **NT Cooking appliances**

Associatively related terms
Add also related terms in different fields or in different facets of the same field.

Examples:

Chefs
  RT Food preparation

Food preparation
  RT Chefs

Restaurant management
  RT Restaurants

Restaurants
  RT Restaurant management

Menus
  RT Diet

Diet
  RT Menus

In the display in Figure 35 the entries appear as follows:

(Personnel)
Catering personnel
  Catering managers
    Chefs
Add **RT Food preparation**

(Operations)
Catering operations
  Catering management
    Food purchasing
    Restaurant management
  Add **RT Restaurants**
  Food preparation
Add **RT Chefs**

(Areas)
Catering areas
  Restaurants
Add **RT Restaurant management**

(Food and meals)
Food
Meals
  Menus
Add **RT Diet**

The related pairs of terms 'Chefs' and 'Food preparation', and 'Restaurants' and 'Restaurant management' are both in the 'Catering' field, but are separated in the detailed display. 'Diet' is under 'Dietetics' in the 'Medical' section. When the 'Medical' section is analyzed, a reciprocal entry will be made from 'Diet' to 'Menus'.

    Diet
        RT Menus

J7.2.1d.

Step D (Figure 35)
In Step D, a conventional alphabetical thesaurus is derived from the terms as analyzed in Step C. A few examples only are shown in Figure 35. A full thesaurus derived from Step C in Figure 35 is shown in Figure 38.

J7.2.1e.

Each subject field must be analyzed in the same way as the Catering field, first by Step A, grouping terms into facets, then by Step B, finding arrays and hierarchies within the facets, and lastly at Step C, adding scope notes and equivalent terms and broader, narrower and related terms in other parts of the display. When all this detail is assembled for each subject field, sufficient information is available for the derivation of a conventional alphabetical thesaurus from the systematic display for the whole thesaurus. (Conventional thesaurus generation from a systematic display is discussed more fully in J8.1.)

J7.2.2. Analysis using a graphic display

An alternative method of analysing the subject field is to use family tree structures, *PRECIS*-type networks, arrowgraphs or terminographs to give a graphic presentation of structure and relationships (see H5). For example, the relationships in the *ISDD thesaurus* (see H5.1) were found through the development of tree structures. If arrowgraphs are compiled as illustrated in Figure 36 facet analysis may be used to determine structure. Facets are displayed together and their arrays indicated by connecting arrows. Associative relationships within the same arrowgraph are indicated either by the code RT (for example, against the term 'Catering equipment' at e5, showing it is not hierarchically related to the main term 'Catering'), or by a dotted line connecting the related terms as between 'Restaurants' at c2 and 'Restaurant management' at e2. Relationships (BT/NT/RT) with terms in other arrowgraphs are indicated by slashed and dotted lines leading to the reference number of the appropriate chart. Equivalence relationships (UF) are given beneath the preferred terms. A conventional alphabetical thesaurus may be derived from the display, and published with or without the accompanying arrowgraphs. If the display and arrowgraph is printed, the coded RTs and the UFs could be omitted to increase the clarity of the layout. The box chart or terminograph display method (H5.3) may also be used during the construction process to display facets, hierarchies and inter-relationships within subject fields.

J7.3. Editing the systematic display

If the systematic display in Figure 35 is to be printed or available to be viewed on line, it must be edited. This consists of adding a notation (see F3), checking the cross-references and adding the correct classmarks to these (see Figure 37).

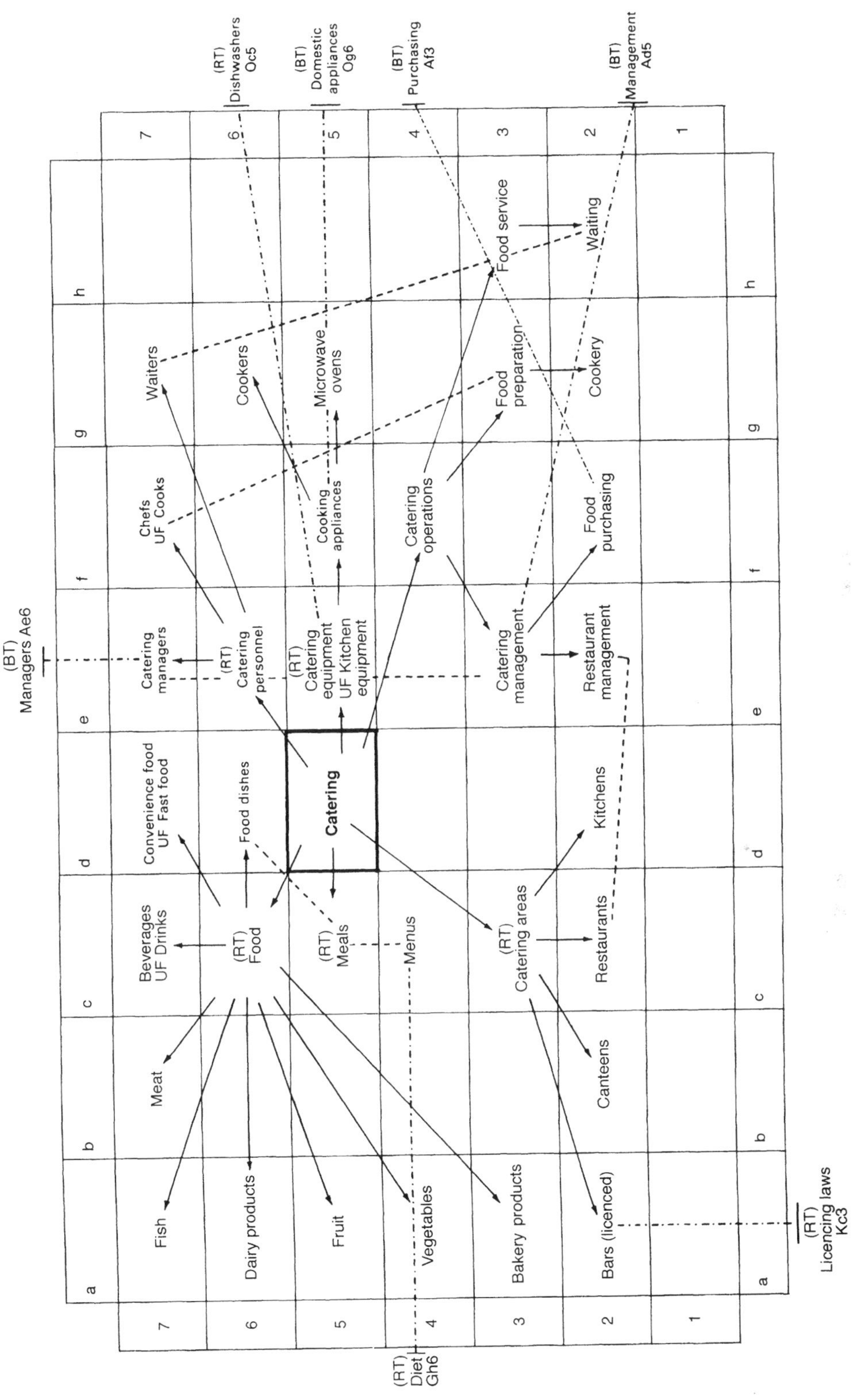

Figure 36. Arrowgraph as a construction tool

It is assumed that it has been decided to use the BSI *ROOT thesaurus* style display which shows polyhierarchies in one preferred place with reciprocal references between the non-preferred and the preferred location (see H4.3.3). For example, the preferred place for 'Cooking appliances' is SJ under 'Catering equipment' and not under 'Domestic appliances' OAD in the 'Household technologies' section (see Figure 37), and 'Food purchasing' TAF is placed under 'Catering management' TA, rather than under 'Purchasing' at AMQ.

As may be seen in Figure 37, cross-references are made between the term and its polyhierarchies elsewhere in the display, using the code *BT and *NT. The asterisk distinguishes these hierarchical relationships from those indicated by the indenting of the narrower term under the broader in the hierarchy.

Examples:

```
AMQ   Purchasing
          *NT Food purchasing   TAF
TAF   Food purchasing
          *BT Purchasing   AMQ
AMB   Managers
          *NT Catering managers   RBC
RBC   Catering managers
          *BT Managers   AMB
```

Cross-references between associatively-related terms in different parts of the systematic display are made using the code *RT. The asterisk distinguishes these associative relationships from those indicated by indenting one term under the other in the array.

Examples:

```
KNF   Licensing laws
          *RT Bars (licensed)   UE
UE    Bars (licensed)
          *RT Licensing laws   KNF
RBM   Waiters
          *RT Waiting   TPD
TPD   Waiting
          *RT Waiters   RBM
```

All these relationships have to be carefully checked and the corresponding notation added. The use of validation programs should ensure errors are reduced to a minimum.

The (RT) in the margin against a term in an array in Figure 37 indicates that the relationship between this term and the term above it will be associative and not hierarchical. In some displays in this style, the (RT) is replaced by a dash '–'.

Figure 37. Systematic display (catering and related subjects)
Edited for printing and alphabetical display derivation

AM	**Management**		**Catering** (cont.)	
	*NT Catering management TA			
			(Equipment)	
	(Personnel)	S *(RT)*	Catering equipment	
AMB *(RT)*	Managers		SN Includes food mixers,	
	*NT Catering managers RBC		cooking ware, tableware, etc.	
	...		UF Kitchen equipment	
			*RT Dishwashers OCD.F	
	(Operations)	SJ	Cooking appliances	
	...		*BT Domestic appliances OAD	
AMQ	Purchasing	SJC	Cookers	
	*NT Food purchasing TAF	SJK	Microwave ovens	
	...			
			(Operations)	
K	**Law**	T	Catering operations	
	...	TA	Catering management	
KNF	Licensing laws		*BT Management AM	
	*RT Bars (licensed) UE		*RT Catering managers RBC	
	...	TAF	Food purchasing	
			*BT Purchasing AMQ	
O	**Household technologies**	TAR	Restaurant management	
	...		*RT Restaurants UM	
OAD *(RT)*	Domestic appliances	TH	Food preparation	
	*NT Cooking appliances SJ		*RT Chefs RBH	
	...	THG	Cookery	
OC	Cleaning technology	TP	Food service	
		TPD	Waiting	
	(Equipment)		*RT Waiters RBM	
OCD *(RT)*	Cleaning equipment			
OCD.F	Dishwashers		*(Areas)*	
	*RT Catering equipment S	U *(RT)*	Catering areas	
	...	UE	Bars (licensed)	
			*RT Licensing laws KNF	
R	**Catering**	UH	Canteens	
		UM	Restaurants	
	(Personnel)		*RT Restaurant management TAR	
RB *(RT)*	Catering personnel	UR	Kitchens	
RBC	Catering managers			
	*BT Managers AMB			
	*RT Catering management TA			
RBH	Chefs			
	UF Cooks			
	*RT Food preparation TH			
RBM	Waiters			
	*RT Waiting TPD			

J8. Alphabetical thesaurus production from a systematic display

The subject display in systematic form as shown in Figure 35 may be used to produce a conventional alphabetical thesaurus (see H2.1) or variations of the alphabetical thesaurus such as the multilevel thesaurus (see H2.2). Equally, as will be seen, it may be used to produce a thesaurus with a systematic display and a full alphabetical thesaurus, or a systematic thesaurus with an index only.

J8.1. Conventional alphabetical thesaurus production

The information in the systematic display in Figure 35 is re-arranged in the standard alphabetical thesaurus format. (See Figure 38 for a full thesaurus derived from the terms in the 'Catering' section.)

Example (a): Details in the systematic display

Catering

(Equipment)

(RT)	Catering equipment			*[Coded RT to superordinate Catering term]*
		SN	Includes food mixers, cooking ware, tableware etc.	
		UF	Kitchen equipment	*[Equivalent term. Needs USE entry]*
		RT	Dishwashers	*[Additional RT]*
(NT)	Cooking appliances			*[Indented term – NT]*
	BT Domestic appliances			*[Additional BT]*
(NT)	Cookers			*[Indented term – NT]*
(NT)	Microwave ovens			*[Indented term – NT]*

Example (b): Conventional alphabetical thesaurus

(Entries for 'Catering Equipment' and 'Cooking Appliances')

CATERING EQUIPMENT
    SN Includes food mixers, cooking ware, tableware etc.
    UK Kitchen equipment
    NT Cooking appliances *[Note that the BT/NTs are to one level only]*
    RT Catering
    RT Dishwashers

COOKING APPLIANCES
    BT Catering equipment
    BT Domestic appliances
    NT Cookers
    NT Microwave ovens

(Reciprocals, excluding the term Catering)

Kitchen equipment
    USE CATERING EQUIPMENT

DISHWASHERS
    RT Catering equipment

DOMESTIC APPLIANCES
    NT Cooking appliance

COOKERS
    BT Cooking appliances

MICROWAVE OVENS
    BT Cooking appliances

If preferred the thesaurus may be in the form of a multilevel display.

Example:

CATERING EQUIPMENT
    UF   Kitchen equipment
    NT1 Cooking appliances
        NT2   Cookers
        NT2   Microwave ovens
    RT   Catering
    RT   Dishwashers

MICROWAVE OVENS
    BT1 Cooking appliances
        BT2   Catering equipment

J8.2. Alphabetical display accompanying a systematic display

If the systematic display is to be retained as part of the published thesaurus, the accompanying alphabetical display may be a simple alphabetical index, or a full alphabetical thesaurus, in a conventional or modified form. The full thesaurus also serves as an index to the systematic display, showing the classmark for each term within the systematic structure.

(a) Alphabetical index
This shows preferred and non-preferred terms only, directing the user to the place for the preferred term in the systematic display (as in Figure 37) via the notation. Details of scope notes, synonyms and broader, narrower and related terms are omitted.

Example:

CATERING EQUIPMENT S
    UF Kitchen equipment

Kitchen equipment
    USE CATERING EQUIPMENT S

(b) Full alphabetical thesaurus
Figure 39a shows a conventional alphabetical thesaurus, derived from the edited systematic display, as shown in Figure 37. This type of thesaurus is the same as the conventional alphabetical thesaurus shown in Figure 38, with the addition of notation. Classmarks are added after the preferred term and to all of its equivalent, broader, narrower and related terms, which are interfiled in one sequence, dropping the asterisks.

Figure 38. Conventional alphabetical thesaurus: catering and related fields
Derived from subject field analysis (Figure 35)

BAKERY PRODUCTS
BT Food

BARS (licensed)
BT Catering areas
RT Licensing laws

BEVERAGES
UF Drinks
BT Food

CANTEENS
BT Catering areas

CATERING
NT Catering operations
RT Catering areas
RT Catering equipment
RT Catering personnel
RT Food
RT Meals

CATERING AREAS
NT Bars (licensed)
NT Canteens
NT Kitchens
NT Restaurants
RT Catering

CATERING EQUIPMENT
SN Includes food mixers,
   cooking ware, tableware,
   etc.
UF Kitchen equipment
NT Cooking appliances
RT Catering
RT Dishwashers

CATERING MANAGEMENT
BT Catering operations
BT Management
NT Food purchasing
NT Restaurant management
NT Catering managers

CATERING MANAGERS
BT Catering personnel
BT Managers
RT Catering management

CATERING OPERATIONS
BT Catering
NT Catering management
NT Food preparation
NT Food service

CATERING PERSONNEL
NT Catering managers
NT Chefs
NT Waiters
NT Catering

CHEFS
UF Cooks
BT Catering personnel
RT Food preparation

CONVENIENCE FOOD

UF Fast food
BT Food

COOKERS
BT Cooking appliances

COOKERY
BT Food preparation

COOKING APPLIANCES
BT Catering equipment
BT Domestic appliances
NT Cookers
NT Microwave ovens

Cooks
USE CHEFS

DAIRY PRODUCTS
BT Food

DIET
RT Menus

DISHWASHERS
RT Catering equipment

DOMESTIC APPLIANCES
NT Cooking appliances

Drinks
USE BEVERAGES

Fast food
USE CONVENIENCE FOOD

FISH
BT Food

FOOD
NT Bakery products
NT Beverages
NT Convenience food
NT Dairy products
NT Fish
NT Food dishes
NT Fruit
NT Meat
NT Vegetables
RT Catering

FOOD DISHES
BT Food
RT Meals

FOOD PREPARATION
BT Catering operations
NT Cookery
RT Chefs

FOOD PURCHASING
BT Catering management
BT Purchasing

FOOD SERVICE
BT Catering operations
NT Waiting

FRUIT
BT Food

Kitchen Equipment
USE CATERING
     EQUIPMENT

KITCHENS
BT Catering areas

LICENSING LAWS
RT Bars (licensed)

MANAGEMENT
NT Catering management

MANAGERS
NT Catering managers

MEALS
RT Catering
RT Food dishes
RT Menus

MEAT
BT Food

MENUS
RT Diet
RT Meals

MICROWAVE OVENS
BT Cooking appliances

PURCHASING
NT Food purchasing

RESTAURANT MANAGE-
MENT
BT Catering management
RT Restaurants

RESTAURANTS
BT Catering areas
RT Restaurant management

VEGETABLES
BT Food

WAITERS
BT Catering personnel
RT Waiting

WAITING
BT Food service
RT Waiters

Example:

CATERING MANAGEMENT TA
    BT Catering operations T
    BT Management AM
    NT Food purchasing TAF
    NT Restaurant management TAR
    RT Catering managers RBC

To produce an alphabetical thesaurus in the style of the BSI *ROOT thesaurus.* (see Figure 39b), the BT/NT/RT relationships would be split into two sequences, one with and one without asterisks, as shown in H4.3.3.

CATERING MANAGEMENT TA
    BT Catering operations T
    NT Food purchasing TAF
    NT Restaurant management TAR
  *BT Management AM
  *RT Catering managers RBC

J9. Final checking with experts

The compilers should have been in contact with subject specialists during all stages of construction (J5.4) and should not finalize and produce the thesaurus before it is approved and accepted by these experts. Relevant sections of the thesaurus should be discussed personally with one or two experts in the appropriate subject fields.

J10. Introduction to the thesaurus

The thesaurus is not complete until a comprehensive introduction has been written covering most, if not all, of the following points.

- The purpose of the thesaurus.
- The subject coverage, with an indication of which are the core and peripheral fields.
- The total number of indexing terms used, with a breakdown showing the number of preferred and non-preferred terms.
- Vocabulary control: the standards used and the rules adopted regarding choice and form of indexing terms.
- Structure and inter-relationships: the standards used and the rules adopted.
- Thesaurus layout and displays: explanation of the function of the individual displays.
- The filing rules used, with reference to the standards used, if any.
- The meanings of all conventions and abbreviations and punctuation marks used in a non-standardized form should be clarified.
- Operational use of the thesaurus; how to use the thesaurus in searching and indexing.
- Updating and maintenance: details of updating policy and the name and address of the agency responsible for maintaining the thesaurus.

Figure 39. Alphabetical display derived from notated systematic display
From Figure 37 (selected entries only)

a. Conventional layout

CATERING MANAGEMENT TA
- BT   Catering operations T
- BT   Management AM
- NT   Food purchasing TAF
- NT   Restaurant management TAR
- RT   Catering managers RBC

CATERING MANAGERS RBC
- BT   Catering personnel RB
- BT   Managers AMB
- RT   Catering management TA

COOKING APPLIANCES SJ
- BT   Catering equipment S
- BT   Domestic appliances OAD
- NT   Cookers SJC
- NT   Microwave ovens SJK

DOMESTIC APPLIANCES OAD
- NT   Cooking appliances SJ
- RT   Household technologies O

MANAGEMENT AM
- NT   Catering management TA
- NT   Purchasing AMQ
- RT   Managers AMB

MANAGERS AMB
- NT   Catering managers RBC
- RT   Management AM

b. ROOT Thesaurus layout

CATERING MANAGEMENT TA
- BT   Catering operations T
- NT   Food purchasing TAF
- NT   Restaurant management TAR
- *BT   Management AM
- *RT   Catering managers RBD

CATERING MANAGERS RBC
- BT   Catering personnel RB
- *BT   Managers AMB
- *RT   Catering management TA

COOKING APPLIANCES SJ
- BT   Catering equipment S
- NT   Cookers SJC
- NT   Microwave ovens SJK
- *BT   Domestic appliances OAD

DOMESTIC APPLIANCES OAD
- RT   Household technologies O
- *NT   Cooking appliances SJ

MANAGEMENT AM
- NT   Purchasing AMQ
- RT   Managers AMB
- *NT Catering management TA

MANAGERS AMB
- RT   Management AM
- *NT   Catering managers RBC

- Acknowledgement of written sources used.
- Personal acknowledgements: addressed to subject experts and others who may have assisted with the compilation.

These points should be well illustrated by examples, wherever possible.

J11. Editing

- Check reciprocal entries: the use of validation programs relieves the compiler of much of this work (see Section K3).
- Check the notation in the systematic display – looking especially for confusion between the letter s and the number 5, and between the letters s and z, u and v.
- Check the form of terms, spelling, etc.: pay special attention to consistency in the use of hyphens.
- Check the alphabetization.
- In the systematic section check the indenting, spacing and layout. Pay particular attention to the indenting, because if it is incorrect, the BT/NT/RT relations

derived from it in the alphabetical thesaurus will be at best misleading and at worst nonsensical.

J12. Testing

Use the thesaurus to index a selection of documents. At least 500–1,000 documents should be indexed before the language is finalized. This may be done by using a semi-published draft of the thesaurus. Test the thesaurus against queries that have been put to the system as well as by document indexing. These exercises are likely to reveal gaps in coverage and will lead to the addition of new terms and an extension of the entry vocabulary, as well as to changes of emphasis in the relationship between the terms.

In some situations the new thesaurus may be used alongside the old system over a period of time to index new accessions. Maintaining this dual system makes heavy demands on the staff but has been reported to be worthwhile (Smith, 1984).

J13. Production for publication

A draft thesaurus should be prepared for discussion and testing before final publication. When the draft is tested and corrected, the amended version should be made available in printed and electronic form (see also K4). Due to the expense of print publication, particularly in the case of a large thesaurus, some thesauri are made available only in electronic form.

Before publishing the thesaurus, a decision has to be made on matters of layout, for example, whether the alphabetical display should have two or more columns. Choice of typestyles has also to be made. When printing a systematic display, the decision on typestyles is especially important, as a wise selection will help to clarify the display, by differentiating between broader and more specific headings, between preferred and non-preferred terms, and between terms and facet indicators. It is useful to provide running headings, and also carry-over headings, when a subject and its subdivisions extend over several pages, as these help the user to establish the context of the terms on a particular page.

J14. Deposit with clearinghouse

A copy of the thesaurus and subsequent editions should be deposited at Aslib in the United Kingdom, and at the appropriate national centre in other countries. If it is appropriate a copy should be deposited with the international clearinghouse at Toronto, which includes thesauri in the English language or multilingual thesauri with English language sections. The address is as follows:

Subject Analysis Systems Collection
Faculty of Library Information Science
University of Toronto
140 St George Street
Toronto
Ontario M55 1A1
Canada

Section K: Thesaurus management

An indexing language is out of date as soon as, if not before, it is published, so that any 'live' thesaurus must be updated regularly. Thesauri with specific vocabularies applied in systems using depth indexing tend to require updating more frequently than those confined to the use of more static, broader concepts. As would be expected, the need for modification increases, whatever the nature of the vocabulary or depth of indexing, as the number of documents that are indexed increases. The thesaurus grows most rapidly in the early stages of database development and levels off subsequently. At a later date, a further burst of growth may occur if the subject coverage of the database is extended.

K1. Maintenance mechanism and routines

Thesaurus updating needs to be managed methodically, otherwise confusion results in indexing and searching, as the thesaurus itself becomes inconsistent, inaccurate and increasingly difficult to use and maintain. The control of a thesaurus should be the responsibility of an editor, possibly assisted by a small team of assistants, and/or advisory subject experts. It is common practice to collect candidate terms from indexers and searchers as they arise from the work in hand. Where the software allows, these candidate terms can be entered into the database as searchable terms, in a separate keyword field. As soon as a decision is made by the editor as to their status, they can be promoted to the indexing term field, deleted or amended and reallocated. It is the job of the thesaurus editor to evaluate each suggestion, taking into account its validity, the need for its implementation and any effects arising from its introduction into the scheme. If the editor has difficulty in coming to a decision, then the panel of experts can be consulted; either informally or at periodical meetings, depending on local circumstances. It is at least courteous, and possibly important, to report decisions back to the person who initially made the suggestion. In some distributed systems, it may be feasible for a rejected term to be adopted locally in a subsystem; though the potential dangers of that should be borne in mind where information transfer is an issue. It is good practice, when accepting a change of term, to record the fact in the thesaurus itself. This record will normally contain the date of the change and the term that was used prior to that date (see also D5.2.2e).

K2. Thesaurus modifications

Changes that can be made fall into six categories, which are briefly discussed below, in ascending order of complexity.

K2.1. Amendment of existing terms

This will occur if an error is found in the spelling or form of a term. In this case, no other terms will be affected, but it is important to remember to alter the term wherever it occurs in the thesaurus.

K2.2. Status of existing terms

This will occur when a lead-in term is raised to a preferred term, and its previously preferred form is downgraded.

K2.3. Deletion or demotion of existing terms

Occasionally a term will be found to be unused or redundant. In such cases it may be deleted altogether, or subordinated to another term as a lead-in term.

K2.4. Addition of new, or deletion of old relationships

Occasionally relationships are found to be either wrong or unhelpful, and should be amended or removed.

K2.5. Addition of new terms

This will become necessary either because more specific terms come into common usage or where an existing generic term becomes over-posted and a greater degree of differentiation is required to enhance precision; or where a concept new to the thesaurus comes to light, or occasionally a neologism enters the language. Great care should be taken to ensure that all existing relationships to existing terms are properly identified and recorded, and that the new term is placed in the correct place of classification, or categorization, where such formats are used. It may be necessary to adjust the structure of the systematic display in the area affected in order to accommodate the new concept.

K2.6. Amendment of existing structure

Amendment of a part of the structure may occasionally be found to be desirable or even necessary, perhaps after a periodic quality audit, where this is part of the maintenance procedure. Such a task should be approached with great care, as there is obviously more chance of introducing error than in the previous examples.

K3. Thesaurus management software

The task of maintaining a thesaurus can be greatly eased by using one of the several thesaurus management packages available on the market. Lists of such packages are maintained on websites, for example, on the websites of the American Society of Indexers (Milstead, 1998), the Australian Society of Indexers (Australian), and Willpower Information, where Leonard Will provides a comparative list of software (Will).

Milstead has discussed the requirements for good thesaurus management software (Milstead, 1991) and concludes that three facilities, not found in conventional databases are necessary:

- control of types of relationship permitted (normally as chosen from those listed in the ANSI Standard)
- checking of reciprocal relationships
- validation of relationships

Software appropriate for monolingual thesauri is not necessarily appropriate for multilingual ones. As Hudon points out, multilingual thesaurus software should not simply perform a translation operation once a preferred record has been created in the source language, as this would result in automatically identical and symmetrical structures in all target languages. Rather it must permit the separation of records for preferred terms in one language from records for preferred terms in another, if language equality is to be ensured (Hudon, 1997).

Other desirable facilities include the identification of orphans (terms carrying no relationships), and a number of fields that can be used for management purposes. It is also, of course, necessary for the package to have good output facilities, either electronic or paper based; and allowing alternative formats to be produced in addition to the normal alphabetical display. It is rare, but greatly advantageous, to have software that is capable of generating a range of formats from classified schedules, where a thesaurofacet approach is used in thesaurus compilation.

K4. The physical form of the thesaurus

It has been noted above that a thesaurus may be used in one or more different physical forms; essentially paper or electronic, though the former may be sub-divided into formally published and locally printed products, and the latter into flat file, database structured and hypertext formats.

K4.1. Print-on-paper

Until relatively recently, print-on-paper was the most usual form of thesaurus. This still applies to some extent, the relatively small number of widely used thesauri being supplied commercially in the form of a bound volume, usually as an alternative to a digital format. Despite the increased capabilities offered to digitised thesauri, in-house systems will still often be used as print-on-paper, if only for convenience of scanning.

K4.2. Electronic thesauri

As noted above, electronic thesauri can be seen, at some risk of over-simplification, as implemented in one of three ways: flat file, database structured, and hypertext.

K4.2.1. Flat file

This is a simple electronic form of a thesaurus, in text processing or ASCII format. It offers no integrative capabilities, and is generally simply a means of storing, communicating and printing a thesaurus.

K4.2.2. Database structured

If the terms of a thesaurus are incorporated into a database structure, particularly if the same structure is used for the files of information which the thesaurus will be used to index, the thesaurus can be invoked much more conveniently for conventional indexing and retrieval; automatic invocation of the thesaurus for indexing and searching is made possible.

The database structure involved may be that of whatever database or text retrieval package is used in the local environment; alternatively, dedicated thesaurus management software may be used, or a thesaurus module of a commercial information management package may be applied.

K4.2.3. Hypertext

Ever since the emergence of hypertext as a tool for information management, the theoretical synergies between it and the thesaurus have been remarked on (Marco, 1996). On a practical level, it has been appreciated for several years that thesauri may be usefully instantiated and made available in hypertext form (Pollard, 1993), particularly in the context of a searching thesaurus (Johnson and Cochrane, 1995).

A more elaborate mode of access to thesauri in hypertext form may be provided by the *Virtual Hyperglossary (VHG)*. This allows glossaries, which may take the form of a full thesaurus, to be created in hypertext form, and associated with existing hypertexts, providing easy look-up of term definitions, synonyms and semantic relations (West and Murray-Rust, 1997).

Section L: Thesaurus reconciliation and integration

L1. The need for reconciliation

Over the last 30 or more years many controlled languages, whether thesauri, classification schemes or subject heading lists, have been published, entirely independent of one another and, even within the same subject field, differing in structure, viewpoint and specialization. This lack of compatibility hampers the transfer of records between systems and searching across databases. Reconciliation or integration of thesauri is a means of overcoming this incompatibility barrier.

The availability of standards for thesaurus construction can only help in a limited way to reduce incompatibilities between controlled languages. The main differences in controlled languages in the same field are as follows.

• Specificity
One thesaurus may contain detailed and precise terminology, while another may consist mainly of broad terms to describe the same subjects.

• Exhaustivity
One thesaurus may omit some areas of the subject field, while another thesaurus may cover all aspects.

• Compound terms
One system may use pre-coordinated (i.e., compound) terms where another will express the same concepts by the combination of separate terms. If the thesaurus construction rules were followed closely on this point, the problem of compatibility would not be so common. As has been seen in paragraph E2.4.2(b), rigid commitment to the Standard is not always practicable, and different interpretations of the rules will result.

• Synonyms
The choice of preferred forms among synonyms or quasi-synonymous concepts differs from thesaurus to thesaurus.

• Inter-relationships
The hierarchies in thesauri may differ in structure and in emphasis. Hierarchical levels occurring in one thesaurus may be absent from another. Associatively-related terms are even more subject to change from one thesaurus to another, since inclusion of a relationship may be influenced by the subject interest or viewpoint of the particular organization for which the thesaurus is compiled.

The pressing need for reconciliation was recognised in September 1995, when the International Society for Knowledge Organisation (ISKO) addressed the problem by holding a Research Seminar on Compatibility and Integration (International, 1996). A number of recommendations were made at the seminar and subsequently published.

It was recommended that there should be research into the principles and methodology of establishing concordances between controlled languages and into the benefits from, and requirements of, compatibility; that there should be emphasis on knowledge organization in the education of information specialists; that there should be international exchange on the principles of knowledge organization, with particular emphasis on cross-cultural comparison of ordering systems; and that an international inventory on software packages and other tools should be compiled for the maintenance of order systems and correspondence among them.

It was also recommended, under the heading of system development and international collaboration, that there should be long-range development of an open, multifunctional, multilingual integrated knowledge base of concepts and terminology that would preserve the integrity of the many sources on which it drew. This open system should allow many contributors and be available for end-users searching on the Internet and other online services in multiple languages, independent of the language used in each database; it would also serve as a dictionary and as a source for the development of specialized controlled languages. Another recommendation was that auxiliary thesauri for geographic names, bibliographic forms and languages, and for names of persons and organizations should be developed. Finally it was recommended that criteria, methodologies, tools and software should be developed for the establishing, maintaining, and harmonizing of monolingual and multilingual controlled languages.

Soergel proposes a blueprint for *SemWeb* (Soergel, 1996b), a multifunctional, multilingual conceptual infrastructure for the Internet, which would serve as a common integrated distributed knowledge base, through which there would be access to information about the concepts and terminology in the constituent controlled vocabularies and dictionaries.

L2. Reconciliation methods

Approaches to the reconciliation of incompatible controlled languages include mapping, switching, merging and integration. Lancaster surveys methods of achieving compatibility and convertibility of thesauri in his *Vocabulary control* (Lancaster, 1986, chapter 19). Papers by Chaplan and Dahlberg include historical reviews of reconciliation projects (Chaplan, 1995, Dahlberg, 1996a), and one by Maniez makes an analytical study of reconciliation methods (Maniez, 1997). An annotated bibliography by Dahlberg of references on the subject between 1960–1995 is included in the papers of the Research Seminar on Compatability and Integration (International, 1996).

L2.1. Mapping, switching and intermediate languages

Mapping links terms directly from one controlled language to another or to multiple vocabularies. The terms in one controlled language point to equivalent terms in the other language. The information may include whether the term is identical, a synonym, or holds some other relationship to the term in the other language. An early example of mapping is the *Table of indexing equivalents* (Hammond, 1962), which maps terms from the *ASTIA thesaurus of descriptors* to subject headings used by the US Atomic Energy Commission (USAEC). A more recent example is the *Bioethics thesaurus* which maps Bioethicsline database terms to *MeSH* (Bioethics, 1987).

A number of projects have been concerned with the mapping of specialised thesauri onto the *Library of Congress subject headings (LCSH)*, which although generally acknowledged to pose retrieval difficulties when used in a specialized field, is a dominant and all-pervasive vocabulary, especially in the United States. The projects include matches between the *Art and architecture thesaurus (AAT)* and *LCSH* (Whitehead, 1990), between *Medical subject headings (MeSH)* and *LCSH* (Muench, 1979), and between *ASFIS (Aquatic science and fisheries information systems) thesaurus* and *LCSH* (Markham and Avery, 1998).

A detailed analysis of problems involve in mapping onto *LCSH* is given in a paper by Chaplan (Chaplan, 1995). The purpose of this project was to facilitate multiple database searching in the Institute of Labor and Industrial Relations Library, University of Illinois at Urbana-Champaign, by mapping terms from the *Laborline thesaurus* used in an in-house database to *LCSH* used in the University of Illinois catalogue. Terms were manually mapped and 19 match codes were created for the types of matches developed, ranging from exact match, partial match (including cross-reference match, plural form, subordination, superordination, part-of-speech difference, spelling variation and homographs), to no match. There were 16.30% exact matches and 21.9% no matches. Only about 40% of terms could be switched automatically due to the present structural limitations of *LCSH*. It was concluded that manual mapping is not impossible if the thesaurus is fairly small.

L2.1.1. Intermediate languages

Switching systems sometimes involve the creation of an intermediate language to which cooperating controlled languages may each be reciprocally mapped. An example of this is the *Intermediate lexicon* researched by Horsnell.

Controlled language A may be switched to controlled language B, C and D via the *Intermediate lexicon X*, and controlled language B to the other three languages, and so on. Research work showed that, to be most effective, the *Intermediate lexicon* must be as specific as the most detailed language to be switched (Horsnell, 1975, Horsnell and

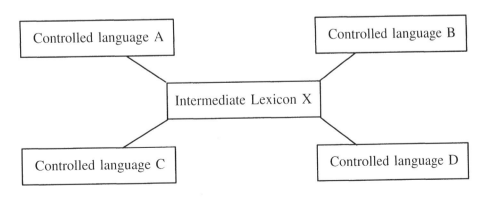

Merrett, 1978). The results also appeared to indicate that the retrieval performance of language B switched to language D was as effective in searching the database D as language D itself.

Another example of a switching language is the *Broad system of ordering (BSO)*. This is a broad-level universal faceted classification, published under the auspices of the International Federation for Information and Documentation (FID) in 1978. After FID gave up ownership of *BSO*, an independent BSO Panel, headed by Eric Coates, one of the three original compilers, continued to develop the scheme and issued it on diskette in 1993 (BSO, 1978). The aim of the *BSO* is to provide a broad subject ordering scheme, which would be used to classify information systems, services and centres, and to act as a switching mechanism between centres using different controlled languages. The classification system is not sufficiently specific for the switching of more than broad categories of records. It is, however, a useful source of broad outline structure for discipline-oriented thesauri (see J7.1).

Ingetraut Dahlberg has proposed that her *Information coding classification (ICC)* should be used as an intermediate language for switching between library classification systems on the Internet (Dahlberg, 1996b). The *ICC* is a universal faceted classification, with main classes in the order of integrated level theory and the detail in the class subdivisions determined by the *Systematifier*, a type of facet formula. (see F2.3.3). Using the compatibility matrix according to the methodology described in Dahlberg's *Guidelines for the establishment of compatability between information languages* (Dahlberg, 1996a), the classes of one classification scheme after the other would be correlated with the subject groups of the *ICC*. This would show where there were gaps or only partial equivalences between the schemes which had to be resolved. The searcher would be led by an alphabetical index to the compatibility matrix where the correlated class marks and captions of the classification schemes included would be displayed. The user would then obtain the corresponding class notations in the other systems to access relevant references.

L2.1.2. Automatic switching

In automatic switching, terms from one vocabulary are transformed automatically to the terms of another. Switching is based on maps, intermediate languages or an algorithm for manipulating the input term. In most cases some human intellectual input is necessary. An early example was a scheme devised in 1969 which used a 42 step algorithm to convert 11 controlled languages to the *Agricultural biological vocabulary* of the National Agricultural Library (Wall and Barnes, 1969).

A later example is a system which has been operating since 1983 to switch terms assigned by Department of Defense indexers using the *DTIC thesaurus* to terms in the *NASA thesaurus* (Silvester and Klingbiel, 1993). A translation table known as the Lexical Dictionary is used, accessed by a program that determines which rules to follow in making the transition from DTIC's to NASA's authorized terms. The candidate terms resulting from the switching are then assessed by the NASA indexers. The system has contributed to the development of the NASA online, interactive machine-aided indexing (MAI), based on the analysis of natural language text in titles and abstracts.

In the medical field there are a number of examples of automatic switching. Martin and Rada reported on switching between *MeSH, SNOMED (Systematic nomenclature of medicine)* and *CMIT (Current medical information and technology)* (Martin and Rada, 1987); Sneidermann and Bicknell on switching between *MeSH, SNOMED* and the *International coding index for dermatology* (Sneidermann and Bicknell, 1992); and Cimino and Sideli on automatic switching between medical vocabularies using an algorithm based on the *UMLS Metathesaurus* (see L3.2.2 below) (Cimino and Sideli, 1991).

In the field of art, Busch and Petersen describe a project for automated mapping of topical subject headings at the Victoria and Albert National Art Library into faceted index strings using the *Art and architecture thesaurus* as the machine-readable dictionary. The computer tools used for the switching process had been developed earlier for matching subject keywords from a variety of art and architectural databases to the *AAT* in order to identify candidate terms (Busch and Petersen, 1994).

L3. Integration and merging

L3.1. Macrothesauri and microthesauri

A situation where there is built-in compatibility between controlled languages occurs when a microthesaurus, a specialized thesaurus, is mapped onto, and is entirely integrated within, the hierarchical structure of some broader thesaurus, the macrothesaurus. For example, a specialized thesaurus on pumps may be included within the fluid-engineering section of a general thesaurus on technology. Indexers in the pumps field would be able to draw on the macrothesaurus for broader fluid engineering and technology terms and for relevant terms in other specialized microthesauri integrated into the macrothesaurus.

A macrothesaurus and its microthesauri may exist as one integrated system, or the macrothesaurus may exist as a separate entity. For example the *Broad system of ordering* (BSO, 1978) mentioned above under Intermediate languages in L2.1.1, has the potential of acting as a macrothesaurus, a structure within which specialized thesauri might be developed.

L3.2. Merged controlled languages

When controlled languages are merged, preferred terms and entry terms, with accompanying thesaural relationships, are brought together into a single alphabetical list, with an indication of which controlled languages contain specific terms, scope notes and relationships. Figure 40 shows an extract from an entry in a proposed descriptor bank consisting of merged thesauri in the social sciences (Aitchison, 1981a), revealing the consistencies and inconsistencies.

The descriptor bank in Figure 40 shows exact matches. For example, six thesauri out of 20 use the term 'Nuptiality'. It also shows that one thesaurus uses the synonym 'Marriage rate' for the term. Figure 40 also shows the matches and discrepancies in the hierarchical and associative relationships in different thesauri and foreign language equivalents for the merged terms.

**Figure 40. Descriptor bank entry
'Integrated thesaurus of the social sciences'**

	IC	IL	IS	MA	PM	SP	UT
NUPTIALITY							
IC : 22230							
IL : 14.01							
IS : 15421							
MA : 14.02.05							
PM : 13.01.00							
UT : R10.71							
F = Nuptialite		IL	IS	MA	PM		
S = Nupcialidad		IL		MA	PM		
= Marriage rate						SP	
< Population dynamics						SP	
< Population events							UT
– Divorce						SP	
– Families						SP	
– Family system						SP	
– Genetic counselling						SP	
– Marriage	IC	IL	IS	MA	PM		UT
– Nuptiality rate					PM		
– Nuptiality table					PM		
– Sexual union					PM		
– Statistical data						SP	

* Codes indicating thesauri included in the descriptor bank, e.g.
MA = *Macrothesaurus*, UT = *UNESCO thesaurus*.

It should be possible, when thesauri are merged, to deduce from relationships between two terms in one thesaurus that these relationships also exist between the same two terms in another. In the example below, thesaurus A uses the term 'Single women' as the preferred term, whereas thesaurus B uses 'Spinsters'. In thesaurus A, 'Spinsters' is a lead-in term to 'Single women', which shows it to be an equivalent term. Although this relationship is not given in thesaurus B, it may be deduced from the cross-references in the merged thesauri that it be present, and that 'Single women' should be added as a UF entry under 'Spinsters'.

Example:

SINGLE WOMEN   *(thesaurus A)*
   UF   Spinsters
   BT   Unmarried people
   RT   Bachelors

SPINSTERS   *(thesaurus B)*
   BT   Unmarried people
   RT   Bachelors

Spinsters
   USE SINGLE WOMEN   *(thesaurus A)*

In merging controlled languages, the purpose may be to abandon the previously independent constituent controlled languages, and to absorb them into a new single tool for indexing and searching. Alternatively, the constituent controlled languages

---

**Figure 41. Vocabulary database for searchers
TERM Record**

TI SPOUSE ABUSE.
ER CONSIDER: BATTERED-WOMEN.
ME SPOUSE-ABUSE.
NC (090A.CC.=SPOUSE ABUSE).
PS FAMILY-VIOLENCE. (1982 +).
**SO CONSIDER: ABUSE. (001050). BATTERED. (051240). (ANDED TO). WIFE.
     (489880). WOMAN (490000).**
**FT SPOUSE ABUSE. BATTERED WOMEN. WIFE BEATING. WIFE ASSAULT. WIFE
     RAPE. ABUSED SPOUSES. ABUSED WOMEN. WIFE BATTERING. WIFE ABUSE.
     CONJUGAL CRIME. WIFEBEATING. SPOUSE ASSAULT. BATTERED HUSBAND.
     VIOLENT HOME. FAMILY VIOLENCE. BATTERED WIFE. BATTERED WIVES.
     BEATEN WOMEN. DOMESTIC VIOLENCE. HUSBAND ABUSE. ABUSIVE HUSBANDS.
     MOTHERS IN STRESS. WOMEN IN CRISIS. VICTIM OF ABUSE BY MATE.
     BATTERED WIFE SYNDROME. VERBAL SPOUSE ABUSE. WIFE BATTERER.
     MENTAL CRUELTY. MARITAL RAPE.**

KEY TO PARAGRAPH LABELS ABOVE:

TI Title	**ME** MeSH Descriptor	**SO** Sociological Ab-
ER ERIC Descriptor	**NC** Family Resources Code	stracts Descriptors
	PS PsycINFO Descriptor	**FT** Free Text Terms

---

may retain their independence and continue to be used for the indexing of the individual databases. In this approach, when searching across the diverse databases, switching is used to transfer between terms in the merged vocabulary. The individual languages may be upgraded, if required, by adding new relationships between terms made obvious from the information in the merged data.

An example of merged vocabularies is the *TERM* database (Knapp, 1984), formerly on the Bibliographic Retrieval Services (BRS), which merges terms and codes from controlled languages used in a number of behavioural and social sciences databases. It includes a series of small subject areas, known as 'titles' covering, for example 'Poverty areas' or 'Battered women' (see Figure 41). Controlled terms and free-text terms which are relevant to each 'title' are gathered under the concept heading.

Other examples of merged vocabularies include the *Integrated energy vocabulary*, which combines index terms and subject headings from 10 vocabularies covering the subject area of energy research and development (Integrated, 1976), and the *Social science and business microthesaurus*, which combines terms from four federal government thesauri with those developed by the National Technical Information Service (NTIS) (Social, 1982).

The *Vocabulary switching system (VSS)* developed by Niehoff at Batelle Columbus Laboratories is an experimental database (Niehoff and Mack, 1985, Chamis, 1988). The *VSS* is an integrated vocabulary consisting of 15 physical science, life science, social science and business vocabularies. The entire vocabularies for all the databases were merged and the linguistic or thesaural relationships existing in each thesaurus were preserved. In response to the input of controlled or natural language terms, the system shows matches and no matches in other vocabularies ranging from exact matches and synonyms, broader, narrower and related terms matches to word matches (i.e., all compound terms and phrases within which the word appears) and word-stem matches. An evaluation of the system, described in the final report (Niehoff and Mack, 1984), showed that the merging of vocabularies for online searching had potentially wide appeal, and that the more vocabularies in the same subject areas are included, the better the performance.

Later examples of merged vocabularies are *Northwestern University online catalogue* which merges and edits *LCSH, MeSH* and *Transportation library subject headings* (Strawn, 1992), and the *AUSTRALIS-PLUS thesaurus*, which merges terms from the controlled languages of several databases of the Australian database service AUSTRALIS (Giles-Peters, 1993).

Soergel and Muraszkiewicz have considered software problems in merging thesauri (Soergel, 1996a, Muraszkiewicz, 1996).

The merging of thesauri in two different specialized fields, agriculture and biomedicine, are described below.

L3.2.1. Unified Agricultural Thesaurus

An alphabetically-merged vocabulary has limitations, in that it may overlook inexact and partial equivalences between terms if these are not indicated by the cross-reference structure of the merged vocabularies. For example, the term 'Heat resistance' in language A may be close in meaning to 'Thermal resistance' in language B, but this will go undetected if there are no relationships recorded in the synonym or related term fields. A method of discovering these equivalences is to plot the merged thesauri against a well-structured master classification. This will bring terms with similar meanings together at the same classmark, where the links between them will become apparent. The use of a master classification was suggested in a design study for the *'Integrated thesaurus of the social sciences'* in 1981 (Aitchison, 1981b), but due to lack of funding the project was never implemented.

A similar classification approach was used more recently in the *Unified agricultural thesaurus* project, involving the agricultural databases, AGRICOLA, AGRIS and CAB ABSTRACTS. Two of these, AGRICOLA and CAB ABSTRACTS, use the *CAB thesaurus*, with 50,000 terms, whilst AGRIS uses *AGROVOC*, a multilingual thesaurus with 15,000 terms. In the course of exchange of input between the databases it became obvious that the two thesauri were not compatible, and efforts were begun to resolve the problem (Hood and Ebermann, 1990). By 1991, the three producers of the databases, the US National Agricultural Library (NAL), the UN Food and Agricultural Organization (FAO) and CAB International (CABI) were cooperating in the production of a *Unified agricultural thesaurus* with the aim of providing users with a comprehensive, automated, multilingual thesaurus system which harmonizes *AGROVOC* and the *CAB thesaurus* (Dextre Clarke, 1996).

The method adopted for integration was first to create a classified structure for both thesauri, into which terms from each thesaurus would be slotted on reorganization.

This would facilitate comparison and analysis on a systematic basis. A high-level classification outline was agreed in September 1991 and later, in 1993, the classification was extended to a structure of about 500 concepts. The form of the classification was a systematic, polyhierarchical thesaurus in the English language, not dissimilar in format to *MeSH* (see H4.2.1), or the *BSI ROOT thesaurus* (see H4.3.3).

The example below, adapted from Dextre Clarke's paper, Figures 4 and 5 (Dextre Clarke, 1996), shows terms from the two thesauri, classified within the same subclass 'Characteristics of Foods and Feeds' of the class 'Applied Human and Animal Nutrition'. This reveals equivalent and non-equivalent terms.

Example:

(Applied Human and Animal Nutrition)
(Characteristics of Foods and Feeds)

CAB Thesaurus	**AGROVOC**
(No equivalent)	Carbohydrate content
Food composition	*(No equivalent)*
(No equivalent)	Keeping quality
Nutritive value	Nutritive value
Digestibility	Digestibility
Energy value	Energy value
Metabolizable energy	*(No equivalent)*
Starch equivalent	Starch equivalent

By the end of 1994, the unification project was by no means complete but the terms of both thesauri had been reorganized according to the classification scheme. Initial efforts had concentrated on the preferred terms and their main hierarchical relationships. The validation of RT relationships of each pair of terms in the context of the new generic hierarchies were left until the next stage. At the higher levels the indexing terms and their BT/NT relationships had been harmonized to the point of becoming identical. At the lower levels considerable differences were still to be resolved.

Once a unified thesaurus is completed and available for use in current indexing, the problem arises of how to deal with back files, which will not be fully retrievable by the new thesaurus. Dextre Clarke recognises this dilemma in the case of the *Unified agricultural thesaurus* and discusses a number of options which are available. Some of these would be costly to apply, including re-indexing the back files and devising switching algorithms between old and new classmarks. A less expensive solution would be to abandon work on a fully integrated thesaurus, continue to index the databases as before with the two separate thesauri, and to switch search statements from one thesaurus to the other, using algorithms facilitated by the powerful master classification.

L3.2.2. Unified Medical Language System

The most well-known of recent examples of a merged thesaurus is the *Unified medical language system (UMLS)*, described in a number of papers (Hoppe, 1996, McCray, 1993, Squires, 1993, Schuyler et al, 1993), and on the website of the *Unified medical language system* (http://www.nlm.nih.gov/research/umls/). The *UMLS* is a long-term research and development project conducted by the NLM (National Library of Medicine) since 1986, with US-national and international cooperation. The aim of the *UMLS* is to provide uniform access to a number of distributed and disparate databases which use different terminologies. The *UMLS* consists of four *Knowledge sources*: the *Metathesaurus*, the *Semantic network*, the *Information sources map* and the *SPECIALIST lexicon*.

(a) *Metathesaurus*

The *Metathesaurus* is a synthesis of existing controlled languages, achieved by linking, merging and integrating them. The thesauri are mapped onto one another, creating pointers from every concept in one thesaurus to the most equivalent concept in the others. This allows a user query to be translated into a search for a given database that is indexed by a given thesaurus. The vocabularies are also merged, creating a more enriched and comprehensive knowledge base. One name is selected as the preferred name for the concept in each component vocabulary (see Figure 42 showing Concept name 'Acquired Immunodeficiency Syndrome' and the matches). This allows

Figure 42. UMLS Metathesaurus
Information for individual concepts

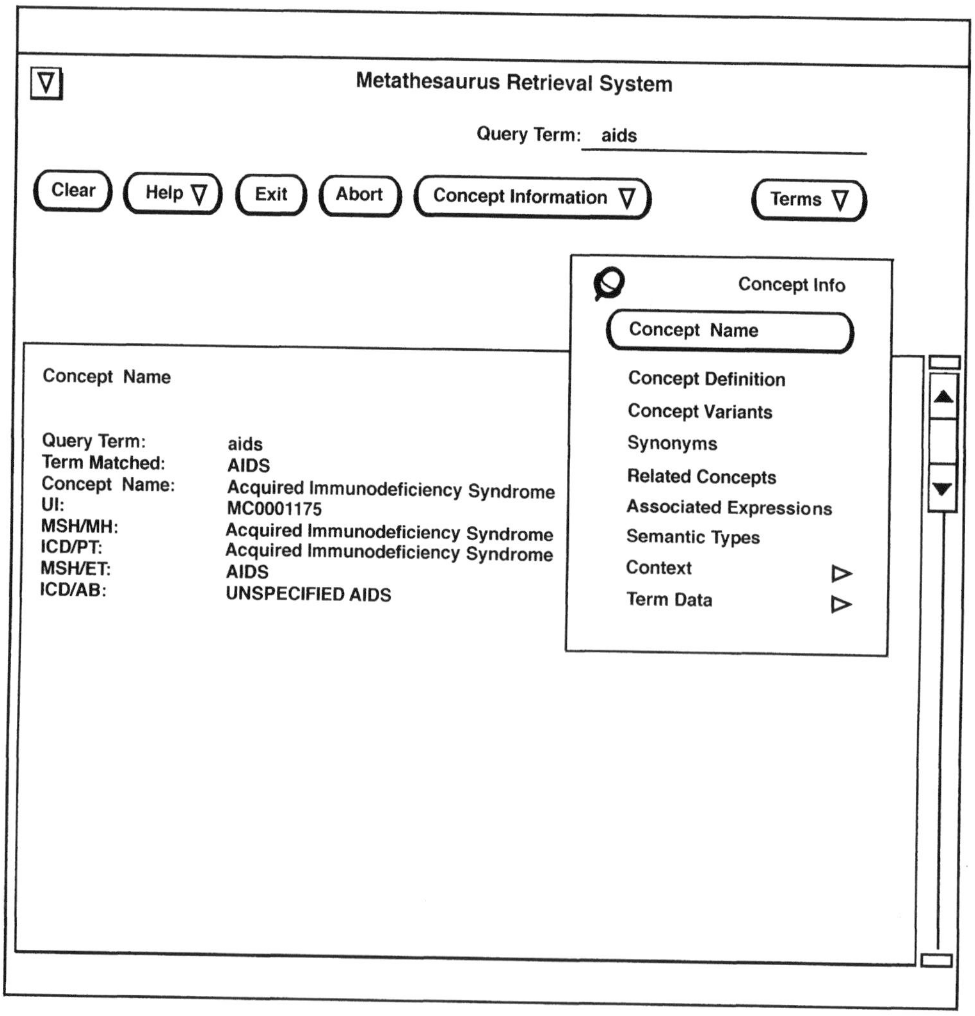

switching between the vocabularies. If the concept exists in *MeSH*, the preferred form of the concept is the form of the main heading in *MeSH*; if not, terms from the other vocabularies are selected in a set order. All other terms, phrases and strings used to express the concept are mapped to the *Metathesaurus* name. The 1999 version of Metathesaurus contained 626,893 biomedical concepts with 1,358,891 different concept names from about 50 source controlled languages. The *Metathesaurus* continues to grow.

(b) *Semantic network*

The second Knowledge source, the *UMLS Semantic network*, provides a consistent categorization of all concepts in the *Metathesaurus* according to Semantic Types or Categories and Relations between these Categories. The 1999 version included 132 Semantic Types, and 53 Relationships. Top levels of the Types are Entity and Event. Major groupings within Entities include 'physical object', 'organisms', 'anatomical structures', 'chemicals' and 'concepts or ideas', and within Events 'Phenomenon or process' and 'biologic function'. The arrangement of the Semantic Types is hierarchical. (Further information on the content of Semantic Types is given in F2.2 and in Figure 3.) Semantic Types help to distinguish different meanings associated with a single term. For example, in *MeSH* 'Osteopathy' is the discipline of 'osteopathic medicine'. In *SNOMED* it is a general expression of 'bone disease'. In the first case the semantic label is 'biomedical occupation or discipline', in the second 'disease or syndrome'.

Relationships are non-hierarchical and divide into five groups; physical relationships (e.g., part of, consists of, contains), spatial relationships, temporal relationships (e.g., precedes, co-occurs with), functional relationships (e.g., causes, produces, affects), and conceptual relationships (e.g., measures, assesses). The relationships are stated between high level nodes of the Semantic Categories, for example, 'process of' between 'Biologic Function' and 'Organisms'. As there exists an 'is a' relation between Semantic Types, this also holds between 'Organ and Tissue Function' (a type of 'Biologic Function') and 'Animals' (a type of 'Organism'). The Relations provided do not represent all possible relationships between the defined Semantic Types but are an initial step in the development of a useful set of relationships. The main uses of the *Semantic network* are in query formulation and interactive query refinement.

(c) *Information sources map* and *SPECIALIST lexicon*

The third *UMLS Knowledge source* is the *Information sources map* which indicates which database may be relevant to a particular question, supplies information to users about particular sources, automatically connects to the sources and conducts a retrieval session on one or more sources. The fourth *Knowledge source* is the *SPECIALIST lexicon*, developed to provide the lexical information needed for the *SPECIALIST natural language processing system (NLP)*. It is intended to be an English-language lexicon with many biomedical terms. The 1999 version included 108,000 lexical records and over 186,000 strings. For each work or term the lexicon contains syntactic, morphological and orthographic information.

The *UMLS* exemplifies how the merging of controlled languages gives the advantage of an end product that is richer in terms and relationships than the constituent vocabularies alone, provides switching between independent vocabularies, and facilitates information retrieval using conventional controlled language terms, and also acts as a tool in efforts to provide access to natural language text in biological databases. It has been named, 'the most important repository of sharable, e.g. re-usable, biomedical experience' (Hoppe, 1996).

L3.2.3.

The task of reconciling thesauri and other controlled languages is one beset by many problems. Among these is that the thesauri to be reconciled are often radically different in structure, and many of them do not follow the ISO or ANSI Standards. There is a greater chance of success if there is some common ground between the thesauri. A frequent experience is that reconciliation is frustrated by the all too common lack of one-to-one correspondence between terms from the different thesauri. The effort is worthwhile, in spite of the difficulties, if the end result of reconciliation is an integrated thesaurus, offering a rich supply of alternative choices to terminology, which the user may apply to free text as well as controlled language searching.

Appendix A: AAT Compound Term Rules

The International Organization for Standardization's guidelines for thesaurus construction state that, 'The establishment of procedures for dealing consistently with compound terms introduces one of the most difficult areas in the field of subject indexing. It can be stated, as a general rule, that terms should represent simple or unitary concepts as far as possible, and compound terms should be factored into simpler elements except when this is likely to affect the user's understanding.'

The following guidelines were established by the AAT for deciding when a compound term should remain intact, or bound, and when the compound term should be factored into unitary concepts, or decoordinated.

Reproduced with permission of the Getty Information Institute from *Guide to indexing and cataloging with the Art and architecture thesaurus*, edited by Toni Petersen and Patricia J. Barnett (New York: Oxford University Press, 1994)

COMPOUND TERMS THAT REMAIN BOUND

1. When one or more of the components of the compound term are not *AAT* descriptors and are not appropriate to add.

1.1) When one or more components of a compound term are too vague to stand on their own.

Examples:

first drafts
official documents
class boats
lost cities

1.2) When the compound includes relational parts of speech.

Examples:

chests with drawers
books of hours
towers of silence
chapels of ease

1.3) When the compound term includes a proper noun or adjective (other than a style term).

Examples

Brewster chairs
Usonian houses
Rangeley boats
Schuetzen rifles

1.4) When one of the components of a compound term is a lead-in term.

Examples:

subway cars
research vessels
emergency currency
clothing stores

2. When the meaning of the expression cannot be accurately reconstructed from the constituent independent parts. Most often this is because the modifier or the focus term changes its meaning in the compound expression.

2.1) When the modifier suggests a resemblance, as in a metaphor, to an unrelated thing or event.

Examples:

rose windows
barrel organs
spade money
saddlebag houses

2.2) When the modifier does not define a subclass of the focus term or when the modifier changes the meaning of the focus term.

Examples:

flying boats
water bombers
clay pigeons
Greek fire

2.3) When the modifier defines a specific shape or type of the focus term.

Examples:

sleigh beds
basket capitals
window seats
ice houses

2.4) When the modifier defines the purpose or function of the focus term, and this purpose or function gives the focus term a specific form.

Examples:

> **prayer rugs**
> **china cabinets**
> **crib barns**
> **measuring cups**

2.5) When the modifier is the governing administrator of the focus term.

Examples:

> **cathedral cities**
> **capital cities**
> **army bases**
> **colonial cities**

3. Where there may be a problem in retrieval or vocabulary control.

3.1) When splitting the compound term would result in confusion in retrieval (too many false drops).

Examples:

> **library science/science library**
> **foreign correspondent**

3.2) When the distinction between two or more compound terms is confused in the field and the distinction would be lost if the terms were decoordinated. (*AAT* clarifies the distinction with reciprocal scope notes.)

Examples:

> **log cabins/log houses**
> **business schools/business colleges**
> **meteorological balloons/sounding balloons**
> **military photography/war photography**

4. When the compound term is in a foreign language.

Examples:

> **lits à la duchesse**
> **cadavres exquis**
> **p'ai-lous**
> **aes rude**

5. When the compound term has a trademark.

Examples:

> **Conte crayon (TM)**
> **Plastic Wood (TM)**
> **Zonolite concrete (TM)**

6. When the compound term has become so familiar in common use, or in the field, that it is considered for practical purposes to represent a single concept.

Examples:

> **data processing**
> **art history**

COMPOUND TERMS THAT ARE SPLIT

Terms are split in the following cases if none of the 'bound' rules apply. They may be brought together when indexing to form modified terms.

1. When the modifier is a style or period term.

Examples:

Medieval + architecture	= modified term: **Medieval architecture**
Impressionist + painter	= modified term: **Impressionist painter**
Baroque + gilding	= modified term: **Baroque gilding**
American + glass	= modified term: **American glass**

2. When the modifier describes a characteristic of the focus term.

2.1) When the modifier is a material term describing what the focus term is primarily made of or what is the support for the focus term.

Examples:

stone + floors	= modified term: **stone floors**
bamboo + flutes	= modified term: **bamboo flutes**
concrete + block	= modified term: **concrete block**
silk + paintings	= modified term: **silk paintings**

2.2) When the modifier is a physical attribute or property.

Examples:

round + photographs	= modified term: **round photographs**
computer-assisted + sculpture	= modified term: **computer-assisted sculpture**
blue + velvet	= modified term: **blue velvet**
automatic + rifles	= modified term: **automatic rifles**

2.3) When the modifier is an activity that had been performed on or with the focus term and is now considered an attribute of the focus term.

Examples:

painted + chairs	= modified term: **painted chairs**
beaded + sheaths	= modified term: **beaded sheaths**
reinforced + tapestry	= modified term: **reinforced tapestry**
corrugated + sheet metal	= modified term: **corrugated sheet metal**

3. When the modifier specifies the scope or content of the focus term.

Examples:

textile + museums	= modified term: **textile museums**
war + photographs	= modified term: **war photographs**
medical + laboratories	= modified term: **medical laboratories**
art + libraries	= modified term: **art libraries**

3.1) When the modifier is the agent who possesses or produces the focus term.

Examples:

potters' + marks	= modified term: **potters' marks**
executioners' + swords	= modified term: **executioners' swords**
policemen's + revolvers	= modified term: **policemen's revolvers**
artists' + houses	= modified term: **artists' houses**

4. When the compound term express a whole/part or part/whole relationship.

4.1) When the focus term refers to a property or part, and the modifier represents the whole or possessor of that property or part.

Examples:

airport + lounges	= modified term: **airport lounges**
aircraft + engines	= modified term: **aircraft engines**
school + libraries	= modified term: **school libraries**
hospital + personnel	= modified term: **hospital personnel**

4.2) When the modifier is a property or part of the focus term.

Examples:

flintlock + revolvers	= modified term: **flintlock revolvers**
pedal + drums	= modified term: **pedal drums**
sheath + knives	= modified term: **sheath knives**

4.3) When the modifier is the location or context of the focus term.

Examples:

coin + inscriptions	= modified term: **coin inscriptions**
furniture + marks	= modified term: **furniture marks**
pottery + marks	= modified term: **pottery marks**
book + illustrations	= modified term: **book illustrations**

Bibliography

Aitchison, Jean (1986). 'Bliss and the thesaurus: the Bibliographic Classification of H.E. Bliss as a source of thesaurus terms and structure.' Paper submitted to the International Conference on Ranganathan's Philosophy. New Delhi, India: November 1985. Subsequently published as: A classification as a source for a thesaurus: the Bibliographic Classification of H.E. Bliss as a source of thesaurus terms and structure. *Journal of Documentation*, vol. 42, no. 3, September 1986, pp. 160–181

Aitchison, Jean (1995). 'Bliss Class R: Politics and public administration: a review.' *The Bliss Classification Bulletin*, vol. 37, 1995, pp. 10–23

Aitchison, Jean (1992). 'Indexing languages and indexing.' In: Patti Dossett (ed). *Handbook of special librarianship and information work*, 6th ed. London: Aslib, 1992, pp. 191–233

Aitchison, Jean (1981a). *'Integrated thesaurus of the social sciences: design study'*, prepared for UNESCO Division for the International Development of the Social Sciences. Paris: UNESCO, 1981. Private publication

Aitchison, Jean (1981b). 'Integration of thesauri in the social sciences.' *International Classification*, vol. 8, no. 2, 1981, pp. 75–85

Aitchison, Jean (1996). *International thesaurus of refugee terminology*, 2nd ed., compiled under the auspices of the International Refugee Documentation Network. New York and Geneva: United Nations High Commissioner for Refugees, 1996

Aitchison, Jean (1992a). *The Royal Institute of International Affairs Library thesaurus*, compiled by Jean Aitchison in association with Nicole Gallimore, Susan Boyde and the staff of the library and press library. London, RIIA, 1992, 2 vols

Aitchison, Jean, Alan Gomersall, and R. Ireland (1969). *Thesaurofacet: a thesaurus and faceted classification for engineering and related subjects*. Whetstone, Leicester, England: English Electric Company Ltd., 1969

Aitchison, Jean et al. (1982c). *Thesaurus on youth: an integrated classification and thesaurus on youth affairs and related topics*. Compiled in association with Inese A. Smith and Susan Thompson. Leicester, England: National Youth Bureau, 1981

Aitchison, T.M. and Peter Harding (1983). 'Automatic indexing and classification for mechanized information retrieval.' *Information management research in Europe. Proceedings of the EURIM 5 Conference, Versailles, France, May 1982*. London: Aslib, 1983, pp. 47–55

American Society of Indexers. 'Thesauri online', prepared by Jessica L. Milstead. (http://www.asindexing.org/thesonet.shtml, accessed 25 September 2000)

American Society of Indexers, *see also* Milstead, Jessica L.

API EnCompass thesaurus. New York, NY: American Petroleum Institute. Annual update

Art and architecture thesaurus, 2nd ed. (1994). New York and Oxford: Published on behalf of the Getty Art History Program by Oxford University Press, 1994. 5 vols. (http://shiva.pub.getty.edu/aat_browser/, accessed 25 September 2000). *Reviewed in: Journal of the American Society for Information Science*, vol. 46, no. 2, March 1995, pp. 152–160

Askew, Colin (1979). *Thesaurus of consumer affairs.* London: The Consumers Association; The Hague: International Organization of Consumers Unions, 1979–1982. 2 vols

Association Française de Normalisation (1981). 'Règles d'établissement en langue française'. NFZ 47–100. Paris: AFNOR, 1981

Austin, Derek (1976). 'The CRG research into a freely faceted scheme.' *In:* Maltby, A. (ed). *Classification in the 1970s: a second look.* London: Clive Bingley, 1976, pp. 158–159

Austin, Derek (1984). *PRECIS: a manual of concept analysis and subject indexing,* 2nd ed. London: British Library Bibliographic Services Division, 1984

Australian Society of Indexers. 'List of packages'. (http://www.aussi.org/resources/software/thesauri.htm, accessed 25 September 2000)

Bates, M. (1989). 'Rethinking subject cataloguing in the online environment.' *Library Resources and Technical Services,* vol. 33, no. 4, 1989, pp. 400–412

Batty, C. David (1981). 'Life begins at 40: The resurgence of faceted classification.' *In: The information community: an alliance for progress.* Proceedings of the 18th Annual Meeting of ASIS p. 36 (abstract), pp. 340–342 (full text)

Batty, C. David (1989). 'Thesaurus construction and maintenance survival kit.' *Database,* vol. 12, no. 1, February 1989, pp. 13–20

Bean, Carol A. (1996). 'Analysis of non-hierarchical associative relationships among *Medical Subject Headings (MeSH)*: anatomical and related terminology.' *In: Advances in Knowledge Organization, vol. 5. Knowledge organization and change. Proceedings of the 4th International ISKO Conference, Washington, DC, 15–18 July 1996.* Frankfurt/Main: Indeks Verlag, 1996, pp. 80–86

Bean, Carol A. (1998). 'The semantics of hierarchy: explicit parent-child relationships in *MeSH* tree structures'. *In: Advances in Knowledge Organization, vol. 6. Structures and relations in knowledge organization. Proceedings of the 5th International ISKO Conference, Lille, 25–29 August 1998.* Würzburg, Germany: Ergon Verlag, pp. 133–138

Beaulieu, M. (1997). 'Experiments of interfaces to support query expansion.' *Journal of Documentation,* vol. 53, no. 1, 1997, pp. 8–19

Betts, R. and D. Marrable (1991). 'Free text vs controlled vocabulary: retrieval precision and recall over large databases.' *In:* David I. Raitt (ed). *Online Information 91. Proceedings of the 15th International Online Information Meeting, London, 10–12 December 1991.* Oxford and New Jersey: Learned Information (Europe) Ltd., 1991, pp. 153–165

Bioethics thesaurus (1987). Washington, DC: Georgetown University, Kennedy Institute of Ethics, Bioethics Information Retrieval Project, 1987

Black, W.T. (1981). *Thesaurus of terms on copper technology,* 7th ed. New York: Copper Development Association, 1981

Bonner, Robin et al. *'Community information classification'.* London: National Association of Citizens Advice Bureaux. Unpublished

British Standards Institution (1987). *BS 5723: Guidelines for the establishment and development of monolingual thesauri,* 2nd ed. London: BSI, 1987

British Standards Institution (1985a). *BS 6723: Guidelines for the establishment and development of multilingual thesauri,* 2nd ed. London: BSI, 1985

British Standards Institution (1985b). *ROOT thesaurus.* 2nd ed. Milton Keynes, England: BSI, 1985. 2 vols

BSO (1978). *Broad system of ordering: schedule and index,* 3rd revision, prepared by the FID/BSO Panel (Eric Coates, Geoffrey Lloyd and Susan Simandi). The Hague/ Paris: FID, 1978. (FID Publication no. 564). Revised ed. 1993. St Albans: BSO Panel Ltd. (On diskette)

BUBL Link/5:15. 'Catalogue of Internet resources: Thesauri'. (http://bubl.ac.uk/link/ types/thesauri.htm, accessed 25 September 2000)

Buchanan, Brian (1979). *Theory of library classification*. London: Clive Bingley, 1979. Chapters 5 and 6, Construction of a faceted scheme

Busch, Joseph A. and Toni Petersen (1994). 'Automated mapping of topical special subject headings into faceted index strings using the *Art and architecture thesaurus* as a machine-readable dictionary.' *In: Advances in Knowledge Organization, vol. 4. Knowledge organization and quality management. Proceedings of the 3rd International ISKO Conference, Copenhagen, Denmark, 20–24 June 1994.* Frankfurt/Main: Indeks Verlag, 1995, pp. 390–397

CAB thesaurus (1999). Wallingford, Oxon, UK: CAB International, 1999

Chamis, A.Y. (1988). 'Selection of online databases using switching vocabularies.' *Journal of the American Society for Information Science*, vol. 39, no. 3, 1988, pp. 217–218

Chaplan, M.A. (1995). Mapping *Laborline thesaurus* to *Library of Congress subject headings*: implications for vocabulary switching. *Library Quarterly*, vol. 65, no. 1, January 1995, pp. 39–61

Chen H. and K.J. Lynch (1992). 'Automatic construction of networks of concepts characterizing document databases.' *IEEE Transactions on Systems and Cybernetics*, vol. 22, no. 5, 1992, pp. 885–902

Chen, H. et al. (1995). 'Automatic thesaurus generation for an electronic community system.' *Journal of the American Society for Information Science*, vol. 46, no. 3, April 1995, pp. 175–193

Chen, H. et al. (1997). 'A concept space approach to addressing the vocabulary problem in scientific information retrieval: an experiment on the worm community system.' *Journal of the American Society for Information Science*, vol. 48, no. 1, 1997, pp. 17–31

Cimino, James J. and Robert V. Sideli (1991). 'Using the *UMLS* to bring the library to the bedside.' *Medical Decision Making 11, suppl. (October–December 1991)*: S116–120

Clarke, Stella G. Dextre, *see* Dextre Clarke, Stella G.

Classification Research Group (1955). 'The need for a faceted classification as the basis of all methods of information retrieval, 1955.' *In:* L.M. Chan et al. *Theory of subject analysis: a source book.* Littleton, CO: Libraries Unlimited, 1985, pp. 154–167, and *In:* Alan Gilchrist (ed). *From classification to 'knowledge organization'. Dorking revisited or 'Past is prelude': A collection of reprints to commemorate the forty year span between the Dorking Conference (First International Study Conference on Classification Research 1957) and the Sixth International Study Conference on Classification Research (London, UK) 1997.* The Hague, Netherlands: International Federation for Information and Documentation (FID), 1997, (FID Occasional Paper no. 14), pp. 1–9

Cleverdon, C.W., M. Keen and J. Mills (1966). *Factors determining the performance of indexing systems: an investigation supported by a grant to Aslib by the National Science Foundation.* Cranfield, England: Aslib Cranfield Research Project, 1966

Coates, E.J. (1960). *The British catalogue of music classification*. London: British National Bibliography, 1960

Cochrane, Pauline A. (1992). 'Indexing and searching thesauri, the Janus or Proteus of information retrieval.' *In:* N.J. Williamson and H. Hudon (eds). *Classification research for knowledge representation and organization. Proceedings of the 5th International Study Conference on Classification Research, Toronto, Canada, 24–28 June, 1991.* Amsterdam: Elsevier Science Publishers BV and FID, 1992, pp. 161–177

Commission of the European Communities (1979). *Food: multilingual thesaurus*, 2nd English ed. London: Clive Bingley, K.G. Saur, 1979

Construction industry thesaurus (1976), 2nd ed., compiled by the CIT at the Polytechnic of South Bank under the direction of Michael J. Roberts. London: Department of the Environment, Property Services Agency, 1976

Cousins, S.A. (1992). 'Enhancing subject access to OPACs: controlled vs natural language.' *Journal of Documentation*, vol. 48, no. 3, September 1992, pp. 291–309

Craven, T.C. (1992a). 'Concept relation structures and their graphic display.' *In:* N.J. Williamson and H. Hudon (eds). *Classification research for knowledge representation and organization. Proceedings of the 5th International Study Conference on Classification Research, Toronto, Canada, 24–28 June 1991.* Amsterdam: Elsevier Science Publishers BV and FID, 1992, pp. 49–60

Craven, T.C. (1992b). 'A general versus a special algorithm in the graphic display of thesauri.' *In:* N.J. Williamson and H. Hudon (eds). *Classification research for knowledge representation and organization. Proceedings of the 5th International Study Conference on Classification Research, Toronto, Canada, 24–28 June 1991.* Amsterdam: Elsevier Science Publishers BV and FID, 1992, pp. 179–186

Craven, T.C. (1997). 'Introductory tutorial on thesaurus construction'. London, Ontario, Canada: University of Western Ontario, Graduate School of Library and Information Science. (http://instruct.uwo.ca/gplis/677/thesaur/main00.htm, accessed 25 September 2000)

Craven, T.C. (1993). 'A thesaurus for use in a computer-aided abstracting tool kit.' *In: Proceedings of the 56th Annual Meeting of the American Society for Information Science.* Learned Information, Columbus, Ohio, 1993, pp. 178–184

Croft, W.B. (1983). 'Experiments with representation in a document retrieval system.' *Information Technology Research and Development (GB)*, vol. 2, no. 1, January 1983, pp. 1–21

Croghan, A. (1971). *Manual on the construction of an indexing language using educational technology as an example.* London: Carburgh Publications, 1971

Crouch, C.J. (1990). 'An approach to the automatic construction of global thesauri.' *Information Processing and Management*, vol. 26, no. 5, 1990, pp. 624–640

Current Awareness Abstracts. 10 issues p.a. London: Aslib, 1984 to date. (http://www.aslib.com/caa/index/html, accessed 25 September 2000)

Dahlberg, Ingetraut (1996a). 'The compatibility guidelines – a re-evaluation.' *In: Compatibility and integration of order systems: Research Seminar Proceedings of the TIP/ISKO Meeting, Warsaw, 13–15 September 1995.* Warsaw: Wydawnictwo SBP, 1995, pp. 32–45

Dahlberg, Ingetraut (1996b). 'Library catalogues in the Internet: switching for future subject access.' *In: Advances in Knowledge Organization, vol. 5. Knowledge organization and change. Proceedings of the 4th ISKO International Conference, Washington, D.C., 15–18 July 1996.* Frankfurt/Maine: Indeks Verlag, 1996, pp. 155–164

Dahlberg, Ingetraut (1978). *Ontical structures and universal classification.* Bangladore, India: Sarada Ranganathan Endowment for Library Science, 1978, p. 42. The Systematifier

Defriez, Philip (1993). *The ISDD thesaurus. Keywords relating to non-medical use of drugs and drug dependence*, 2nd ed. London: Institute for the Study of Drug Dependence, 1993

Deutsches Institut für Normung (DIN) (1987). *Richtlinien für die Herstellung und Weiterentwicklung von Thesauri. DIN 1563 – Pt. 1 1987, Pt. 2 1993*. Berlin: DIN, 1987–1993

Dextre, Stella G. and T.M. Clarke (1981). 'A system for machine-aided thesaurus construction.' *Aslib Proceedings*, vol. 33, no. 3, March 1981, pp. 102–112

Dextre Clarke, Stella G. (1997). 'The construction of a multilingual thesaurus based on a classified structure.' *In: Knowledge organization for information retrieval. Proceedings of the 6th International Study Conference on Classification Research, University College London, 16–18 June 1997*. The Hague, Netherlands: International Federation for Information and Documentation, 1997, (FID 716), pp. 120–128

Dextre Clarke, Stella G. (1996). 'Integrating thesauri in the agricultural sciences.' *In: Compatability and integration of order systems. Research Seminar Proceedings of the TIP/ISKO Meeting, Warsaw, 13–15 September 1996*. Warsaw: Wydawnictwo SBP, 1996, pp. 111–122

Dextre Clarke, Stella G. (2001). 'Organizing access to information by subject'. *In:* Scammell, A. (ed). *Handbook of special librarianship*, 8th ed. Aslib: 2001 (not yet published).

Dextre Clarke, Stella G. (2000). 'Thesaural relationships'. *In:* Bean, Carol A. and Green, Rebecca (eds). *Relationships in the organization of knowledge*. Dordrecht: Kluwer, 2000, pp. 37–52

DIAL UK Classification (1996). (Classification/thesaurus for use in disability information services). Doncaster, England: DIAL UK, 1996

Doszkocs, T.E. (1978). AID, an Associative Interactive Dictionary for online searching. *Online Review*, vol. 2, no. 2, June 1978, pp. 163–173

Doszkocs, T.E. and B.A. Rapp (1979). 'Searching *Medline* in English: a prototype user interface with natural language query, ranked output and relevance feedback.' *Proceedings of the ASIS Annual Meeting*, vol. 16, 1979, pp. 131–139

Dubois, C.P.R. (1987). 'Free text versus controlled vocabulary: a reassessment.' *Online Review*, vol. 11, no. 4, 1987, pp. 243–253

Dubois, C.P.R. (1984). 'The use of thesauri in online retrieval.' *Journal of Information Science Principles & Practice (Netherlands)*,vol. 8, no. 2, March 1984, pp. 63–66

Ellis, David and Ana Vasconcelos (1999). 'Ranganathan and the Net: using facet analysis to search and organise the World Wide Web'. *Aslib Proceedings*, vol. 51, no. 1, 1999, pp. 3–10

EMTREE thesaurus. Amsterdam: Elsevier Science BV, Excerpta Medica Publishing Group. Annual publication

EURATOM thesaurus (1966), 2nd ed. Brussels: European Atomic Energy Community, 1966–70. 2 vols

European education thesaurus (1991), produced by the Council of Europe in collaboration with the Commission of the European Communities. English version, 1991 edition. Luxembourg: Office for the Official Publications of the European Communities, 1991

Fidel, Raya (1991). 'Searchers' selection of search keys: 2. Controlled vocabulary or free-text searching.' *Journal of American Society for Information Science*, vol. 42, no. 7, August 1991, pp. 501–514

Foskett, A.C. (2000). 'The future of faceted classification'. *In:* Marcella, Rita and

Arthur Maltby (eds). *The future of classification*. Aldershot: Gower, 2000, pp. 69–80

Foskett, A.C. (1996). *Subject approach to information*. 5th ed. London: Bingley, 1996

Foskett, D.J. (1974). *Classification and indexing in the social sciences*. 2nd ed. London: Butterworth, 1974

Foskett, D.J. (1981). 'Thesaurus.' *In: Encyclopaedia of Library and Information Science*, vol. 30. New York: Marcel Dekker, Inc., 1981

Fugmann, Robert (1982). 'The complementarity of natural and indexing languages.' *In:* Perreault, J.M. and I. Dahlberg, (eds). *Universal classification II: subject analysis and ordering systems, Proceedings of the 4th International Study Conference on Classification Research, FID/CR, Augsburg, 28 June–2 July 1982.* Frankfurt: Indeks Verlag, 1982/83, pp. 86–89

Fugmann, Robert (1988). 'Grammar in chemical indexing languages.' *In:* W.A. Warr (ed). *Chemical structures; the international language of chemistry.* Berlin, Heidelberg: Springer Verlag, 1988, pp. 425–439

Gilchrist, Alan (1994). 'Classification and thesauri'. *In:* B.C. Vickery (ed). *Fifty years of information progress: a Journal of Documentation review.* London: Aslib, pp. 85–118

Gilchrist, Alan (1997). 'The subject approach in managing information', *In:* Scammell, Alison (ed). *Handbook of special librarianship and information work.* 7th ed. London: Aslib, 1997, pp. 51–79

Gilchrist, Alan (1971). *The thesaurus in retrieval.* London: Aslib, 1971

Giles-Peters, A. (1993). 'Experiments in the mechanical construction of cross-database thesauri.' *In: Online Information 93, Proceedings of the 17th International Online Information Meeting, London, 7–9 December 1993.* Oxford and New Jersey: Learned Information (Europe), 1993, pp. 137–145

Green, Rebecca (1996). 'The development of a relational thesaurus.' *In: Advances in Knowledge Organization, vol. 5. Knowledge organization and change. Proceedings of the 4th ISKO International Conference, Washington, DC, 15–18 July 1996.* Frankfurt: Indeks Verlag, 1996, pp. 72–79

Hack, John (1984). 'Search aids for American Petroleum databases.' *Database*, vol. 7, no. 4, December 1984, pp. 84–88

Hammond, William and Staffen Rosenbord (1962). *Experimental study of convertibility between large technical indexing vocabularies – with table of indexing equivalents.* Silver Spring, MD.: Datatrol Corp., 1962

Hanani, U. (1996). 'Intelligent hypertext: a framework for automatic search guidance system.' *In: Proceedings of the 19th International Online Information Meeting, London, 5–7 December 1995.* Oxford: Learned Information, 1995, pp. 219–229

Hood, Martha W. and Christine Ebermann (1990). 'Reconciling the *CAB thesaurus* and *AGROVOC*'. *Quarterly Bulletin of the IAALD*, vol. 35, no. 3, 1990, pp. 181–185

Hoppe, Stephan (1996). 'The *UMLS* – a model for knowledge integration in a subject field'. *In: Compatibility and integration of order systems: Research Seminar Proceedings of the TIP/ISKO Meeting, Warsaw, 13–15 September 1995.* Warsaw: Wydawnictwo SBP, 1996, pp. 97–110

Horsnell, V. (1975). The *Intermediate lexicon:* an aid to international cooperation. *Aslib Proceedings*, vol. 27, no. 2, February 1975, pp. 57–66

Horsnell, V. and A. Merrett (1978). *Intermediate lexicon research project: Phase 2. Evaluation of the switching and retrieval performance of the Intermediate Lexicon for information science.* London: Polytechnic of North London, School of Librarianship, 1978

Hudon, Michèle (1997). 'Multilingual thesaurus construction – integrating the views of different cultures in one gateway to knowledge and concepts'. *Information Services and Use*, vol. 17, no. 2/3, 1997, pp. 112–123

Hudon, Michèle (1998). 'A preliminary investigation of the usefulness of semantic relations and of standardized definitions for the purpose of specifying meaning in a thesaurus'. *Advances in Knowledge Organization, vol. 6. Structures and relations in knowledge organization. Proceedings of the 5th ISKO International Conference, Lille, France, 25–29 August 1998.* Würzburg, Germany: Ergon Verlag, pp. 139–145

Hudon, Michèle (1996). 'Preparing terminological definitions for indexing and retrieval thesauri: a model.' *In: Advances in Knowledge Organization, vol. 5. Knowledge organization and change. Proceedings of the 4th International ISKO Conference, Washington, DC, 15–18 July 1996.* Frankfurt/Main: Indeks Verlag, 1996, pp. 363–369

Hunter, E.J. (1988). *Classification made easy.* Aldershot: Gower, 1988

INSPEC thesaurus. London: Institution of Electrical Engineers. Biennial

Integrated energy vocabulary (1976). Springfield, VA: National Technical Information Service, 1976

International Bureau of Education (1984). *UNESCO:IBE education thesaurus: a list of terms for indexing and retrieving documents and data in the field of education, with French and Spanish equivalents*, 4th revised ed. Paris: UNESCO, 1984

International Labour Organization (1998). *ILO thesaurus*, 5th ed. Geneva: ILO, 1998

International Organization for Standardization (1986). *ISO 2788: Guidelines for the establishment and development of monolingual thesauri*, 2nd ed. Geneva: ISO, 1986

International Organization for Standardization (1985a). *ISO 5964: Guidelines for the establishment and development of multilingual thesauri.* Geneva: ISO, 1985

International road research documentation (IRRD) thesaurus (1985b). 2nd ed. Paris: OECD, 1985. 2 vols

International Society for Knowledge Organization (ISKO), Polish Librarians Association and Society of Professional Information (TIP) (1986). *Compatibility and integration of order systems: Research Seminar Proceedings of the TIP.ISKO Meeting, Warsaw, 13–15 September 1995.* Warsaw: Wydawnictwo SBP, 1996

Johnson, E. and P.A. Cochrane (1995). 'A hypertextual interface for a searcher's thesaurus.' *In: Digital Libraries '95 Proceedings, 1995*, pp. 77–86

Johnston, S.M. (1982). 'Effect of thesaurus indexing on retrieval from machine-readable databases.' *Quarterly Bulletin of IAALD*, vol. 27, no. 3, 1982, pp. 90–96

Jones, S. (1993). 'A thesaurus data model for an intelligent retrieval system.' *Journal of Information Science*, vol. 19, no. 2, 1993, pp. 167–178

Jones, S. et al. (1995). 'Interactive thesaurus navigation. Intelligence rules OK?' *Journal of the American Society for Information Science*, vol. 46, no. 1, 1995, pp. 52–59

Knapp, S.D. (1984). '*BRS/TERM*, a vocabulary database for searchers.' *Database*, vol. 7, no. 4, December 1984, pp. 70–75

Knowledge Organization. Copenhagen, Denmark: International Society for Knowledge Organisation (ISKO). General Secretariat, Royal School of Librarianship. Published quarterly, Würzburg: ERGON-Verlag. Each issue includes a section on Knowledge Organization Literature including new classification systems and thesauri

Koch, Traugott. 'Controlled vocabularies, thesauri and classification systems available in the WWW'. (http://www.lub.lu.se/metadata/subject-help.html, accessed 25 September 2000)

Kristensen, J. (1993). 'Expanding end-users' query statements for free-text searching with a search-aid thesaurus.' *Information Processing and Management*, 1993, vol. 29, no. 6, pp. 733–744

Krooks, D.A. and F.W. Lancaster (1993). 'The evolution of guidelines for thesaurus construction.' *Libri*, vol. 43, no. 4, 1993, pp. 326–342

Lambert, N. (1995). 'Of thesauri and computers: reflections on the need for thesauri.' *Searcher*, vol. 5, no. 8, 1995, pp. 18–22

Lancaster, F.W. (1986). *Vocabulary control for information retrieval.* 2nd ed. Arlington, Virginia: Information Resources Press, 1986

Lancaster, F.W. (1989). 'The perspective: natural language versus controlled language: a new examination.' *In:* C. Oppenheim, et al, (eds). *Perspectives in information management, vol. 1.* London: Butterworth, 1989, pp. 1–23

Lopez-Huertas, M.J. (1997). 'Thesaurus structure design: a conceptual approach for improved interaction.' *Journal of Documentation*, vol. 53, no. 2, 1997, pp. 139–177

McCray, A.T. et al. (1993). '*UMLS* knowledge for biomedical language processing'. *Bulletin of the Medical Library Association*, vol. 81, no. 2, April 1993, pp. 184–194

McIlwaine, I.C. and Nancy J. Williamson (1994). 'A feasibility study on the restructuring of the *Universal decimal classification* into a fully-faceted classification system.' *In: Advances in Knowledge Organization, vol. 4. Knowledge organization and quality management. Proceedings of the 3rd International ISKO Conference, Copenhagen, Denmark, 20–24 June 1994.* Frankfurt/Main: Indeks Verlag, 1994, pp. 406–413

Macrothesaurus for information processing in the field of economic and social development. (1998). 5th ed., OECD, 1998, Paris, France. HTML Version: (http://info.uibk.ac.at/info/oecd-macroth/, accessed 3 October 2000)

Maltby, A. (1968). 'Faceted classification'. *In:* K.C.G. Bakewell (ed). *Classification for information retrieval.* London: Bingley, 1968. pp. 33–41

Maniez, J. (1997). 'Database merging and the compatibility of indexing languages.' *Knowledge Organization*, vol. 24, no. 4, 1997, pp. 213–224

Maniez, J. (1988). 'Relationships in thesauri: some critical remarks'. *International Classification*, vol. 15, no. 3, 1988, pp. 133–138

Marco, J.G. (1996). 'Hypertext and indexing languages: common challenges and perspectives'. *In: Advances in Knowledge Organization, vol. 5. Knowledge organization and change. Proceedings of the 4th International ISKO Conference, Washington DC, 15–18 July 1996.* Frankfurt/Main: Indeks Verlag, 1996, pp. 87–94

Markey, Karen et al. (1979). 'An analysis of controlled vocabulary and free text search statements in online searches.' *Online Review*, vol. 5, no. 3, 1979, pp. 225–236

Markham, J.W. and B.F. Avery, (1998). 'LCSH and the ASFIS Thesaurus: an update'. *Looking to the electronic future, let's not forget the archival past. Proceedings of the 24th Annual Conference of the International Association of Aquatic and Marine Science Libraries and Information Centres (IAMSLIC) and the 17 Polar Libraries Colloquy, Reykjavik, Iceland, 20–25 September 1998*, pp. 347–353

Maron, M.E. et al. (1959). *Probabilistic indexing: a statistical technique for document identification and retrieval.* Los Angeles, California: Thompson Ramo Woodridge, 1959

Martin, Brian K. and Roy Rada (1987). 'Building a relational database for a physician document index.' *Medical Informatics*, vol. 12, July–September 1987, pp. 187–210

Medical subject headings (MeSH). Bethesda, MD: National Library of Medicine. Annual update (http://www.nlm.nih.gov/mesh/ and http://www.nlm.nih.gov/mesh/changes2000.html, accessed 3 August 2000)

Metallurgical thesaurus (1975). Luxembourg: Système de Documentation et d'information Metallurgique des Communautés Européenes (SDIM), 1975

Miksa, F.L. (1998). 'The DDC, the universe of knowledge and the post-modern library'. Albany, New York: OCLC Forest Press, 1998

Mills, J. and V. Broughton (1977–) *Bliss bibliographic classification*. 2nd ed. *Introduction and auxiliary schedules; Class A/AL Philosophy and Logic; Class AM/ AX Mathematics, Statistics and Probability; Class AY/B General science, Physics; Class H Anthropology, Human biology, Health sciences; Class I Psychology and Psychiatry; Class J Education; Class K Society; Class P Religion; Class Q Social welfare; Class R Politics and Public administration; Class S Law; Class T Economics and Enterprise management*. Classes in preparation include Class 2/9 Generalia, Phenomena, Knowledge, Information science and technology; Class C Chemistry; Class D Astronomy and Earth Sciences; Class E/GQ Biological sciences; Class GR/GZ Agriculture; Class L/O History; Class U/V Technology; Class W Recreation and the Arts; Class X/Y Language and Literature. Bowker-Saur, 1977–. In progress

Milstead, Jessica L., ed. (1998). *ASIS thesaurus of information science and librarianship*, 2nd ed. Medford, NJ: Published for the American Society for Information Science by Learned Information, Inc., 1998. (ASIS Monograph Series.) (http://www.asis.org/Publications/Thesaurus/tnhome.htm, accessed 3 August 2000)

Milstead, Jessica L. (1996). 'How do I build a thesaurus'. *In*: American Society of Indexers. Thesaurus information. (http://www.asindexing.org/thesauri.shtml, accessed 4 August 2000)

Milstead, Jessica L. (1995). 'Invisible thesauri: the year 2000.' *Online and CDROM Review*, vol. 19, no. 2. 1995, pp. 93–94

Milstead, Jessica L. (1994). 'Needs for research in indexing.' *Journal of the American Society for Information Science*, vol. 45, no. 8, September, 1994, pp. 557–582

Milstead, Jessica L. (1991). 'Specifications for thesaurus software.' *Information Processing and Management*, vol. 27, no. 2/3, 1991, pp. 165–175

Milstead, Jessica L. (1998). 'Thesaurus management software', prepared for the American Society of Indexers. (http://www/asindexing.org/thessoft.shtml, accessed 4 August 2000)

Milstead, Jessica L. (1997). 'Thesaurus in a full-text world'. *In*: Cochrane, Pauline Atherton and Eric H. Jones (eds). *Visualizing subject access for 21st century information resources. Proceedings of the 1997 Clinic on Library Applications of Data Processing, 2–4 March 1997*. Urbana-Champaign, Illinois: Illinois University at Urbana-Champaign, Graduate School of Library and Information Science, 1998, pp. 28–38

Molholt, Pat (1996). 'Standardization of inter-concept links and their usage.' *In: Advances in Knowledge Organization, vol. 5. Knowledge organization and change. Proceedings of the 4th International ISKO Conference, Washington, DC, 15–18 July 1996*. Frankfurt/Main: Indeks Verlag, 1996, pp. 65–71

Muench, Eugene V. (1979). *Biomedical subject headings: a reconciliation of National Library of Medicine (MeSH) and Library of Congress subject headings*, 2nd ed. Hamden, Conn: Shoe String, 1979

Muraszkiewicz, H. et al. (1996). 'Software problems of merging thesauri.' *In: Compatibility and integration of order systems: Research Seminar Proceedings of the TPI/ISKO Meeting, Warsaw, 13–15 September 1995*. Warsaw: Wydawnictwo SPB, 1996, pp. 58–67

NASA thesaurus (http://www.sti.nasa.gov/thesfrm1.htm, accessed 4 August 2000). Fig 9 is taken from a browsable PDF version of the hierarchical display, 24 Oct 1997. A later version is found at (http://www.sti.nasa.gov/98Thesaurus/vol1.pdf, accessed 4 August 2000).

National Information Standards Organization (1994). *ANSI/NISO Z39.19:1993. Guidelines for the Construction, Format and Management of Monolingual Thesauri. ANSI/NISO Z39.19-1993.* Bethesda, MD: NISO Press, 1993. An American National Standard, developed by the National Information Standards Organization, approved August 30, 1993 by the American National Standards Institute, Bethesda, MD: NISO Press, 1994

Nestel, B. et al. (1992). 'A minithesaurus as an aid to the management of agricultural research.' *Quarterly Bulletin of the International Association of Agricultural Information Specialists*, vol. 27, no. 4, 1992, pp. 215–223

Niehoff, R.T. and G. Mack (1984). *Final report on evaluation of the Vocabulary Switching System. NSF Grant IST-7911190 and IST-8111497 for National Science Foundation, Division of Information Science and Technology.* Columbus, Ohio: Battelle Columbus Laboratories, 1984. Summary in: *International Classification*, vol. 12, no. 1, 1985, pp. 2–6

Nielson, L. M. (1998). 'Future thesauri: what kind of conceptual knowledge do searchers need?' *In: Advances in Knowledge Organization, vol. 6. Structures and relations in knowledge organization. Proceedings of the 5th International ISKO Conference, 25–29 August 1998, Lille, France.* Würzburg, Germany: Ergon Verlag, pp. 153–160

Orna, Elizabeth (1983). *Build yourself a thesaurus: a step-by-step guide.* Norwich: Running Angel, 1983

Perez, Ernest (1982). 'Text enhancement. Controlled vocabulary v. free text.' *Special Libraries*, vol. 73, no. 3, July 1982, pp. 183–192

Perreault, Jean (1965). 'Categories and relators: a new schema.' (originally published in Rev. Int. Doc., vol. 32, no. 4, 1965, pp. 136–144). *Knowledge Organization*, vol. 21, no. 4, 1994, pp. 189–198

Peters, Thomas A. and Martin Kurth (1991). 'Controlled and uncontrolled vocabulary subject searching in an academic library online catalog.' *Information Technology and Libraries*, vol. 20, no. 3, September 1991, pp. 201–211

Petersen, Toni and P.J. Barnett (1994). *Guide to indexing and cataloging with the Art and architecture thesaurus.* New York and Oxford: Published on behalf of the Getty Art History Information Program by Oxford University Press, 1994. Reviewed in the *Journal of the American Society for Information Science*, vol. 46, no. 2, March 1995, pp. 152–160

Pollard, R.A. (1993). 'Hypertext-based thesaurus as a subject browsing aid for bibliographic databases.' *Information Processing and Management*, vol. 29, no. 3, 1993, pp. 345–357

Pollitt, A. Steven (1994). 'HIBROWSE for bibliographic databases.' *Journal of Information Science*, vol. 20, no. 6, 1994, pp. 413–416

Pollitt, A. Steven (1996). 'Taking a different view. What can the design of a view-based searching technique offer libraries? *Library Association Record, Library Technology*, vol. 1, no. 1, 1996, p. 20

Pollitt, A. Steven et al. (1996). 'Empowering users for improved database access and analysis through the application of knowledge structure views, progressive refinement techniques and a design approach driven by usability.' *In: Advances in Knowledge Organization, vol. 5. Knowledge organization and change. Proceedings of the 4th International ISKO Conference, Washington, DC, 15–18 July 1996.* Frankfurt/Main: Indeks Verlag, 1996, pp. 231–241

Queensland University of Technology. 'Controlled vocabularies guide', prepared by Michael Middleton. (http://www.fit.qut.edu.au/InfoSys/middle/cont_voc.html, accessed 4 August 2000)

Ranganathan, S.R. (1987). *The Colon classification*, 7th ed. Bangalore: Sarada Ranganathan Endowment for Library Science, 1987

Roberts, N. (1984). 'The pre-history of the information retrieval thesaurus.' *Journal of Documentation*, vol. 40, 1984, pp. 271–285

Robinson, L. and D. Bawden (1999). 'Internet subject gateways'. *International Journal of Information Management*, vol. 19, no. 6, 1999, pp. 511–522

Rolling, L. (1971). 'Computer management of multilingual thesauri.' *Aslib Proceedings*, vol. 23, no. 11, November 1971, pp. 591–594

Rowley, J.E. (1994). 'The controlled versus natural indexing language debate revisited: a perspective on information retrieval practice and research.' *Journal of Information Science*, vol. 20, no. 2, 1994, pp. 108–119

Rowley, J.E. (1992). *Organizing knowledge: an introduction to information retrieval*, 2nd ed. Aldershot: Gower, 1992

Royal Pharmaceutical Society of Great Britain (1990). *Martindale online: drug information thesaurus.* 2nd ed. London: Pharmaceutical Press, 1990

Salton, G. (1989). *Automatic text processing.* Reading, MA: Addison-Wesley, 1989

Salton, G. and M.J. McGill (1983). *Introduction to modern information retrieval.* New York: McGraw Hill, 1983.

Salton G. et al. (1975). 'A theory of term importance in automatic text analysis.' *Journal of the American Society for Information Science*, vol. 26, no. 1, 1975, pp. 33–44

Schmitz-Esser, W. (1999). 'Thesaurus and beyond. An advance formula for linguistic engineering and information retrieval.' *Knowledge Organization*, vol. 26, no. 1, 1999, pp. 10–29

Schoonbaert, D. (1996). 'SPIRS, WinSPIRS and OVID: a comparison of three MEDLINE–on CD-ROM interfaces.' *Bulletin of the Medical Library Association*, vol. 84, no. 1, 1996, pp. 63–70

Schuyler, P.L. (1993). The *UMLS Metathesaurus*: representing different views of biomedical concepts. *Bulletin of the Medical Library Association*, vol. 81, no. 2, April 1993, pp. 217–222

Shapiro, C.D. and P.F. Yan (1996). 'Generous tools: thesauri in digital libraries.' *In: Proceedings of the 17th National Online Meeting, May, 1996, New York.* Medford, New Jersey: Information Today Inc., 1996, pp. 323–332

Sievert, Mary Ellen, and Bert R. Boyce (1983). 'Hedge trimming and the resurrection of the controlled vocabulary on line.' *Online Review*, vol. 7, no. 6, 1983, pp. 89–94.

Silvester, J.P. and P.H. Klingbiel (1993). 'An operational system for subject switching between controlled vocabularies.' *Information Processing and Management*, vol. 29, no. 1, 1993, pp. 47–59

Smith, Inese A. (1984). 'Development of indexing systems at the National Youth Bureau.' *Catalogue and Index*, no. 74, Summer 1984, pp. 1–4

Smith, M.P. and Pollitt, A. Steven (1996). 'Ranking and relevance feedback extensions to a view-based searching system.' *In: Proceedings of the 19th International Online*

Information Meeting, London, December 1996. Oxford: Learned Information, 1996, pp. 231–240

Sneiderman, C.A. and E.J. Bicknell (1992). 'Computer-assisted dynamic integration of multiple medical thesauruses.' *Computers in Biology and Medicine*, vol. 22, no. 1/2, January–March 1992, pp. 134–145

Snow, Bonnie (1985). 'Why use a database thesaurus?'. *Online*, vol. 9, no. 6, November 1985, pp. 92–96

Social science and business microthesaurus (1982) : *a hierarchical list of indexing terms used by NTIS*. Springfield, Va: National Technical Information Service, 1982

Soergel, Dagobert (1974). *Indexing languages and thesauri: construction and maintenance*. Los Angeles, California: Melville Publishing Co., 1974

Soergel, Dagobert (1996a). 'Data models for an integrated thesaurus database.' *In: Compatibility and integration of order systems: Research Seminar Proceedings of the TIP/ISKO Meeting, Warsaw, 13–15 September 1995*. Warsaw: Wydawnictwo SBP, 1996, 47–57

Soergel, Dagobert (1996b). '*SemWeb*: Proposal for an open, multifunctional, system for integrated access to knowledge about concepts and terminology'. *In: Advances in Knowledge Organization, vol. 5. Knowledge organization and change. Proceedings of the 4th ISKO International Conference, Washington, DC, 15–18 July 1996*. Frankfurt/Main: Indeks Verlag, 1996, pp. 165–173

Song, Min (2000). 'Visualization in information retrieval: a three-level analysis.' *Journal of Information Science*, vol. 26, no. 1, 2000, pp. 3–19

Sparck Jones, K. (1974). *Automatic indexing, 1974; a state-of-the-art review*. Cambridge: University of Cambridge, 1974

SPINES thesaurus (1976) : *a controlled and structured vocabulary of science and technology for policy making, management and development*. Paris: UNESCO, 1976

Spiteri, L. F. (1997). 'Use of facet analysis in information retrieval thesauri: an examination of selected guidelines for thesaurus construction'. *Cataloging and Classification Quarterly*, vol. 25, no. 1, 1997, pp. 21–37

Squires, S.J. (1993). 'Access to biomedical information: the *Unified medical language system*.' *Library Trends*, vol. 42, no. 1, Summer 1993, pp. 127–151

Starr, Jennie (1999). 'Content classification: leveraging new tools and librarians' expertise.' *Searcher*, vol. 7, issue 9, 1999, pp. 10 (+ 8 pages)

Strawn, Gary L. (1992). 'Multiple thesauri and Northwestern University Libraries' NOTIS 5.0 Online Public Catalog'. *Paper presented at the 1992 NOTIS Users' Group Meeting*

Stevens, M.E. (1980). *Automatic indexing: a state-of-the-art review*. Washington, DC: National Bureau of Standards, 1980

Strong, G.W. and M.C. Drott (1996). 'A thesaurus for end-user indexing and retrieval.' *Information Processing and Management*, vol. 22, no. 6, 1996, pp. 487–492.

Svenonius, Elaine (1997). 'Definitional approaches in the design of classification and thesauri and their implications for retrieval and for automatic classification.' *In: Knowledge organization for information retrieval. Proceedings of the 6th International Study Conference on Classification Research, University College London, 16–18 June 1997*, The Hague, Netherlands: International Federation for Information and Documentation, 1997, (FID 716), pp. 12–16

Svenonius, Elaine (1987). 'Design of controlled vocabularies.' *In: Encyclopaedia of Library and Information Science*, vol. 45, Supplement 10: New York: Marcel Dekker Inc., 1987, pp. 82–109

Svenonius, Elaine (1986). 'Unanswered questions on the design of controlled vocabularies.' *Journal of the American Society for Information Science*, vol. 37, no. 5, 1986, pp. 331–340

Taylor, A.G. (1999). *The organization of information*. Englewood, CO: Libraries Unlimited, 1999

TDCK circular thesaurus system (1963). The Hague: Netherlands Armed Forces Technical Documentation and Information Centre, 1963

Thesaurus guide: an analytical directory of selected vocabularies for information retrieval, 1992, prepared for the Commission of the European Communities, by Eurobrokers, 2nd ed. Luxembourg: Office for Official Publications of the European Commission, 1993. (EUR/92/14006); (Rapports EUR 14006). (The 1985 edition was prepared by Gesellschaft für Information und Dokumentation (FID)).

Thesaurus of engineering and scientific terms (TEST) (1967): a list of scientific and engineering terms and their relationships for use as a vocabulary in indexing and retrieving technical information. New York: Engineers Joint Council and US Department of Defense, 1967

Thesaurus of ERIC descriptors (1995). 13th ed., edited by James E. Houston. 13th ed. prepared for the US Department of Education. Phoenix, Arizona: Oryx, 1995. ERIC Search Wizard, (http://ericae.net/scripts/ewiz/, accessed 15 August 2000)

Thomas, A. R. (1997–98). 'Bibliographic classification: the ideas and achievements of H.E. Bliss', *Cataloguing and Classification Quarterly*, vol. 25, no. 1, 1997, pp. 51–104; addenda, vol. 26, 1998, no. 2, pp. 73–75

Townley, H.M. and R.D. Gee (1980). *Thesaurus-making: grow your own word-stock*. London: Andre Deutsch, 1980.

UNESCO (1981). *Guidelines for the establishment and development of monolingual thesauri for information retrieval*. 2nd rev. ed. PGI-81/WS/15. Paris: UNESCO, 1981

UNESCO thesaurus (1995) : *a structured list of descriptors for indexing and retrieving literature in the fields of education, science, social and human science, culture, communication and information*. Paris: UNESCO, 1995, (http:/www.ulcc.ac.uk/unesco/index.htm, accessed 3 October 2000)

Unified medical language system. The National Library of Medicine's UMLS. (http://www.nlm.nih.gov/research/umls/, accessed 15 August 2000)

Vickery, B.C. (1975). *Classification and indexing in science*, 3rd ed. London: Butterworth, 1975

Vickery, B.C. (1960). *Faceted classification: a guide to construction and use of special schemes*. London: Aslib, 1960

Vickery, B.C. and A. Vickery (1992). *Information science in theory and practice*, rev. ed. Bowker-Saur, 1992. Chapter 6. Semantics and retrieval

Wall, Eugene and J.M. Barnes (1969). *Intersystem compatibility and convertibility of subject vocabularies*. Technical Report no. 1582-100-TR-5. Philadelphia: Auerbach, 1969. (NTIS Document PB 184 144)

Ward, Joyce (1999). 'Indexing and classification at Northern Light'. *NFAIS newsletter*, vol. 41, no. 10, 1999, pp. 138–140

'Web thesaurus compendium', prepared by Barbara Lutes, Darmstadt University of Technology. (http://www.darmstadt.gmd.de/~lutes/thesauri.html, accessed 15 August 2000)

West, L. and P. Murray-Rust (1997). 'Steps towards the global linking of knowledge.' *Managing Information*, vol. 4, no. 4, 1997, pp. 36–39

Whitehead, Cathleen (1990). 'Mapping *LCSH* into thesauri: The *AAT* Model.' *In:* Toni Petersen and Pat Molholt (eds). *Beyond the book: extending MARC for subject access.* Boston: Hall, 1990, pp. 81–98

Will, L. (1996). 'Thesaurus principles and practice'. (http://www.willpower.demon. co.uk/thesprin.htm, accessed 15 August 2000). Revision of a paper *In: Thesauri for museum documentation: the proceedings of a workshop held at the Science Museum, London, 24 February 1992,* Museum Documentation Association, Terminology Working Group, Cambridge. (MDA occasional paper 18)

Will, L. 'Software for building and editing thesauri'. (http://www.willpower. demon.co.uk/thessoft.htm, accessed 15 August 2000)

Willets, M. (1975). 'An investigation of the nature of the relations between terms in thesauri'. *Journal of Documentation,* vol. 3, no. 3, 1975, pp. 58–184

Williamson, Nancy J. (1996). 'Deriving a thesaurus from a restructured *UDC.*' *In: Advances in Knowledge Organization, vol. 5. Knowledge organization and change. Proceedings of the 4th International ISKO Conference, Washington, DC, 15–18 July 1996.* Frankfurt/Main: Indeks Verlag, 1996, pp. 370–377

Williamson, Nancy J. (1996a). 'Standards and rules for subject access'. *Cataloguing and Classification Quarterly,* vol. 21, no. 3/4, 1996, pp. 155–176

Willpower Information. 'Publications on thesaurus construction and use', prepared by Leonard and Sheena Will. (http://www.willpower.demon.co.uk/thesbibl.htm#lists, accessed 25 September 2000)

*word*HOARD. Museum Documentation Association (MDA). 'A guide to terminology resources relevant to museums'. It includes links to a selection of online thesauri, classification systems and other authority files. (http://open.gov.uk/mdocassn/ wrdhrd1.htm, accessed 25 September 2000)

Zoological Record online thesaurus. Philadelphia, PA: BIOSIS

Index

References are to paragraph codes and not to page numbers. An asterisk following a code indicates that the subject is covered not only in that paragraph but also in its subdivisions.